EASTERN LIGHT IN WESTERN EYES

BY THE SAME AUTHOR

YUGA: An Anatomy of Our Fate
The Sandstone Papers

MARTY GLASS

EASTERN LIGHT IN WESTERN EYES

❀

A PORTRAIT OF THE PRACTICE OF DEVOTION

SOPHIA PERENNIS

HILLSDALE NY

First published in the USA
by Sophia Perennis
Series editor: James R. Wetmore

Series editor: James R. Wetmore

For information, address:
Sophia Perennis, P.O. Box 611
Hillsdale NY 12529
www.sophiaperennis.com

Printed in the
United States of America

Library of Congress Cataloging-in-Publication Data

Glass, Marty, 1938–
Eastern light in western eyes : a portrait of the practice
of devotion / Marty Glass.—1st ed.

p. cm.
ISBN 0 900588 52 7 (pbk. : alk. paper)
1. Hinduism. I. Title
BL1202.G53 2003
294.5'4—dc22 2003027276

Bhaktya mamabhijanti yavanyascasmi tattvatah
Tato mam tattvato jnatva visate tadanantaram. . . .
Sarvadharmanparityajya mamekam saranam vraja.

To love is to know Me,
My innermost nature,
The Truth that I am:
Through this knowledge he enters
At once to my Being…
Abandoning all dharmas.
Take refuge in me alone.

Bhagavad Gita XVIII.55.66

For my
family and
friends; all those I love
and those I might fall
in love with at
first sight

CONTENTS

Part Two

PREFACE

EARTHLY AFFAIRS & CONNECTIONS

About thirty years ago I looked up from the Prabha-vananda-Manchester translation of the *Upanishads* I was reading, said to myself 'This is clearly and obviously the truth,' looked down again and continued reading. Nothing dramatic, nothing emo-tional. Simply a fact to be recorded. A single drop of rain fell from a blue sky, hit the ground, and it was a whole new ballgame.

Now the sacred texts of India, among which the *Upanishads* is central, speak very often about the indispensable role of the guru, "the knower of Brahman," who will be your teacher. Somewhere I had heard about the Vedanta Society, an overseas branch of the Ramakrishna Monastic Order of India, which had temples, or centers, in American cities run by people called 'swamis'. There was one in Berkeley run by a Swami Swananda. Perhaps he would be my guru.

I went to an evening sermon at the temple. I sat, as I had planned, in the first row (alone, as it turned out), because I wanted to be close enough to get a solid sense of who, or what, the swami was. I wanted to read his face and mannerisms, his style, even if a fixed scrutiny might seem impertinent. I wanted to know if he was for real. The guru is supposed to be quite different from us.

It took about two seconds for me to see that Swami Swananda was indeed different from us. Very different. A total departure.

Later that week I phoned the center and asked a secretary or acolyte of some kind for an appointment with the swami. I was going to ask him if he thought a guru was necessary. If he said yes I would ask him to be my guru.

I wasn't sure how I would say it. (Am I worthy? Does this sort of thing still go on? How much do you charge?) In India a thousand years ago I would have brought him firewood and prostrated myself.

As it turned out, his answer was no. You could, in his opinion, 'do it' without benefit of a formal guru/disciple relationship. He answered a few questions I had, recommended some reading. Over the next few years, before he was reassigned, I met with him from time to time for dinner and discussions in the small library. I knew he was a saint. Once he read to me, at my request, from the *Gita* in Sanskrit. I wept; he said he'd never met anyone like me before; I hadn't either. He told me I was 'no longer a beginner'. About a year ago I learned he had 'left the body.'

Since then the Vedanta Retreat in Olema (or the Vedanta Advance, as Vedananda likes to call it), a monastery of the Ramakrishna Order, has become my 'earthly' connection with the religion of India. I love the guys there—the monks and residents, the community of 'regulars', many of them Indian, who turn out to help prepare the annual Memorial Day Program, I am blessed in knowing them. This book, however, is about the 'heavenly' connection within all of us. The Axis within theomorphic humanity, *imago dei*, uniting the finite with the Infinite. Vedanta, *Sanatana Dharma*, the Eternal Truth.

INTRODUCTION

Religion is direct experience of the Divine Reality, direct experience of the Truth. It's an event. It *happens*: happens in the lives of people. Has happened to others, can happen to you. And though there are certainly other ways we might legitimately define 'religion', other perspectives, other dimensions, this is the one that really matters. Why? Because we could replace 'religion' in that first sentence with 'human fulfillment', or 'the purpose of life', or 'the goal of existence'.

Two things immediately.

First, the Divine Reality, the Truth we directly experience, may or may not be experienced as God, a personal deity. Usually is, but not always. It could be Nirvana; It could be Infinite Peace or Absolute Beauty or Pure Bliss. It could be The Tao That Cannot Be Named or a Name that is God. It could be the Self of the Universe, Life Eternal or 'the Love that moves the sun and the other stars,' as Dante put it in his last line. It could be a moment when we smiled a faint smile because we knew we'd seen into the heart of things. Or simply a fleeting inarticulate intuition. And It is One: endless and inexhaustible, but still and forever One. 'Truth is One; the sages call It by many names.'

Second, this 'event', this direct experience in its gorgeous variety, occurs outside of time. It abolishes time. It is an eternal Event in an Eternal Now. Behind the shifting scenes, the 'phantom flux of life', behind the 'ego', the tenacious illusion of personality, It is the Eternal Reality. It's all there ever was, is or ever will be and all 'you' ever were time out of mind, world without end. This is known, always, seen with clear and vivid certitude, in the experience.

And it happens, usually, when we have prepared ourselves for it, made ourselves receptive. When we *sit*. We can't *make* it happen, but we can *wait* for it to happen: create a space for it by emptying our minds of the trash and the racket and trying to face in the direction from which It might enter. This is why we meditate, pray and practice Invocation of a Holy Name. We're announcing our candidacy for an experience.

❁

So: In 56 medium-sized reader-friendly pieces, many short ones, the 'Glints and Glimpses', 'A Sequence on Identity' and 'A Sequence on the Heart', and in 'Fourteen *Mantras* in Praise of the Light', this book tries to describe direct experience of the Divine Reality. Direct experience of rewarded practice. It is discourse on that experience. Evocation of that experience, reflection upon that experience, examination and celebration of It, joyous Immersion in It. Definitely a 'proof of the pudding' enterprise.

I'm a wordsmith. I try to write English Prose. My goal has been, through the employment of that Instrument—vocabulary and syntax, verbal orchestration, the magic of language, the culture of the English-speaking peoples—to convince you that direct experience of the Divine Reality actually happens. To make that experience *real* insofar as the resources of language have the power to do that, which means never *really* real, of course—that's the eternal Event in the lotus of your heart—but as close as we can get to it, as *I* can get to it with humbling fading memories of Conrad, James, Melville, Hawthorne and Forster in the back of my mind, on the printed page. And also to whet your appetite, make you want it. (What appetite? Why, the appetite that you *are*, of course!) Want it very much. (As you already do, of course! You're human, aren't you?) To know or at least suspect what that experience is, know it's real, and want it. My hope for you.

❁

Now the timeless Event, if it Is to overcome transience, occurs, and is defined, sustained and nourished, within a tradition. A spiritual tradition. The tradition that informs this book is the tradition of

India. We can use Hinduism as the general term, Vedanta as a metaphysical specific. Direct experience of the Divine Reality, the Truth, is here invoked—petitioned, solicited, comprehended, encompassed, explored, interpreted, received with inexpressible humility and gratitude—within the framework and categories of that particular Revelation. That particular Grace. That particular 'form of the Formless', 'manifestation of the Principle', crystallization of the Light. That translation of the eternal Word. And since that framework and those categories are presented and elaborated throughout the text, I will concentrate in this Introduction, following a brief summary of Hinduism's Basic Statement, on the aspect of Vedanta most relevant to us here and now: *a Truth or Supreme, a focus of spiritual practice aspiration and realization, which is both personal and impersonal.* There it is. That, I believe, is the decisive element, the highest 'achievement' of Vedanta. For us, today, inhabitants of the twentieth century.

Why so? What's this all about? What does this mean, 'personal and impersonal'?

✲

Let's take a few steps back. Let's consider the great success, compared with other spiritual imports, of Buddhism in this country. Why is there so much more Buddhism here than Hinduism? Why are there so many Buddhist claimants and Buddhist groups among the countless lapsed Christians, disaffected Jews and spiritual seekers of all shapes and sizes wandering around in this culture?

First the secondary reasons, just for the record.

Buddhism is a 'doctrine of Realization', emphasizing the evidence and sufficiency of direct experience, the attainment of a state, called Enlightenment, which is experienced as proof of Itself, and therefore Buddhism has exercised a powerful appeal to many Christians who have balked at being required to 'believe in' a God whose existence is to be accepted 'on faith' and in miracles they have never personally witnessed (and which seem, to serious seekers at any rate, 'beside the point') and who have had serious difficulties with a religion approached through perfunctory attendance, sacramental intervention and creedal affirmations; a religion, moreover, whose institutions appear to be so thoroughly, suspiciously and hypocritically enmeshed in earthly affairs as to present a barrier rather than an avenue to emancipation from worldliness.

Buddhism, furthermore, emphasizes peace and compassionate reconciliation in a time when anger and violence are continuously erupting, in reality and as 'entertainment', virtually everywhere we look, and Buddhism teaches love of Nature and empathy with all living things in a time of global ecocide. Buddhism employs a psychology plausible and attractive in our nerve-wracking culture: the first of the Four Noble Truths is the Truth of Suffering, a Truth which rung a loud bell in a society plagued by anxiety, depression and gnawing malaise, and which translated smoothly into the language of psychotherapy, into stress reduction techniques, a wide variety of yoga classes, and innumerable 'healing' and 'centering' fads. The vicissitudes of geopolitical displacement have carried into our communities teachers and Masters from Tibet and Vietnam. Buddhist Masters from Japan, a 'westernized' country much closer to us in many respects than 'underdeveloped' India, are able to 'speak our language' with sympathetic insight and shrewd discernment, and the romance of Zen, martial arts and even the Japanese cinema have played their role in bringing the beauty, depth and refinement of Buddhism to spiritually hungry people in the West.

And now the major reason, the decisive reason, for Buddhism's success: Buddhism, in its dimension that has addressed Westerners so compellingly, is non-theistic. It demands no belief in a 'Personal God', so none of the insuperable vexing dilemmas posed by biblical literalism and the existence of evil and divine 'partiality' that originate in the anthropomorphism of western theistic religions, the Abrahamic monotheisms, in their exoteric forms. As FRITHJOF SCHUON puts it (and if you are familiar with his work you know that the way he puts it is the way it is):

> The Buddhist 'non-theism' offers the advantage of avoiding an impression of an interested God; this advantage is evidently a relative and conditional one, but it has its importance for the sake

> of certain mentalities. As Buddhists see things, moreover, the religious dissensions of the monotheist world are bound up with a dogmatic and anthropomorphic theism as such; no God with-out a party, no party without struggle against another party . . .
> What modern man is no longer willing to admit is above all the idea of an anthropomorphic, 'infinitely perfect' God, creating the world 'out of goodness' while foreknowing its horrors—creating man 'free', while knowing he would make bad use of his freedom; a God who, despite His 'infinite goodness', can punish man for faults which He, the 'omniscient' Creator, could not fail to foresee. . . .
> The Vedantic and Buddhist solution, which avoids the obstacles of anthropomorphism, is certainly unsuited to the monotheistic collectivities; however, by a tragic paradox, some answer of this nature has become indispensable to meet the demand in respect of ultimate causality among these same collectivities once they have lost the religious instinct and have started wrestling with the logical contradictions then inescapably bound up with anthropomorphism.

❁

However, and this is truly a massive However, two things, two immense reservations:

First: the Absolute, as a matter of fact, is both personal and impersonal. God and Godhead. 'Thou' and 'It'. Presents Itself to us 'here below' as such. No doubt about that. The theistic religions are not fantasies, allegories or concessions to the simpleminded and their saints and sages were not deluded and the 'problems' of evil (or theodicy: the vindication or defense of God in the face of 'evil', one of which is the answer given to Job), predetermination and divine 'inconsistency' seem 'problems' only to those who misinterpret their stature in the scheme of things.

> The Absolute of necessity takes on, in relation to man, aspects that are more or less human, without however being intrinsically limited by these aspects.
> ~ SCHUON again

Second: the overwhelming majority of humanity requires a personal God if they are to have any God at all: a *Thou* they can worship and adore and to Whom they can pray and in Whom they can find refuge. This includes you. Realization of an impersonal Absolute—such as Suchness, Emptiness, Nirvana, the Void, Buddha-Nature; or *turiya*, OM, Pure Consciousness, Atman and Brahman of Vedanta—is hard, hard to understand, hard to enact, hard to sustain. Even great 'non-dualists' like Shankara and Ramana Maharshi turned regularly to God. Buddhism, then, in its western forms where the innumerable Bodhisattvas worshipped in the East play practically no role—it's almost purely 'intellectual' here—excludes a great many people: excludes, specifically, that (equally) supreme Realization called 'the love of God.'

What Hinduism offers, and which meets, there can be no doubt, a need that Buddhism does not directly address, is the path of *bhakti* or *devotion*. The love of God. The experience of the love of God, the experience of *loving God*, is a spiritual absolute, an ultimate: there is nothing beyond it: it is supreme, because it is the Oneness: God is Love, and in our love for God, in that experience, we disappear into that Oneness, that infinite Bliss, *ananda*, which is the Reality. Many Indian worshippers repeat the familiar slogan, 'I would rather taste sugar than be sugar'—meaning rather be 'lost' in the love of God than 'extinguished' in the being of God—but as it turns out, the tasting is the being anyway. 'Thou art my Beloved' and 'I am Nirvana', 'Dearest of the Dear, my very Heart' and 'I am Brahman', 'All is Krishna' and 'There is Nothing'—these are spiritual epitomes identical in their metaphysical realization, accuracy and prestige, and differ only in the flavor, the emphasis, in the inclinations of temperament and even of the moment. At the highest stages of both, Hindu and Buddhist Enlightenment are essentially indistinguishable. In the classic analogy, the Paths up the mountain may look very different and appear very distant from one another (especially near the bottom) but they all arrive at the same pinnacle.

✲

Now for that 'brief summary of Hinduism's Basic Statement' I promised.

The Ten Principle Upanishads chosen by Shankara celebrate, primarily and not without a certain inescapable ambiguity, an impersonal Absolute: Brahman Supreme. (This is the Vedanta Schuon had in mind in the passage quoted above.) 'Vedanta' means the end or goal of the Vedas, the Hindu scriptures, an end or consummation which is described in the Upanishads, the concluding portions of those texts. The essence of the Upanishadic message, or *sanatana dharma*, Eternal Truth, is summarized *Brahman satyam, jagan mithya*: *Ayam Atma Brahman*. Brahman is real, the world is not: this Self is Brahman. Which means that only the Absolute or Brahman, the impersonal Ground of all Being, is truly Real, all else being an *appearance*, called *maya*, superimposed upon that Reality, and the innermost Self of each of us, called the Atman, is identical with that Absolute: *Aham brahmasmi*, I am Brahman. Atman and Brahman are One. This great spiritual truth is to be directly experienced in meditation, or ecstatic states of consciousness, as it was directly experienced by the nameless *rishis* who described their experience in the Upanishads. Religion is Realization. In the words of the great modern saint Ramana Maharshi, 'The essential aim of the Veda is to teach us the nature of the imperishable Atman and show us that we are That.'

Without a doubt. However, I said 'primarily and not without a certain inescapable ambiguity' because most of the remaining extant Upanishads (there are 108 in all) have strong theistic elements, especially Svetasvatara (one of the six others recognized by Shankara as authentic and authoritative), and even in Mundaka, one of the Ten, we read:

> The Imperishable is the Real. As sparks innumerable fly upward from a blazing fire, so from the depths of the Imperishable arise all things. To the depths of the Imperishable they in turn descend.

> Self-luminous is that Being, and formless, He dwells within all and without all. . . .
> Heaven is his head, the sun and moon his eyes, the four quarters his ears, the revealed scriptures his voice, the air his breath, the universe his heart. From his feet came the earth. He is the innermost Self of all. . .
> In him the seas and mountains have their source; from him spring the rivers, and from him the herbs and other life-sustaining elements. . . .
> Self-luminous is Brahman, ever present in the hearts of all. He is the refuge of all, he is the supreme goal. In him exists all that moves and breathes. In him exists all that is. . . . Adorable is he. Beyond the ken of the senses is he. Supreme is he. Attain thou him!. . . .
> Affix to the Upanishad, the bow incomparable, the sharp arrow of devotional worship; then, with mind absorbed and heart melted in love, draw the arrow and hit the mark—the imperishable Brahman. . . .
> The knot of the heart, which is ignorance, is loosed, all doubts are dissolved, all evil effects of deeds are destroyed, when he who is both personal and impersonal is realized.
> ~ Prabhavananda, Manchester translation

And so on. You see the blend here? Doesn't this sound very much like 'God'?

This blurring of 'personal' and 'Impersonal' is found throughout the Upanishads.

Impersonal Anthropomorphism, Theistic Absolutism.

❁

But as soon as we move *outside* the Upanishadic literature, to the *Bhagavad Gita* and the *puranas* or epic literature and elsewhere in the tradition, and above all to the experience of the countless millions who practice the religion, the emphasis is overwhelmingly theistic or mingled.

In other words:

Two great Paths, or *margas*, are recognized by the religion of India: *Bhakti*, or the Path of Love, and *jñana*, the Path of Knowledge. Both lead to the same indescribable Realization, and each is present in the other. The first emphasizes union with the Personal God through Love, the second emphasizes identity with the Impersonal Absolute through Knowledge, through discrimination between the Real and the Unreal and dis-identification with the non-Self or ego. The first is the experience of a relationship with a Thou, the second the experience of identity with an It. Brahman is actually either both or neither, for these are merely our ways of seeing and talking about what actually transcends our minds and our languages. Nor does it matter, because both Paths are walked simultaneously anyway, since the Thou and the It are actually One.

> The lives of saints constantly pass from the personal to the impersonal, and vice versa; moments of passive characterless consciousness alternate with deep devotion to a Personal God. . . . The finite proves, on analysis, to be the infinite; the Personal to be the Impersonal; the many with forms and attributes to be the Absolute Real.
>
> ~ B. V. N. Swami, *Life and Teachings of Sri Ramana Maharshi*

As the Maharshi Himself affirms, 'Jñana Marga and Bhakti Marga are one and the same.' One and the same, a single simultaneous journey. That's what I tried to write about.

❁

And now I want to summarize it one last time. The happy resolution of the 'personal-impersonal' dilemma in Hinduism.

Love and knowledge, Thou and It, Union and Identity, God with attributes and God without attributes, 'formful' and formless, *bhakti* and *jñana*, dualism and non-dualism, devotional meditation and sapiential or gnostic meditation, Hari and Brahman, and so on: these complementary pairs, dynamic duos, diametrical antitheses, 'two sides of the same coin,' define the Two Great Paths, the theistic and the impersonal, whose criss-crossings, interpenetrations and ultimate unity compose the great theme, the symphony—I suppose it would be more accurate to call it a Duet—of the tradition.

Vedanta, in other words, provides both what is absent, love for a personal God, and what is present, intellection, in Western Buddhism. (Absent because *unnecessary*, it should be clear. Buddhism is complete, and its salvific perfection, exquisite beauty and matchless refinement is in no way being impugned in these pages. We're talking about an historical anomaly here, the specific 'situation' of Western seekers in a culture they experience as spiritually bankrupt, not a defect—there are none—in Buddhism. We can all, periodically in our meditation, 'measure time' from the Buddha's Nirvana as well as the Incarnation of Our Saviour.) And the unity or simultaneous treading of those Two Great Paths, sometimes called the *bhagavata dharma*, the experience of integration within that particular 'spiritual universe', is what this book seeks to celebrate. Both Paths, as we have seen, are acknowledged, both sanctioned, by scripture. The impersonal Absolute and the personal God are both real, neither subordinate, and they are ultimately non-different. *Jñana* and *bhakti* lead to the same goal. The Advaitic or 'non-dual' position perhaps enjoys the greater prestige, but it does not deny, nor does it seek to, the authenticity of theistic experience. Indeed, the endless variety of interplay, mutual transformation and 'exchange of roles', the dazzling and ingenious reciprocity between *jñana* and *bhakti*, the path of knowledge and the path of love and devotion, is the unique glory, and unique delight, of the Hindu religion and surely its supreme contribution to humanity's spiritual hope. As a matter of fact, it's clearly divine: only God could have thought of it.

❁

Let's take a look at some textual citations, authoritative commentary—who am I?—on this matter. Not so much to 'drive the point home' but rather to get a preliminary 'feel' for it, for the richness of it, for the idioms in which the great personal-impersonal unity is expressed and explained. (One of which is the present submission.) So I will now slip into the background, emerging only to introduce the illustrious speakers. (And don't just read the first few and then skip ahead thinking you got the point. It's not a matter of 'getting the point' but of letting something sink in. Soak in.)

Swami Prabhavananda, citing 'the idea of an impersonal-personal God which we find in the teachings of the Indian scriptures,' writes:

> Both aspects of the Godhead—the personal and the impersonal—are realized and experienced by those whose eyes have been opened.

In the Swami's commentary on Narada's *Bhakti Sutras* he writes:

> Brahman or God is Sat-chit-ananda—Existence or eternal Reality, pure Consciousness, and pure Love and Bliss. These, however, are not attributes of Brahman. That which is Sat is the same as Chit, and the same as Ananda. Sat is identical with Brahman, Chit is identical with Brahman. Ananda is identical with Brahman. In the path of knowledge, emphasis is laid upon Chit, pure Consciousness; and in the path of devotion, emphasis is laid upon Ananda—Love or Bliss. When the aspirant reaches the end, there is no longer any distinction between the Chit and Ananda. Then supreme love and unitive knowledge of Godhead become one and the same.

In his masterful Introduction to *Bhakti Ratnavali* of Vishnu Puri, a selection from the *Srimad Bhagavatam* in which the *bhagavata dharma* reaches the summit of its expression (you can read the complete translation in two volumes, each about 700 pages, or the excellent abridgement by Swami Prabhavananda), Swami Tapasyananda writes:

> True jñana Yoga is only Bhakti with a higher degree of intellectual, and less of sentimental, element in it—a form of 'intellectual love of God' and absorption in Him. The Jnani looks upon the Lord as his own Higher Self and seeks communion with Him through the 'I' sense.

SRI RAMAKRISHNA PARAMAHAMSA:

> The true knower knows that he who is Brahman is the personal God; that he who is impersonal, attributeless, and beyond the gunas, is again the personal God, the repository of all blessed qualities.... Pure Knowledge and pure Love are both one and the same.... The same Being whom the Vedantins call Brahman, is called Atman by the Yogis and Bhagavan by the Bhaktas.... My Divine Mother (the personal phase of Brahman) has declared that She is the Brahman of the Vedanta. It is within Her power to give Brahma-jñana.... Jñana is like a man and Bhakti is like a woman. Knowledge has entry only up to the drawing-room of God, but Love can enter His inner apartments.

The classic statement on this subject by the PARAMAHAMSA OF DAKSHINESWAR goes as follows:

> Think of Brahman, Existence-Knowledge-Bliss-Absolute, as a shoreless ocean. Through the cooling influence, as it were, of the bhakta's love, the water has frozen at places into blocks of ice. In other words, God now and then assumes various forms for His lovers and reveals Himself to them as a Person. But with the rising of the sun of Knowledge, the blocks of ice melt. Then one does not feel anymore that God is a Person, nor does one see God's forms.

From RABINDRANATH TAGORE's introduction to his translation, *Songs of Kabir*:

> Kabir belongs to that small group of supreme mystics—amongst whom St. Augustine, Ruysbroeck, and the Sufi poet Jalalu'ddin Rumi are perhaps the chief—who have achieved that which we might call the synthetic vision of God. These have resolved the perpetual opposition between the personal and impersonal, the transcendent and immanent, static and dynamic aspects of the Divine Nature; between the Absolute of philosophy and the 'sure true Friend' of devotional religion. They have done this, not be taking these apparently incompatible concepts one after the other; but by ascending to a height of spiritual intuition at which

> they are, as Rukysbroeck said, 'melted and merged in the Unity,' and perceived as the completing opposites of a perfect Whole. . . . He is the omnipresent Reality, the 'All-pervading' within Whom 'the worlds are being told like beads.' In His personal aspect He is the 'beloved Fakir,' teaching and companioning each soul. Considered as Immanent Spirit, He is 'the Mind within the mind.' But all these are at best partial aspects of His nature, mutually corrective . . . so Kabir says that 'beyond both the limited and the limitless is He, the Pure Being.'

But KABIR, 'a weaver, a simple and unlettered man, who earned his living at the loom,' 'settled' the question simply with:

> The formless Absolute is my Father, and God with form is my Mother.

The words of SHRI DADA SANGHITA, as recounted by Hari Prasad Shastri in *The Heart of the Eastern Mystical Teaching*:

> My sisters from Bengal, devotion is the easiest way to prepare the heart for achieving identity with God within. In fact what we call 'jñana' or 'identity of the individual Self with the Supreme Self', is only a higher form of devotion. Love strikes at the root of duality and finally brings about absorption of the lover in the being of the Beloved.
>
> Devotion to God is first expressed in the third person; the devotee says: 'He of whom the Vedas sing, Who incarnated as the son of Vasudeva and played in the woods of Brindavana, is my sole Lord and Master. . . .' Then follows the second phase of devotion, in which Hari is worshipped in the second person:
>
> 'Thou art my Lord, and I am Thy servant. . . . In Thee I take refuge.' In this stage the devotee sees Hari in every being. A true lover loves the world. . . . The devotee now begins to lose consciousness of his individuality. In the third stage he worships Hari in the first person. Hari becomes his own Self and all duality comes to an end; the veil of samsara is lifted and there is no longer 'I' or 'my', 'thou' or 'thine', but only one cosmic Consciousness in which universes rise and fall like bubbles in the sea.

> My sisters, this is the consummation of devotion. 'Vasudeva is all'; the Mahatma who knows this is rare. Thus you will see there is no difference between devotion and jñana.

From the PRABHAVANANDA abridged translation of the *Srimad Bhagavatam*. This is Scripture. Direct from Heaven:

> The wise call Thee the impersonal, without attributes; They also call Thee personal God with divine attributes; Thou art both, and Thou dost manifest Thyself as the one or the other, according to our understanding.
>
> Love is divine. But love is expressed differently and in different degrees according to the evolution of the individual human soul. There are people who still have hatred, jealousy, anger and pride in their hearts. To such, God is above, beyond and apart. They also may love God, but their love is selfish. This love is Tamasika. That, too, is a low form of love by which people love and worship God as a separate being, and pray to Him for the fulfillment of their material desires. Such love is known as Rajasika love. But the love which seeks God for the sake of love alone and by means of which we offer ourselves whole-heartedly to Him—this love we call Sattvika love. But when the love, the lover and the beloved have become one, when we see God and love Him as the innermost Self in all beings, and when there is a continuous current of love flowing in the heart, then is it that we realize divine love. When such divine love fills the heart, we transcend the three Gunas and become united with Brahman.

SWAMI YATISWARANANDA, from his Introduction to *Universal Prayers* and his magisterial *Meditation and Spiritual Life*:

> With the march of time, it has been recognized with greater clearness that the impersonal Principle forms the background of all personal aspects of God, and is the source of all divine personalities worshipped through various symbols. Indeed, according to Advaita (non-dualistic) Vedanta, whatever be the symbol one may adopt or the personality one may adore to begin with, the highest goal of spiritual life lies in the ultimate experience of the Impersonal, the One-without-a-second, in

> which the worshipper is merged and becomes one with the Infinite. . . .
> Besides this lofty conception of the absolute transcendent Reality, the One-without-a-second, there developed in ancient India the ideas of an immanent impersonal divine Principle, which manifests Itself through finite forms and yet remains infinite and formless. . . .
> Even in the concept of a personal God itself there is the distinction between anthropomorphic and non-anthropomorphic aspects. In Islam God is personal but not anthropomorphic, i.e. God does not have a human form. . . .
> The Impersonal is beyond the reach of the devotee, while the Personal does not satisfy his philosophic sense. Hence the worship of the Personal-Impersonal has been most popular in Hinduism in almost all forms of spiritual practice. . . . Thus the conception of the Personal-Impersonal, of the One in the many, permeates the entire Hindu religious consciousness—a fact that will be clearly understood by those who are able to enter into that true spirit of the Hindu scriptures.

From Narasimha Swami's *Life and Teachings of Sri Ramana Maharshi*:

> A question may be considered at this stage about the relation of emotion to illumination, of devotion (bhakti) to realization (jñana). Even about the time of Maharshi's leaving Madurai he would remain at times absorbed in the Self, lost in samadhi and at times visit the temple and pour out his soul in tears. These tears of devotional fervour continue to flow even today when occasions for them arise. . . . Maharshi, explaining these facts, says that devotion (bhakti) and realization (jñana) are the same and not different. In the devotional path one starts by dwelling intently on the Personal God whom one worships and proceeds till one loses oneself or merges in Him. In the path of inquiry one starts by dwelling on oneself, which one loves most, and proceeds till one loses oneself in that.

And in the words of the MAHARSHI Himself:

> Bhakti and Self-Enquiry are one and the same. The Self of the Advaitins is the God of the bhaktas. . . . The meaning or significance of 'I' is God.

From SWAMI TYAGISANANDA's brilliant and scholarly commentary on his translation of the *Narada Bhakti Sutras*:

> Thus love of God is nothing but love of the Reality or the higher Self of man which he has forgotten. . . . The individual gradually acquires all the fundamental characteristics of his Ideal, and in course of time feels himself as part of God and finally realizes Him as his own Self. . . . But Parabhakti or the higher Love is possible only when the Chosen Ideal is loved after the realization of the Divine as one's own very Self . . . one who has realized this Parabhakti is the same as the Jivanmukta. . . . Bhakti is thus no loss of individuality, but only a supreme transcendence of the limitations of individuality and regaining of the true status of the Self. . . . Bhakti is the supreme goal of man's endeavour; it is incomparable and unalloyed bliss. . . . To the Vedantin, whether he is a Jnanin or a Bhakta, the summon of existence is the regaining of the natural blissful state of the Atman, as well as freedom from the miseries of the transmigratory cycle. Narada emphasizes this double aspect of Vedantic Release. The emphasis of the Bhakti schools is always on the positive aspect. . . . There is not much difference between the Parabhakti (Supreme Love) accepted by the Bhakti teachers and the Jivanmukti of Shankara. . . . The Bhakta never craves for Mukti; he is quite satisfied to enjoy the love of God for love's sake. Still Mukti comes to him by the grace of God. . . . The love, which brought him nearer and nearer to the Lord, would not have finished its function until there is no separation at all between the two. Even this duality is to be transcended through love. . . . The state of the Bhakta after the final realization is called Jivanmukti by Jnanins and Parabhakti by Bhaktas. But there is no difference between Jivanmukti and Parabhakti except in name. . . . The Lord of his heart who had been such an entirely different and separate being from

> himself, the Bhakta now finds to be one with his own Higher Self. The object of his love now is not the personal God with an individuality of His own but the Absolute.

From Swami Satprakashananda's lyrical essay, 'Divine Love':

> Love of God is the very essencc of spiritual life. . . . The one purpose of all religious disciplines is to develop love of God within the heart of the aspirant. . . . This love of God is the one supreme ideal of life as taught by all the great teachers of the world. . . . It is through love alone that we can be united with Him and attain eternal life, light, and joy. . . . Love of God is bliss itself. . . . As the love of God grows within, the devotee's entire being becomes vibrant with divine life, light, and sweetness. Fascinated and intoxicated with the nectar of divine love, he lives in a state of ecstasy. He finds within himself a perennial spring of joy welling up from that fountainhead of all blessedness. . . . Love culminates in complete union with God. As it grows deeper, the devotee feels an ever-increasing longing for the realization of God. It becomes the sole concern of his life. His entire being centers upon this one idea. He feels God's presence nearer and nearer, until he comprehends Him as the supreme spirit shining within his heart as the very soul of his soul. . . . As love intensifies, the devotee's individual self becomes so completely unified with God that he realizes the divine being as his very Self, and as the Self in all beings. . . . Through devotion is also attained the know-ledge of Brahman, the Impersonal, absolute being. Sri Krishna declares. 'To love is to know me, my innermost nature, the Truth that I am. Through this knowledge he enters at once to my Being.'

Enough! Citations to the same effect, with innumerable variations in shading, emphasis and approach, could be multiplied through many more pages than you need anymore to read. The relations between jñana and bhakti, impersonal and personal, non-dualism and theism, are clearly a fundamental theme of the Vedanta. And one more passage comes to my memory! I can't resist. It's this beautiful moment in the great masterpiece *Jnaneshvari*, the song-sermon on the Bhagavad-Gita by the Marathi saint, Jnanadeva:

> 'Moreover, were I to reveal the whole secret of the Eternal which casts out all thought of duality, then the joy of my affection for Arjuna would be destroyed.' Therefore Krishna did not tell Arjuna everything but drew a thin veil over it. He allowed the sense of his mind being separate to remain with Arjuna in order that Arjuna should be able to enjoy the experience. For this enjoyment oneness with Brahman is an obstacle. . . . 'If this state of union with Me were reached, with whom could I speak of the precious secret that cannot be contained in the heart?' With this compassionate thought Krishna reached out with His mind to draw to Himself the mind of Arjuna in conversation, under the pretext of this exposition.
>
> If, hearing this, it seems difficult to understand, remember that Arjuna is but an image moulded out of the bliss of Sri Krishna.

And so are you and me.

❋

The last two extracts referred to Krishna. Shri Dada's phrase, 'Vasudeva is all'— *Vasudeva sarvamiti*, a Sanskrit *mantra*, is probably how he said it—also refers to Krishna; Vasudeva is one of His Names. The *Srimad Bhagavatam* (the quotation I introduced as 'direct from Heaven') is the other great scriptural text, along with the *Bhagavad-Gita*, in which the Krishna Incarnation is revealed to us. His Teaching, His Truth.

I'd like to recommend Krishna to you. It's in the figure of this Hindu Avatar, Krishna, that we find the most perfect synthesis of personal God and impersonal Absolute. In all three hypostases, or divine 'presentations': *anthropomorphic*—with human form and superhuman attributes (exquisite iconography here); *immanent*—divine attributes but no form; and *transcendent*—without form or attributes, the inexpressible Supreme, the Absolute. Avatar or Incarnation, God, Brahman Supreme.

Consider this one quotation from Swami Prabhavananda's excellent abridgement of Srimad Bhagavatam, in which Krishna responds to the request of his faithful disciple, Uddhava, 'Please teach me how to meditate':

> Then, with your mind intent, behold within thy heart my benign form. Meditate on Me as the Supreme Cause, in whom the whole universe exists and from whom the whole universe evolves.
> Then, last of all, meditate on the oneness of the Self with God, the one blissful existence, the one I AM.
> With mind thus absorbed, a man sees Me alone in himself, and sees himself in Me, the Self of all – light joined to light.
> A Yogi, thus practicing meditation regularly, with intense devotion, soon rises above all limitations of knowledge and action by realizing the one, all-pervading Reality.

This really happens. Vedanta is Reality.

Krishna was Kabir's choice. (It was actually the other way around, of course.) As Tagore wrote, 'The one figure which he adopts from the Hindu Pantheon and constantly uses, is that of Krishna, the Divine Flute Player.' (What more could you want? The Lord of Love, Who is actually 'Brahman within this body,' Who draws you to Him with irresistible divine music!)

He was also 'the choice' of Madhusudana Sarasvati (16th century), the 'great Advaitin', who, despite his rigorous and uncompromising non-dualism, apparently burst out—at some point in his life, we're not told when—with the following hymn, described, in 'the humble opinion' of his translator, as 'Madhusudana's greatest contribution to the religious thinking of the country':

No truth I higher hold
Than Krishna, my beloved Lord!
With the glint of fresh raincloud hue
And smiling eyes of lotus blue,
Clad in robes, saffron-dyed,
He holds His enchanting flute
To luscious lips of cherry red.

In MADHUSUDANA's more rigorous mood, the great Advaitin wrote, in his commentary (*Gudhartha Dipika*) on the *Bhagavad-Gita* (XII, 6–7):

> The worshippers of Lord Krishna . . . merge in Supreme Reality, the Reality hidden in the niche of their awn hearts, in their own essence. The Complete, the Inmost, the Unique, the Undifferentiated Supreme Essence is revealed to them. They realize it with the help of Vedantic truths which appear to them without any effort on their part. They finally attain to supreme disembodied liberation. They become one with Reality. Thus those who know God in His Aspect with Qualities reach the same goal, through Divine Grace, as those who contemplate the Absolute.

A commentary which should sound familiar enough to us now. Devotion leads to, or is equivalent to, Knowledge. Worship of the Personal leads to Realization of the Impersonal. Bhakti and jñana are One. Notice the little extra twist here, however. Through the love of God, devotional worship, we actually *learn* things, learn *truths.* Gnosis, divine wisdom, spiritual knowledge, and 'without any effort.' Just sitting there with your eyes closed lost in the rapture of love. That's what happens in the 'eternal Event' I talked about at the beginning of the Introduction, and it's a principal theme of this book.

The fact is, Krishna *discusses* Himself—identifies Himself, explains Himself, teaches His worship and the Path to union or identity with His Being—in precisely the terms we have been reviewing and citing here. It is Krishna Himself Who teaches us that devotion to the Personal God—to Him, Krishna—or the approach to the Infinite through devotion to the Personal God, is the easier Path. Very very few, as the saints and sages unanimously agree, can make it to the mountaintop without recourse to God, to a Thou the love of Whom draws them there, and none without His Grace. And as we shall soon be seeing, it's not only 'the easier Path' but the Path expressly indicated for our age. But I anticipate.

Here's the passage from the *Bhagavad-Gita.* It's in chapter 12:

> ARJUNA: Some worship you with steadfast love. Others worship God the unmanifest and changeless. Which kind of devotee has the greater understanding of yoga?

> Sri Krishna: Those whose minds are fixed on Me in steadfast love, worshipping Me with absolute faith. I consider them to have the greater understanding of yoga.
> As for those others, the devotees of God the unmanifest, indefinable and changeless, they worship that which is omnipresent, constant, eternal, beyond thought's compass, never to be moved. They hold all the senses in check. They are tranquil-minded, and devoted to the welfare of humanity. They see the Atman in every creature. They also will certainly come to Me.
> But the devotees of the unmanifest have a harder task, because the unmanifest is very difficult for embodied souls to realize.

Quickly I come
To those who offer Me
Every action,
Worship Me only,
Their dearest delight,
With devotion undaunted. . . .

Be absorbed in Me,
Lodge your mind in Me:
Thus you shall dwell in Me,
Do not doubt it,
Here and hereafter.

Krishna's 'partiality' to the Path of devotion is expressed throughout the *Srimad Bhagavatam*. Here's just one passage, from Book II:

> Neither Yoga, nor Samkhya, nor Dharma, nor scriptural study, nor austerity, nor renunciation can attract and dominate Me as deep-rooted devotion can. By means of loving devotion, which is constant and deep-rooted, man attains to Me, the Supreme Master of all the worlds, the First Cause and Brahman, in whom creation, preservation and destruction of the worlds take place.
> Many are the means described for the attainment of the highest good, such as love, performance of duty, self-control, truthfulness, sacrifices, gifts, austerity, charity, vows, observance of moral precepts. I could name more. But of all I could name, verily love is the highest: love and devotion that make one forgetful of

> everything else, love that unites the lover with Me. What ineffable joy does one find through love of Me, the blissful Self! Once that joy is realized, all earthly pleasures fade into nothingness... Those only who have pure love for Me find Me easily. I, the Self dear to the devotee, am attainable by love and devotion. . . . O Uddhava, of all the paths to Me, Who am the goal of the sages, the path of love is happiest and best.

❁

I think I'm going to slip into the background again, yield the stage to the sages. You know why? It's because I really believe that the love of Krishna, that particular option of the Hindu religion, the love of that particular 'figure from the Hindu Pantheon' adopted by Kabir and so many others, that 'bhagavata-dharma' Path I have referred to, and which certainly should be taking shape for you, may be your best bet. The Answer for you. It was for me. So I should present it a little more fully.

All the following selections are from Introductions to the *Bhagavad-Gita*, (usually by the translator), except the concluding one by Swami Tapasyananda, which is excerpted from his brilliant Introduction to Vishnu Puri's selection from the *Srimad Bhagavatam*, the classic text of the *bhagavata dharma*. Then we'll move into the home stretch.

Swami Nikhilananda:

> The teacher of the Gita is Krishna, who is regarded by the Hindus as the supreme manifestation of the Lord Himself. . . . From the human standpoint Krishna and Arjuna are friends and companions; but in a deeper sense they are one soul in two bodies, two aspects of the one Reality, each incomplete without the other. . . . They are worshipped as Nara-Narayana, Arjuna as Nara, Man, and Krishna as Narayana, God. The two, God-Man, form the total picture of the Godhead. The Gita is written in the form of an inspired dialogue; it is that living dialogue which the

eternal knowledge all other highest teaching is but the various reflection and partial word, this the Voice to which the hearing of our soul has to awaken.

Swami Tapasyananda:

In the view of the Bhagavata there was a fuller manifestation of Divine excellences in Krishna than in any other Incarnation. It discovers all the majesties of God in Sri Krishna the Incarnate, and therefore equates Him with the Bhagavan Himself in the sense of fullness of manifestation. He is depicted as an expression of the redeeming love of God. . . . The Puranas in general, and the Bhagavata in particular, accept the Supreme Being as both Murta (Formful) and Amurta (Formless), with a greater stress on the Murta aspect and call Him the Bhagavan. . . . The Bhagavan is the term specially used to indicate that God is the Supreme Person but not an individual, that He is the Absolute Being but is yet responsive to worship and prayers. . . . The Deity it depicts is the all-inclusive Absolute Being as He presents Himself to the illumined minds of the sages. . . . 'On this form of Vishnu residing in one's own heart. let one meditate with the mind melting in love and feeling attraction for nothing else'. . . . At least as far as the Bhagavata is concerned, no metaphysics seems to be obnoxious to it, if it does not question the ultimacy of the Bhagavan and the supremacy of Bhakti. . . . And of all divine forms, Krishna is the most versatile manifestation, as every form of loving relationship could be established with Him. . . . Devotion of this type also can end in the sense of unity, in the understanding 'I am He'. . . . According to the Bhagavata, perfect spiritual realization consists in experiencing the Non-Dual Reality as Impersonal-Personal Being.

✲

OK. So much for the Impersonal-Personal Symphony of Hinduism (of the universe, I could just as well say), the role of *bhakti* or the love of God in the lives of those who hear or wish to hear that music, and the *bhagavata dharma* starring Sri Krishna which is its supreme rendition. This is the 'tradition within the Tradition' in which direct experience of the Divine Reality is invoked and celebrated ('petitioned, solicited, comprehended, encompassed, explored, interpreted, received with inexpressible humility and gratitude,' as you will recall from page 5 of this Introduction) in these pages, in this book. I have, however, in this final draft, 'played down' the Krishna Avatar (which often meant simply replacing the word 'Krishna' where it appeared in the original draft with 'God' or another equivalent) to avoid any suggestion of (Vaishnavite) sectarianism—there are other great Avatars in the Tradition—and in recognition of the broader appeal and universality of language which Hinduism offers. Krishna is my heart. We don't know yet whether He will be yours.

So allow me to conclude my 'recommendation' of Krishna with this little poem in which I tried to capture and preserve the memory of a priceless moment alone with Him.

The bluejay folds its wings, swoops,
Snaps them out and darts off again.
I watch the mist, I watch the trees.
I am far from the world of men.

And women. I mean both of course,
No slight intended: au contraire.
To this peace each absence donates
An exactly equal share.

I watch the mist, I watch the trees.
But this 'I' isn't really 'me'.
There is no 'me'. This 'I' is the Light.
And the Light we are is the world we see.

Krishna, Krishna, my very heart!
Thou art the Light, the One and the All:
The Universe, this very Self.
The Paradise before the Fall.

❁

Now to the other main order of business of this Introduction. I'll present it in three Statements:

1. We live in the Kali-Yuga: the end of the cosmic cycle.
2. The Path indicated for the Kali-Yuga, is *bhakti*.
3. The specific practice for the Kali-Yuga is Invocation of a Holy Name, or, in Hindu terminology, *mantra-japa*: repetition of a Holy Name or *mantra*.

Statement One is attested by traditional Hindu cosmology (and in 'sacred science', the sapiential dimension or principial Truth that informs all the world's religions and is elaborated quite fully in the publications of the contemporary traditionalist school—René Guénon, Ananda K. Coomaraswamy, Frithjof Schuon, Seyyed Nasr, et. al). Statement Two is also attested within the Hindu tradition but not unanimously. Statement Three is attested by some but not all of those who agree with Statement Two. And all of these attestations come with variations of emphasis.

Statement One can be dealt with quite briefly. The Hindu tradition simply assumes it: presents it as doctrine, takes it for granted, probably regards it as self-evident to the intuition of sages and plain as the nose on your face to anyone with eyes to see and ears to hear. A continuously escalating 'viciousness' of humanity, an ever-expanding irreligion (secularism, atheism, scientism, materialism, relativism, chauvinist 'humanism'—all that), an ever increasing defection and departure from *dharma*—the modern world, in other words—is perceived, regarded as sufficient evidence, and tranquilly accepted as being in the providential nature of things. It has happened an infinite number of times before, will happen again and forever, and that's the way of the world we inherit: the only way things can go in a manifested universe.

Now you can think what you wish about Statement One. It doesn't matter. Statements Two and Three advocate specific spiritual practices whose efficacy is interrogated in direct experience independent of our agreement or disagreement with the ancient

Hindu doctrine of comic cycles. Nor does confirmation of Two and Three prove One anymore than difficulties with the recommended practices disprove it. Statement One hovers in the background of our lives, a mystery beyond us, a haunting presentiment, a feeling in the air, in our troubled hearts. Maybe a Truth. Certainly a suspicion. Something we'll never know for sure.

❁

Lets take a look again at some testimony —always keeping in mind, however, that what matters here is the practice itself: whether it 'works.' What is 'interrogated' in other words, is simply the efficacy of the practice in your own experience, not the claim of the Statement. The Statements, when all is said and done, ought really to be regarded merely as suggestions.We always want to keep our feet on the ground: heads in the clouds, perhaps, but feet on the ground.

So. With regard to Statement Two:

Sri Ramakrishna remarks, 'The jñana Yogi longs to realize Brahman—God the Impersonal, the Absolute and the Unconditioned. But, as a general rule, a soul would do better, in this present age, to love, pray, and surrender himself entirely to God' (Saying 800). And elsewhere: 'The best path to union with God is to follow the way of divine love as taught by Narada.' 'Sri Ramakrsnaparamahamsa has stressed again and again that for *Kali-Yuga* the Path of Devotion as described by Narada is indeed the best and the easiest,' as we read in Swami Tyagisananda's Introduction to his translation of the *Narada Sutras*. 'Kali Yuga has its own advantages,' Shri Dada Sanghita points out, 'and the greatest of them is that devotion fructifies much quicker than in other ages.'

We find the fullest treatment, however, in DR. V. RAGHAVAN'S learned Introduction to *The Spiritual Heritage of Tyagaraja*:

> It has been held that with the gradual deterioration in the faculties and abilities of men, as ages pass on towards Kali, the sages devised further and further easier paths, for the salvation of suffering humanity. It is with this purpose in view that the path

> of Bhakti or devotion was developed. Kali is predominantly an age of emotion and it is through this emotion that man has to be saved. This is achieved by turning the flow of his emotion in the direction of a Supreme saving Personality. To draw man's heart in love towards the Supreme Being, the emphasis was shifted from knowledge to devotion and from an abstraction to a Personality endowed with infinite excellences, in fact another human form itself in which Divinity frequently incarnated. When Bhakti was thus evolved and developed, further processes of simplification were introduced, so that anybody and everybody, in whatever standard of equipment of mind and character, might have some means to take to. Along with temples, worship of images, adoration with acts of worship, the singing of the Lord's glory, the reading of or listening to writings on His glory or even the mere recitation of His Names developed. Thus were the Himalayan waters of the Upanishads brought to the plains, to irrigate the hearts of the masses of the entire country. . . .

The literature of Bhakti bearing in particular on the doctrine of the Lord's Name as the supreme means of salvation is considerable.

Which brings us to Statement Three.

❁

Dr. Raghavan continues:

> Besides some of the later Saguna Upanishads, portions of the Mahabharata, the Gita, and the Vishnu Sahasranama, the Puranas, and especially the Vishnu and the Bhagavata Puranas, form the main authorities in this school of thought. A number of religious writers contributed treatises on the theory of the subject of Nama-mahatmya in which they seek support not only in the above mentioned texts, going up to the later minor Upanishads, but also to the Rig Vedic hymns themselves. . . .
>
> Of the Upanishads referred to, I shall mention briefly here only one, the Kalisantaranopanishad, which specially concerns itself

> with the means of salvation appropriate or most efficacious in Kali or to get over Kali. According to this text, at the end of Dvapara and the opening of Kali, Narada asked his father Brahma how he could cross over Kali. Brahma gave him the remedy: 'You can shake off Kali by reciting the Name of the Lord Narayana, the Prime Being.'
>
> The Gita added its weight to this school of thought when it said that of all forms of Yajna, the Lord was of the form of Japa-yajna. . . .
>
> So, the expiation of all expiations is the thought of the Lord with the uttering of His Name.

Invocation in the Kali-Yuga is affirmed also in the RAMAYANA:

> In the first age of the world men crossed the ocean of existence by their spirit alone. In the second age sacrifice and ritual began, and then Rama lived, and by giving their every act to him men lived well their ways. Now in our age what is there to do but worship Rama's feet? But my friend, the last age of this world shall be the best. For then no act has any worth, all is useless . . . except only to say Rama. The future will read this. Therefore I tell them, when all is ruin around you, just say Rama.
>
> We have gone from the spiritual to the passionate. Next will come ignorance, Universal war. Say Rama, and win! Your time cannot touch you.

We might recall that Gandhi's last words, when the assassin's bullets struck, were 'Ram! Ram!'

The doctrine of the Name is affirmed, of course, throughout the SRIMAD BHAGAVATAM. I cite only a few instances.

> In this degenerate age of Kali, when all religious observances and ethical conduct have disappeared from society, those who are whole-heartedly devoted to Vasudeva will certainly attain the goal of life (Moksha).
>
> High-minded men, who have insight into the nature of the Kali age, and the discrimination to seize the essence, regard it highly, since then one may obtain all that one values most by simply singing the praises of the Lord and reciting His Names. . . .

> In Kali, too, they worship Him according to the modes prescribed in various Agamas; let me describe them. Men of enlightenment worship Him . . . according to modes of worship in which the singing of His praises and the recital of His Names play a predominant part. . . . Thus occupied, they came to love the Lord intensely, from incessant repetition of the Name of Him Who is dear to them.

The position of Statement Three is summarized (once and for all, one feels) in Swami Tapasyananda's conclusion to his Introduction to the *Bhakti Ratnavali* of Vishnu Puri, in a chapter he titles 'The Glory of the Divine Name':

> Among these devotional disciplines there is one which the Bhagavata emphasizes specially through the lives of several devotees. It consists in the utterance of the Divine Name (Nama), the unique power of which finds a place among the most important teachings of the Bhagavata. . . . The uniqueness of the Name is that its utterance is the most powerful expiatory discipline for men suffering from sin-consciousness, and also the most effective practice for gaining concentration, remembrance and devotion to God. Sri Ramakrishna also advocates this as the Sadhana (spiritual discipline) par excellence for man. . . .

Further, the Bhagavata states that the continuous repetition of the Lord's Names and excellences is the best and the most potent of spiritual disciplines in the age of Kali. 'In this age of Kali,' says the Bhagavata, 'they indeed are the fortunate and the blessed who themselves remember the Names of Hari and help others to remember the same. Though the age of Kali is dominated by evil, it holds forth one great advantage. What an aspirant attains in Krita Yuga through meditation, in Treta Yuga through sacrifices, in Dvapara through service of holy images, the same is attained in Kali Yuga through mere chanting of Sri Hari's Name.'

> It may be said that the whole teaching and philosophy of the Bhagavata is compressed in the doctrine of the infinite power of the Divine Name, which is veritably an Avatara (Descent) of God for everyone with faith to commune with—whether he is a saint

or a sinner, a learned man or one in ignorance. The Lord has made Himself easy of access to everyone through His Name.

✿

Whitall Perry's magnificent compilation, *A Treasury of Traditional Wisdom* (Preface by Huston Smith, Foreword by Marco Pallis), is without a doubt, as Pallis without reservation praises it, that 'summa of the Philosophia Perennis' called for by Ananda Coomaraswamy in the final note of his *Hinduism and Buddhism.* The final section of this priceless anthology, beginning on page 1001, is titled *Colophon: Invocation.* There are about 350 quotations in this Colophon, gathered from all the spiritual traditions of the world, celebrating the miracle of invocation of the Holy Name. I quote from Perry's introduction to that section:

> The cyclical opportuneness of invocation as a method relates to the place in spiritual practice for a corrective which can silence the unruly elements in the soul and burn out the negative aspects, while nourishing simultaneously all that is positive and orienting the soul towards its true felicity. Man is rightly a temple of the Holy Spirit, but fallen man houses a throng of idols—disordered reason, luciferian imagination, misplaced faculties of the soul, inordinate desires, inferior psychic entities, and demonic intruders—which have usurped his temple and turned its service more into a perpetual carnival. One becomes what one thinks upon; and as the mind is incessantly on the world in this period of the Kali Yuga, a method is needed that can continually and rhythmically and inexorably turn the mind away from its habitual worldly dementia, re-minding it in the Truth. A Name of God, divinely revealed, legitimately bestowed by the proper spiritual authority, and constantly invoked, reconsecrates the altar of the temple or heart of the aspirant and, functioning as a direct support, reanimates the Holy Spirit or Divine Breath still latent but despirated within.
>
> The facility of invocation derives from the prototypal simplicity of the Name itself . . . each repetition of the Name acts as a fresh

initiation into the spiritual life, being a renewal of one's aspiration, and at the same time a stabilizing of one's inward center. a fixing of consciousness on Reality.

❁

And last now, with regard to Statement Three, something that happened to me personally. Presented not as 'proving' anything, of course, but as an experience that contributed to the shaping of the spiritual assumptions and methods that inform this book. I wrote the following piece several years ago, and I'm including it here without revision. 'The above quotation' to which it refers at the end of the first paragraph was the passage from BHAGAVATA with which Swami Tapasyananda concludes the 'once and for all' textual citation above (pp30–31). Here it goes:

> Astronomers, anthropologists, historians, economists, scientists and cultural critics, dealing in events, personalities and the appearance, transformations, inter-relations and dissolution of institutions—all inseparable by rigorous definition from their dates or geological periods, since intelligibility here derives solely from succession—combine forces to provide us with the official diagram of 'the past' and with our (linear) sense of the meaning of time. We learn the contents and sequence of the temporal continuum, which is equivalent to reality itself, and locate and define ourselves within by reference to their work. This point of view commands massive prestige, to say the least; in its immense shadow, the above quotation must indeed appear quaint.
>
> There is no reason to confront the Indian cosmology of cyclic yugas with the linear temporality of the West, nor to defend the former's independent plausibility. The two emerge from different spiritual universes, having different priorities and different goals, and are not rivals. The passage from the Bhaga-vatam, like Western historicity, also 'locates' us; but in a different kind of continuum, one that is landmarked by soteriological alternatives rather than causes and effects.

No one knows, or cares, who wrote the Srimad Bhagavatam; we know approximately when it 'appeared', but again no one really cares; it's irrelevant. Nor does anyone care when the events it describes occurred, or even whether they occurred at all. The approach to Indian documents like the puranas finds no parallel in the West. They provide us with spiritual knowledge, with timeless truths and wisdom, and cogent verifiable instruction about how we may attain our salvation, and that is all that matters to the mentality which produced and resorts to them. The quoted passage informs us that the sadhana of the Kali-Yuga is mantra-japa, or repetition of a Holy Name—a conclusion echoed, oddly enough, by the hesychastic branch of the Eastern Orthodox Church. Who knew this, or how they knew it, is neither important nor knowable. The point is to verify, by direct experience, its truth.

About twenty-five years ago I was lying in bed one night preparing for sleep. For some reason, with no expectations, almost idly, I said to myself the word 'God'. I am not trying to recreate the experience here, so I will simply appeal to a sufficiently hackneyed descriptive metaphor: instantly I felt as if had be hit by lightning, within myself. I writhed to a half-upright position, leaning on one elbow, utterly shaken, stunned, wild-eyed I believe, and said it again. This time it hit me even harder. Half-choking, groping, sitting bolt-upright now, I felt that I was in danger of losing control of myself in some sense. I knew I couldn't withstand any more of what had struck me, and a third repetition died on my lips. I sank back, overwhelmed by the staggering, stupendous and undeniable reality of the Being Who was, in that moment, identical with His Name. I knew I had learned what mantra meant (I had always been curious about it, but had dismissed it as one of those numerous Eastern techniques which could only be practiced by Eastern people), and I knew that that lesson had been the point of the experience, immanent intention being obviously inherent. Ten years went by before I decided to use the word again as a mantra. I think I wanted to hold it in reserve in some sense, as an ultimate

> recourse to be drawn upon only in some kind of spiritual extremity. That extremity never came, and gradually the need to hold something in reserve disappeared. 'God' is the most powerful mantra in the English language. The Name is worshipped because He is present in His Name.

There are landmarks like that. Surprise gifts.

> The Divine Name, revealed by God Himself, implies a Divine Presence which becomes operative to the extent that the Name takes possession of the mind of the person invoking. Man cannot concentrate directly on the infinite, but by concentrating on the symbol of the Infinite he attains the Infinite Itself: for when the individual subject becomes identified with the Name to the point where all mental projection is absorbed by the form of the Name, then its Divine Essence manifests spontaneously, since this sacred form tends towards nothing outside of itself. It has a positive affinity with its Essence alone, wherein its limits finally dissolve. Thus it is that union with the Divine Name becomes Union with God Himself.
>
> ~ Titus Burckhardt

❁

But the use of verbal formulas, or *mantras*, is not restricted to repetition of a Holy Name, nor to theistic realizations. We may be inspired, 'moved towards Enlightenment,' by an inexhaustible variety of spiritual statements, affirmations, insights, truths, comments, reminders, associations, *expressed in words*. What we're talking about here is the use of verbal formulas in meditation as a means of focussing the mind and 'penetrating the Veil'. These 'extended' *mantras* are known in the Tibetan Buddhist tradition as *dharanis*.

Already the early Mahasanghikas possessed a special collection of mantric formulae in their Canon under the name Dharani or Vidyadhara-pitaka. Dharanis are means for fixing the mind upon an idea, a vision or an experience gained in meditation. They may represent the quintessence of a teaching as well as the experience of a certain state of consciousness, which hereby can be recalled or re-created deliberately at any time. Therefore they are also called supporters, receptacles or bearers of wisdom (*vidyadhara*). They are not different from *mantras* in their function but to some extent in their form, insofar as they may attain a considerable length and sometimes represent a combination of many *mantras* or 'seed-syllables' (*bija-mantras*), or the quintessence of a sacred text. They were a product as well as a means of meditation: 'Through deep absorption (samadhi) one gains a truth, through a dharani one fixes and retains it'.

From *Foundations of Tibetan Mysticism* by Lama Anagarika Govinda (a Western scholar-traveler-practitioner who once identified himself as a reincarnation of a German poet with a Latin name, presumed to have been Novalis).

The words of a *dharani* are something like a 'packaging' for a basic spiritual Truth: they may simply say it, or they may, in addition, convey the tone, the flavor, the attitude, the angle on it, the 'feel' of it, the access to it, the accompanying emotion with its power to reawaken the insight. *Dharanis* provide a focus: a 'snapshot' of a Truth, one way of experiencing that Truth. A *dharani* may be regarded as an epitome or essence or verbal crystallization, or simply a minimal description, of what we perceive or realize in a state of 'super-consciousness'. If, in meditation, the vision starts to fade, we can summon it back, nudge it into sharper focus, or 'fix' it, by repeating the *dharani* silently in our minds. Or out loud. Sometimes it works, sometimes your mind wanders off again. Back to Go.

In his Introduction to Swami Rama Tirtha's *Yoga and the Supreme Bliss*, A.Z. Alston writes:

> The chief spiritual discipline he taught was affirmation of and mentally dwelling upon the final metaphysical truth, followed by the chanting of the holy syllable OM. He suggested the use of very simple formulae, including such alternatives as: 'All power am I,' 'All joy am I,' 'All Knowledge I am,' 'All truth I am.' 'Fearless, fearless I am.' 'No attachment or repulsion, I am the fulfillment of all desires.' 'I hear in all ears.' 'In all minds I think.' 'Sages aspire to know only the truth which is myself.' 'The Life and Light that

shine through the sun and stars am I.' The Swami attached great importance to the chanting of OM three times on each occasion the affirmation was made. These are obviously Upanishadic affirmations aimed at realization of the impersonal Absolute, Brahman Supreme. The technique, however, is the same as the devotee's repetition of the Holy Name of the personal God.

Where *mantra-japa* or *dharani-japa* end and meditation begins is really impossible to say. Absorbed repetition, focussing the mind on a divine Truth, shades off into wordless absorption in that Truth, which is meditation. If extraneous thoughts intervene, meditative concentration is restored by resumed repetition.

There's good material on this subject in SWAMI SATPRAKASHANANDA's excellent book, *Meditation: Its process, Practice, and Culmi-nation.* He stresses the continual abbreviation of prayerful verbal formulas until they finally culminate by zeroing in on the Holy Name. This 'progressive' interpretation is true in principle, of course—the Holy Name really is the 'Divine Essence', 'God Himself', as Burckhardt explains—but not necessarily in practice. 'The Spirit bloweth where It listeth': if there's one room in our lives where the linear and the mechanistic have never entered and never will, its the meditation room—the Oratory of the Heart. *Dharanis* have a very great value, function, power and 'finality' of their own – as Tibetan Buddhists, and I'm sure the Swami, were well aware—and should not be regarded, *in the event*, as nothing more than approximations or rungs on a ladder.

Let's listen to his inspired words. He was obviously a saint:

It is to be noted that prayer does not necessarily mean asking God for something. In a restricted sense prayer means that. But in a wide sense, prayer means a verbal approach to God. You may chant the glory of God; it arouses devotional feeling within you. This is also a prayer. You may sing devotional songs without asking for anything. They are also prayers. So, any verbal approach to God is a prayer. You may say, 'Thou art my Mother, Thou art my Father, Thou art my Friend, Thou art my Companion, Thou art my Knowledge, Thou art my Treasure, Thou art my All-in-all, O God of gods!' without begging for anything. Or you may simply say, 'I bow down to Thee, o Lord. I bow down to Thee, O Lord.'

In the beginning a seeker of God may use many words in his prayer; but as his understanding becomes clearer, as his spiritual feeling deepens and his faith becomes intense, he realizes that all he needs is devotion to God. So he prays to God only for devotion. He simply says, 'O Lord, may I have true love for Thee!'. . . . The prayers become shorter, the devotee does not use too many words. . . . As his spiritual feeling deepens, his prayers become shorter. . . . One or two ideas become the keynote of his spiritual life. . . . Later one or two words became sufficient. . . . 'Have mercy on me'; 'May I see Thee.' Sri. Ramakrishna says God's name is the potent seed of spiritual consciousness.

In case you understand the true significance of the life of Jesus Christ and have devotion to Him, just the word Jesus will be enough for you. . . . Similarly if a person understands the true significance of the life and teachings of Krishna, then the word Krishna will be enough for him. The word Krishna will give rise to all the spiritual thoughts and feelings connected with the spiritual understanding.

The repetition of a single word signifying the Lord, the Holiest of the Holy, just a single word indicative of Divinity, becomes the focal point of one's spiritual life. Then the person continually repeats that Name.

And not only an actual Name. Epithets are also 'names' in their fashion.

As the English word God is signified by different synonyms such as Divinity, Providence, the Almighty, the Omnipresent, the Omnipotent; so there are many words in Vedantic scriptures signifying the Divine Being, such as Vishnu, Narayana, Hari, Bhagavan. They have different shades of meaning, each word fits the particular inner attitude of a devotee.

The supremacy of a Holy Name is certainly not contested. But, as I hope this book will show, there are many other ways, countless ways, of 'naming' the Divine Reality, 'naming' That. For the simple reason that It is Infinite. Infinite and everywhere, within and without, it has even been called, for the very reason that It is Infinite, thc Nameless. Every Name, then: a Name of the Nameless.

> The ones who know say that Allah has three thousand names: one thousand He has revealed to His angels; one thousand He has revealed to His prophets; three hundred are in the zabur—the psalms of David; three hundred are in the Torah; three hundred are in the Gospel; ninety-nine are in the Holy Koran. One, the name of His Essence, He has kept for Himself and hidden in the Koran. . . . There are further names attributed to Allah in the Koran and infinite others which He has revealed to His choice creation.
>
> ~ Sheikh Tosun Bayrak al-Jerrahi al-Halveti

You could even say that anything whatsoever—a flower, a shaft of sunlight, the sound of the stream or the silence of the stars—that reveals God to us is, in that moment of Grace, one of His Names. The whole world sings His Name.

❁

I've gone at some length into the subject of 'extended' *mantras* or *dharanis* because they were instrumental, actually central, in the experience that led to the writing of this book.

Most if not all of the 'chapters' in this book were inspired by, and are commentaries upon, *dharanis* that came to me in meditation—'a product as well as a means of meditation,' as Anagarika Govinda explained. They can equally well be seen as instances of those 'Vedantic truths which appear to them without any effort on their part' that are, according to Madhusudana, offered to 'the worshippers of Lord Krishna.' I offer no apologies (I can't see that I owe any) or explanations (I have none). It just happened. Over a period of some fifteen years. Usually, but not always, I quote the *dharanis* at some point in the chapters, which are really simply commentaries, subsequent reflections upon, interpretations or explorations of the meaning, content and extended implications of the meditative insight epitomized in the *dharani*. Often, as I already mentioned, I substitute the Word 'God' for the Name 'Krishna'. Feel free to replace It. And insofar as the *dharanis* 'worked' for me, and continue to work, they may work for you.

The fact is, I must confess, I learned about *dharanis*, the *bhagavata dharma*, the Personal-Impersonal theme of Vedanta and many other essentials of the Hindu tradition long after, years after, they had already become operative realities in my mind and my practice. That confessed, I have to hope that what you have read so far of the Introduction to this book is sufficient evidence of the commitment to orthodoxy that informs it; in all truth, I see nothing 'personal' in these pages.

❁

But, of course, that depends on how you define 'personal'. Lot's of latitude here.

Let's try a test.

The passage that follows was originally going to be one of the chapters. I decided to incorporate it in the Introduction instead to illustrate the point that the 'practice' this book is about isn't restricted to the meditation room but can become, should become, the drama of our life. The relationship to a Divine Reality, 'Personal-Impersonal', is what our life is all about anyway, already is our real life, 'behind the scenes', whether we know it or not. The thing is to know it. Live it.

Here's the passage:

> Driving the dirt road down the hill early in the morning in the truck ('Old Brown', 1965 Ford half-ton pick-up), curving around by Big Sue's I get the first quick glimpse of the mist floating in the Eel River valley, shimmering in the bright sun like a lake with island hills rising up through its radiant surface, silhouetted against the vivid blue, then under the trees again till I come out in the short steep bumpy stretch heading down to the Four Corners where the log pile has all but returned to the soil, now almost level with the mist trailing by in tendrils across the

meadow below Peter's abandoned windmill, Bear Butte rearing up in the north like a mountain with its peak sliced off, more beautiful things going on with colors and light and clouds and shapes and shadows than I ever have time to take in before I finally plunge into the lake of mist myself on the rutted stretch down Perry Meadow, my son alongside me reading out loud from 'Where the Sidewalk Ends', struggling with the big words. It's about an hour since the end of morning meditation which is always followed immediately by the whirlwind impact of domestic mornings, family life—clothing, breakfast, last minute information, instructions from my daughters, homework business, washing dishes, phone calls, problems, arrangements, looking for things, lunch money or preparation, car keys, cat food, dog food—and this time in the truck is really the first chance I get to recover myself and think again of Krishna. I repeat His Name, my eternal Beloved. The eternal smiling glory beneath the silly, lightweight, inescapable and—because they are the path allotted to us, God's Will—welcome responsibilities of our karma, smiling eternally behind the earth clothed with the beauty of the morning, changeless behind everything and within my own heart. My God, my God. I chant His blessed Name to myself, suppressing tears of joy, carefully correcting my son's errors of pronunciation.

Out by the pump in the afternoon I realize that this moment is all there is and I stop dead in my tracks: this moment is all that can be said now to be 'my life', nothing more, nothing else, nothing left, this is what it's all come to, the rest gone, gone forever except for this and this is a dream: there never was any 'me', there never was anything but this one moment continually assuming different guises in its masquerade as Time. No 'me'! Just this indescribably contentless Now! What is it? It's nothing. And how beautiful it is! I stand, transfixed, my eyes filling with tears of bliss. The sunlight filters down through the gently weaving branches of madrone. I hear the water dripping into the spring box, the sounds of birds. I watch the tremor of the leaves. I am no one. There never was anyone, always no one, never anything but This, Now. Krishna: this is Thy Being, this is the Self. There has never been anything but Thee. The Eternal Beloved, the Self. My God. Walking for the thousandth time down the path by my 'cell' I perceive for the first time the identity of my foot hitting the ground with the ground rising up to meet my foot. I look at the trees and the trees enter my look. I move through the air and the air embraces and gives shape to my movement. I was just a momentary piece of all this, this earth, like a leaf, just one more among the myriad innumerable reflections of the all-pervading Consciousness that give their imaginary containers the fleeting illusion of a separate existence. I feel no different from the mass of soil ten feet beneath the ground. I see my form trudging along as if from a great height, a speck moving across the immense surface of the dream world. There was never anything to worry about, never anything at stake. I am nothing. There is only the Eternal Beloved, the One I love, my Krishna, my God. He is the All.

Back in the kitchen, cooking dinner. I turn on the tape deck and listen to 'My Fair Lady', the Graceland Concert, the Mamas and the Papas, the Jefferson Airplane, Peter, Paul and Mary. Frag-ments of memories of the sixties drift by . . . we thought we were building a new world, a wonderful new world for everyone. We were the future. I chuckle to myself: what 'world'? Indeed we had a lot to learn. I wonder: was God more at home at the Graceland Concert or in Vatican City? Crazy thought! Was it blasphemy? I experience gratitude for the richness of my particular strand of the Cosmic Dream. Then I remember that there is really only one Dreamer. Saute the onions. Cube the tofu. Turn down the flame under the vegetables. They're singing 'California Dream-ing'. I love that tune. I sing along. The dream of 'California'. The dream of 'me'. The Dream that is the All. Krishna, Krishna. All this, and it's all Thee. My Beloved. My God. I say to myself, 'Thou Eternal Beloved, my God.'

Between 'Thou Eternal Beloved' and 'My God' there's a pause. In that pause consciousness descends to the heart and I feel the great Joy, the Silent Presence there, where It always was and always is. I think the words 'My God'. And then it's wordless, and complete, and everything else disappears.

Now, did that seem 'personal'? Sure it did. But was it?

Our lives are a perpetual oscillation between forgetting and remembering the Truth. What Truth? Which Truth? The Truth that there is absolutely no one. That's the Good News! On that Truth the sages are quite comfortably, quite blissfully unanimous. The individual ego is the illusion we have to see through, the dream from which we are to awaken. When we forget the Truth, the illusion of the 'personal' arises; when we remember, the illusion is dispelled. 'The only thing which a man must renounce if he wishes to attain the Supreme Truth is the notion of individuality—nothing else.' (SWAMI RAMDAS) And there's no way to see through that notion until there's no one to see through it. Far out!

There is only the Self. That's the Vedantic revelation, the Truth to which we bear witness. Nothing personal.

So: who wrote that passage?

But this is to anticipate.

✽

Some final details, winding it up.

1. Repetition of a Holy Name, Invocation, *mantra-japa*, is enormously facilitated and enhanced (in mysterious ways) by the use of a *mala*, the Hindu rosary of 108 beads. (Remember that number? The number of the extant Upanishads?) You can buy them in Indian outlet shops; look for the *saris* in the windows. I delight in making my own, go crazy in those amazing bead stores; I have about a dozen. It's a good idea to always be wearing one around your neck. I also carry a 'pocket mala' (my own invention) of 18 beads (18 for the number of chapters in the Gita and also because it's 108 with nothing removed. Get it?) for surreptitious invocation (remembering that Truth) at any time in the day. You don't want to call attention to your piety. The number 108 is divisible by 2, 3, 4, 6, 9, and 12. This makes for great variety of patterned repetitions of combinations of *mantras*.

2. If you're going to be serious about spiritual practice—serious

about being human, in other words—you'll need a special place for daily meditation. Set aside for that purpose alone. And also, with a certain flexibility, a special regular time. This is basic.

3. Joining the group? Group meditation? This is a matter of your own preference, inclinations and circumstances, and your spiritual temperament. If you were the last person alive in the world, or marooned on an island, you might have a hard time being a Christian, but Vedanta would come naturally.

4. We do not enter a spiritual Path in the pursuit of happiness, to relax, to 'center' ourselves or to relieve stress, nor for any other airhead 'New Age' goal. We enter a spiritual Path because we were made for the Truth. The Path is not therapy and it is not easy. It's for people who mean business. People with strength of will. As you will discover, there's something like an 'all the way' you have to go: in prayer, Invocation and meditation particularity, and in the way you gradually restructure your inner life and 'self' definition. You want to be real in this.

5. This book is filled with quotations from the world's spiritual traditions, the other religions. So while it originates in, and seeks to convey, the experience of Hinduism—the great Eastern spirituality to which it pays homage, or tries to pay homage, and which is, I believe, as valid an explanation now, and as glorious and exhilarating a discovery, as it always has been and always will be world without end—it is also a text in comparative religion, from which, I hope, 'the transcendent unity of religions', (title of a book by Frithjof Schuon) and therefore of humanity gradually emerges. We are all One in God, and through divine Love may know that Oneness, and that God.

❁

Without a doubt, anyone trying to write about spiritual experience is on uncertain and very treacherous ground. The only 'hard fact' in a religious universe is Revelation itself, Holy Writ: there are no 'new discoveries' or 'advances' to be made, nothing 'new' in any sense:

accommodations to changing circumstance, but no concessions. We have to continually test and pursue our experience by reference back to the methods and Goals as they have been revealed in Scripture and verified in the practice and testimony of the saints and the sages. The element of uncertainty enters because spiritual experience is not, and cannot be, planned or outlined in advance to accord with doctrine, no matter how traditional the method and aims. It is assessed after the fact.

Nor can we confidently appraise the purity of our own hearts, or even the sincerity of our prayer for that purity. What we can know without doubt in our spiritual experience is, in a sense, confined to that experience itself as it is lived in our aloneness before God. Religious certitude, in other words, is synonymous with religious experience. When we bring that experience out of the shrine, out of the oratory of the heart, and into the light of the common day, even in obedience to what we believe to be the Will of God that we share it, we immediately encounter our own limitations, both of skill and character, the limitations and temptations of language, and the bland ineffaceable ambiguity of the relative world.

The answer to all this is taught in the *karma yoga*. We offer our work to God, without attachment to the results, without concern or investment in the fruit of our labor, its success or failure, and try to perform our work in a sacramental consciousness, our hearts, as it says in the *Gita*, 'fixed on the Supreme Lord.'

I have kept the foregoing provisos in mind, throughout the writing of this book, and struggled both for precision and rectitude. Where I may have fallen short of the mark, I hope the Truth of the Hindu tradition, *sanatana dharma*—and indeed of the Primordial and Universal tradition, Lex Aeterna, Hagia Sophia, Sophia Perennis et Universalis, the Perennial Philosophy—shines through anyway: for It is the Light of the World.

PART ONE

WHAT'S IN A WORD? WHERE ARE MY THOUGHTS?

'The love of God'

What does that mean? What does it look like, feel like? What are we even talking about here? This is the twentieth century. We've come a long way.

We're talking about a self-evident direct experience. It happens in devotional meditation. As practiced by serious people.

In devotional meditation our minds are intensely concentrated upon *the thought of God*, the idea of God, and if we don't know what to think of and have no idea just the *word* 'God'. It's a direction, as it were, a direction of our thought. An attempt, a reaching out into darkness. Our eyes may be closed or we may be contemplating an image or symbol. We're in our meditational setting, the special time and place we've set aside for this purpose, inaccessible, as far as that's possible, to distraction and intrusion.

And something happens. The 'thought' becomes a Presence.

There are many possibilities at this point, We may find ourselves, in this priceless aloneness before God, murmuring a phrase, or just thinking it—'My Beloved', or 'My God', or 'Heart of my heart': whatever—as we often do in response to anything sudden and remarkable. Or maybe we just sit there in rapt silence, stunned, shaking our head in smiling disbelief: this is incredible, this joy, infinite peace, overwhelming love, is absolutely incredible.

We feel actual amazement, gratitude too great to be expressed or gratitude hopelessly unequal to the transcendent immensity of the gift: God's gift of Himself as a Presence which we recognize immediately, with absolute certitude, as that 'Beloved One' Whom the scriptures, saints and sages of the theistic traditions have proclaimed. God's gift of Himself as the revelation of what 'the love of God' means. Amazed relief: we feel the lifting of a burden which was nothing less than our entire life, leaving us now weightless, 'selfless': we *are* 'the love of God'. The love of God, we see clearly, is the Truth. The Answer.

The experience becomes wordless, thought ceases. We dwell in it, float in it, till it fades, then repeat the phrase that originally came to our lips, turn again toward the Presence, toward peace, calm bliss, reunion. And maybe it's there, maybe it's not.

At such times in the back of our minds, or later in retrospect, we know that our love for God is all we have, really, the only thing we can fear to lose, and yet we don't even really 'have' it because it doesn't depend on us. Sometimes it comes, sometimes it doesn't, sometimes the love of God fills our hearts, sometimes we are 'dry'. It vanishes and reappears for no reason we can ever discover. When we try to imagine what it would be like to lose it permanently we feel something like terror, the apprehension of an unendurable desolation: in some sense we would die. It becomes quite natural, urgently obvious, to conclude every meditation with a prayer, a plea, for the continued genius of the name or words which were drawn from us by the love of God always present in our hearts, and which, by His Grace, have the power to reawaken it.

We pray, in other words, for the miracle of *mantra*. Invocation is the spiritual technique for God-Realization specific to the present Age, the 'iron age', or 'kali-yuga', in which the cosmic cycle comes to a close. The love of God is a transfiguring event. There is nothing more precious than the words with which that event was articulated in our souls.

BACK TO REALITY!

If we're in the right mood or worshipful state, the love of God can blossom in our hearts, suddenly fill our hearts with joy, when we pronounce a word or name referring to Him—Jesus, Krishna, Allah, or simply the word 'God'. This has been the direct experience of worshippers for millennia, the *dhikr* of Islam, the *japa* of Hinduism, the Jesus Prayer of the Eastern Orthodox Church, the whole world of *mantras* and invocations. God is mysteriously 'present' in these words and names when they are pronounced with devotion.

Sometimes it goes further. Love of God seems to carry with it a consciousness or intuition of what is genuinely real, meaning changeless and eternal, and not, like everything else we encounter in our vivid baffling lives, merely transient, as well as a profound sense of being real ourselves, being in that moment what we really are and have been all along beneath some kind of ephemeral and insubstantial surface self.

So saying these words and names is like suddenly remembering who we are and what the world really is. We become aware of an infinite blissful beatitude pervading everything, within and without. An eternal invisible Being known as God—now complacently, but perhaps occasionally somewhat uneasily regarded, of course, as a fiction of humanity's fearful ignorant childhood—is felt as our only true Beloved and in that love we inhabit and are one with Reality.

WE'RE ALL IN THIS TOGETHER

Consider the canonical invocation, certainly a *mantra*, 'Blessed be the Holy Name of God.'

The spirit here is impersonal. We invoke the God of all of us, not the personal Beloved prefixed with the possessive pronoun 'my'. We become representative, advocates for all humanity, and praise God's presence among us in His Name—that felt presence which is a ray of the divine beatitude piercing the darkness of our customary semi-consciousness wherever His Name is uttered with devotion.

In the same representative vein, there is also the sense of a collective 'despite all' in this *mantra*. Despite all we go through, all the whole world has gone through, all the absurdity and apparently needless suffering, all the disappointment and tragedy, the dispensing authority of a wisdom beyond our capacity to question is quietly affirmed. 'Thy will be done.' The Name is unconditionally blessed. This orientation to life is implicit in our mortality, in our finitude and ephemerality, and most of us, sooner or later, come to it gracefully and gratefully. Our maturity in spirit is the understanding and acceptance of our true status, of what certain masters refer to as 'the nature of things.'

We bless the Name of God because the Name is His presence among us, in our very hearts. *Mantra* makes that presence as effortlessly available as the thought of a word, like a wish that comes true instantly upon the mere voicing of it. We have to call it a miracle, because it originates beyond the world we physically inhabit, beyond what is explicable according to the ways of that world. Even more to the point, this presence of God in our hearts is what we call Grace, because it's a gift, not an attainment, it's bestowed, not earned. All we can do for our part is turn in the right direction and wait.

GOD GIVES US *INFINITELY* MORE THAN WE ASK FOR!

In the path of devotion we often find ourselves feeling the need to request that our worship be acceptable. *May my worship be acceptable to Thee.* And in the plea, coming from the depths of our hearts, that our worship be acceptable to God, we find a deep peace. We define ourselves and understand ourselves as worshippers, finite, incomplete and dependent—in other words, simply and definitively human—in need of grace, and take our rest in that identity. We can't really know, as a fact, whether our worship is acceptable, or even what that would mean; we are envisioning and petitioning a state which, although we do not doubt its reality, is beyond the scope of our understanding. But we know that to hope for that state, to will it and long for it, is sufficient. No more is asked of us, and when we are doing all that is asked of us we are at peace.

Here, as so often in spiritual life, what counts is a kind of sincerity which is also humility. Our own sincerity can be our refuge. There are times when we realize, right there in the living moment before God, that we are nothing but a plea for His acceptance, that that's all we are.

Sometimes the weight of spiritual aspiration, because the goal is so infinitely beyond us, becomes too great, and we want to place ourselves entirely in the hands of God—a state of soul often called self-surrender. It's as if we're saying, 'I've done, I think, everything I can up to this moment. I place it all before Thee. Now I want to disappear, to exist only in Thy wisdom. I know I'm always there anyway.' We acknowledge the transcendence of the authority that contains the hidden meaning of our lives, our helplessness without grace, our non-existence here below and our real existence in heaven. Our truth is always beyond us, out there in the infinite from which we have only apparently been separated.

Meditation and contemplative prayer, the 'prayer of the heart', are, on one level, an attempt to realize what we are: to stop being what we really aren't, the ego, and become what we really are—a consummation for which every tradition has its own vocabulary. The 'acceptability of our worship' is a metaphor or symbolic expression of that return to our own reality. An approximation, because it is still dualistic, of what is called Self-Realization: the realization, in direct experience, that the worshipper and the Being Who is worshipped are one and the same. It's a renunciation: a confession: an abandonment. A glance at the dazzling radiance on the mountain top.

THE DEFINITION OF GOD: INDISPENSABLE, MIND-BOGGLING, FUTILE

Who, or what, is God?

What follows is the answer of Vedanta, the core spiritual tradition of India, and the background, as it were, the inspiration, of all meditation in that tradition.

God is simultaneously all things, the universe, and the 'uncreated' light of awareness in which all things are suspended. There is only this great Oneness. It's the All. What we see as the ever-unfolding drama of life is actually the dream of an eternal Person, the God we love, Who in His impersonal aspect is the Brahman Who is Atman: the Self of the universe which is also our own true Self—it is in this sense that we are 'made in His image'—the infinite Pure Consciousness in which everything exists, which *is* everything, and which is our consciousness as well.

Beneath and within the spell-binding spectacle, visible to 'the eye of the heart', is the Changeless, the Silence, the absolute Absence that is eternal Presence, the Bliss, *ananda*, in which all things originate: the one I AM: God. Personal and impersonal, Self and world, are One, separable in the discursive mind, inseparable in the Reality which is their Oneness.

The realization that 'God is everything' casts God into the phenomenal multiplicity: the world is divine manifestation. The realization that 'Everything is God' resolves the multiplicity back into God: the world is an illusion, the divine *maya*.

All of which is merely words pointing to the inexpressible. 'Mind and speech return baffled from That,' we read in the Upanishads. And since tradition is unanimous that words are unable to express the divine truths, and tradition is delivered to us by words above all, it is fair to say that language is the insignia both of our divinity and our separation from it—the two sides of our coin and our whole story in a nutshell.

These observations are contradicted by the flat, one-dimensional and purely material experience of daily life in these times, and by the worldview that reflects and reinforces that experience, which is why divine wisdom has about it the air of a comforting secret.

✽

GLINTS & GLIMPSES I

'May Thy Will and My Life be One'

A plea for self-extinction, for the removal of the burden of a false life. (As if it weren't already accomplished!) 'Thy Will is our peace,' as the author of *La Commedia* pointed out.

❁

'May I give myself to Thee utterly'

A variant. The emphasis here is on purity of life. We don't want any part of our life to be claimed by or surreptitiously reserved for manifest deviations from rectitude, behavior clearly reprehensible, shameful, immoral, dishonorable, dishonest, vulgar. Sex and Fun, Wine and Good Cheer and Good Humor, and all the wonderful innocent pastimes, are fine! Life is worth living! But there's a little candle in the background that should always be burning, an awareness of that candle that should never be lost. 'Give Me your whole heart, Love and adore Me, Worship Me always, Bow to Me only, And you shall find Me: This is My promise, Who love you dearly.' Krishna's promise. The gates of heaven were built for us.

❁

'May I serve Thee'

Another variant. We know we have a 'life', on some level, *karma* exists, in its fashion, and we want this life and *karma* to be His, an instrument of His Will. We want to be servants—'slaves of Allah'. Every moment and aspect of an act would be radiant, unchallengeable, exemplary, pure peace, if it were an act in His service. We always feel right, for example, when we are taking care of children, or aged parents, or anyone in need, because we know it would be His Will for us according to His great cosmic law of self-sacrifice. Bearing witness to God is another way of serving Him. 'May I serve Thee' emerges from a profound intuition that everything I do for myself alone, i.e. at the instigation of the ego, the lower self, is worthless. Not sinful, not even 'selfish', but simply unnoted, unrecorded. Not denounced, simply not registered, not registered in heaven. Therefore not an event, nothing at all.

❁

'Thou art the Sovereign Good'

There's a kind of enthusiastic, even *voracious* sadhana that wants to affirm all the divine hypostases, all the 'faces' of God—although since He is fully present in each of them this 'comprehensiveness', while commendable, is in an individual perspective redundant. Knowing even one Name is sufficient.

But richness is still richness. The Name 'Sovereign Good' testifies that the ultimate Reality and creative Source of manifestation is good, and that it rules or prevails in the universe. Therefore God is known as the Sovereign Good. There is an element of awesome majesty here, suggestive of the divine Rigor and Law, but mitigated or balanced by the 'softness', warmth and generosity in the word Good; the legislative and judgmental aspect is permeated by Mercy. When we say 'Thou art the Sovereign Good,' enter the feeling of it, we experience the certitude that the universe is 'in good hands' and comfortably invulnerable to permanent damage, to wounds that will not, no matter how painful, obscene or initially insupportable, heal in the fullness of time: appearances to the contrary notwithstanding. Certitude, and also Joy: a Joy from which a certain hard-edged detachment from earthly affairs is not excluded. Things are as they must be. Or, if they aren't, we know the explanation, the error, the particular submission to Ignorance. The eclipse of the spiritual in our times has drastically simplified the problem of tracing responsibility.

You think of Psalm 19: 'The heavens declare the glory of God, and the firmament showeth His handiwork.' And the Koran: 'All that is in the heavens and the earth glorifieth Allah; and He is the Mighty, the Wise.' To know this order of Truth, and to acknowledge it, is emancipation from the world. If you follow it through to the end. It's a road with hurdles.

❁

'Thou art the Source of all Good'

The good we know, or at least believe we know, here below, in this world. He is its Source, and that is a truth we can know directly, not because we read it somewhere, but because we can see that the presence or quality that inheres in earthly good, that defines it as such for us, is identical to His Presence to us in meditation: a manifestation of It. In meditation we learn what the word means. What is good for us is what He is. It originates in Him and is one form of His Presence among us. Again and again, we come to see how meditation teaches us things, reveals the truths tha8mt tie all things together, that make sense of it all, and one of those truths is that 'good' is His Will. That's why we say 'Thy Will be done,' why Aquinas wrote 'The greatest good for man is to become conformable to the will of God.'

But in the absence of the spiritual experience provided by techniques of the sacred or residence in a traditional society, by entering upon a Path or embracing a doctrine of realization, such an assertion can only seem a mere 'religious' sentiment: one of those 'matters of faith' or soft-headed pieties resorted to by 'religious' people and which are therefore, by contemporary definition and consensus, 'objectively' meaningless. And so be it. To suggest that a return to Divine Wisdom will provide solutions to the galaxy of dilemmas that plague the world is, in present circumstances, sufficiently laughable. Even the gentle intimation that a departure from Wisdom might lie at the root of our dilemmas is clearly discountable because just as clearly translatable to the naivete of maligning Progress, of wilfully dissenting from or failing to grasp the obvious basic truth of our times implicit in the phrase 'the *price* of Progress'.

Misguided worlds become genuinely beyond remedy, things can get out of hand, go too far. 'So foul a sky clears not without a storm'. A memorable line from one of the history plays.

❁

'How can I love Thee enough?'

A rhetorical question, wrenched from our hearts in the blazing clarity of the knowledge, revealed by love itself, of our limitations. We can't. We located (or were located by) an Infinity. His Infinity was revealed by our love, and we want to rise to the occasion, but we know we can't. A love commensurate to what we have received and what He is, commensurate to the relationship, commensurate to the immeasurable, is utterly beyond the speck of nothingness we feel ourselves to be.

But then think this: 'Thou art all my love, All the love I have is Thine.' It's not 'enough', but it's all we have. We declare His exclusivity, our total self-giving, our complete surrender to His infinite irresistible attraction. There are no competitors, no rivals. Our love is really our selves, our very hearts, offered to Him without reservation. We find our rest in Him, in His Peace, in His unique identity with the absolute immortal Reality.

The syntax supports a second meaning here. God *is* our love, He is the love with which we love Him. The first interpretation is self-surrender, the second invokes His presence within us.

Non-dualism, the Vedantic *advaita*, is the only answer to 'How can I love Thee enough?' *Bhakti* culminates in self-extinction, union, identity. The question disappears with the questioner.

❁

'To have known Thee...'

What can anything else matter? To have known God, to have known *of* God, is all that counted. Everything else was, comparatively speaking, nothing, everything else was transient, it simply came and went, but this was eternal, this was *real*. To have known God is the one and only victory, the one and only true joy, and there, in meditation, we can see it clearly, we can know without a doubt that 'we' made it. (More accurate, of course, to say 'it happened.') There's nothing to sum up about a human life but 'God was known' or 'God wasn't known': this seems an inescapable conclusion. (From our side of the river. We may or may not know God, but God certainly knows us, and our truth in the final analysis is His Knowledge, not ours. In other words, His Mercy is infinite, and mysterious are His ways.) We dwell upon our indescribable good fortune, a stroke of simply incredible good luck. We were blessed. What can compare with it? Nothing.

So we linger, in the silence and the candle-light, in the sense of blessedness in God, a blessedness that simply annuls everything else in the biography, and marvel over the miracle of gnosis, spiritual knowledge. In this identity alone, as knowers of God, did we truly exist: such is His gift to us: existence: the true existence, our true existence, what is alone existence, which He is: Life Eternal. By stating it in the past tense, 'To have known Thee,' as if we are reviewing our life story at the moment of death, the *mantra* generates the whole picture, the whole truth of our lives. To have known God was everything. It's that genuine knowledge, the only true knowledge there is, gnosis, in which we, who never really existed, disappear into the Unutterable we always were.

DEVELOP A GOOD MEMORY

To see God, to love God, to be with God.
To see Thee, to love Thee, to be with Thee.

This is the goal, this is what we long for. To remember that it has actually happened, that it's possible, and to know that it can happen again—this is joy. We linger over the memory, we dwell upon the true purpose of our lives. This is all we ask for, this is all we want, nothing more. This is everything to us.

We may think:

> In the silence of my shrine, in the candlelight, you have come to me, I remember it. You were a Presence, an image made of stars, an infinite radiance. You were heaven. You were the Lord.

We may meditate upon the definition of the goal, upon the eternal possibility of the divine vision, as a strategy for realizing it. We know, with absolute certainty because it's 'worked' before, that the thought of the consummation can *become* the consummation if we can hold it steadily in our minds, thinking of nothing else. The memory can become a present reality if we can focus upon it, immerse ourselves in it: we gaze at it with a shining unwavering wonder, dwell in the marvelling at it. The feeling is something like, 'What could be more wonderful? What can hope to compare with this?' Knowledge of the goal, the arrival at certitude, is already a foretaste of the joy it will bring, A part of us is at peace simply in knowing what peace is, in being able to define it. Memory of the Presence is an edge of it, a faint flickering thrill in the heart, a spark.

THAT VERY HEAVY *TULSI* LEAF

The legend has it that Krishna, the Hindu avatar of God, placed Himself in one pan of a balance and the Holy Name, written on a *tulsi* leaf, was placed in the other pan. And the Holy Name went down.

Repeating a name of God and experiencing the love of God can become so inseparable that we actually find ourselves loving the Name itself. Love of God and love of the Name became identical, or at least indistinguishable. We may even, at times, find ourselves unable to 'locate' God anyplace else outside of His Name. If love of God and love of the Name—which always means *saying* it, mentally or audibly—become identical, than God and the Name become identical also. And that this is what actually happens is precisely what tradition and immemorial experience affirm.

But the power of the Name is not autonomous. An intuition of the Love that pervades the universe—and, as we may ultimately realize, *appears as* the universe—is the precondition for successful invocation. The Name will not 'work' if the love of God, or the desire to love God, is not present already to a degree. *Mantra* practice is definitely not mechanical; in the absence of devotion, or at least some kind of feeling, the Name will fall quite flat, reduced to a mere sound. But if love is latent, waiting to emerge, if your heart is in it, the Name then focuses and expresses that love: liberates and expands it. The love was like a smouldering ember and the Name a fan. Then it happens: the love, in turn, flows back into the Name, donating more power to it. The Name fills our hearts, the love of God fills our hearts, and a current flows in both directions between the two, ever stronger, till love of God and the Name of God, together filling the universe, become One. They become the All.

In the practice of invocation, we feel that we only know God, only know we love Him, only know what He can be in our direct experience, if the Name 'works': if we are profoundly moved, to the very depths, and a Presence, both within our hearts and mysteriously 'everywhere', shines through the Name. We feel then that we only met God through His Name, were drawn to God by something in that very word, some resonance or aura. In a way, it is through the love of God in His Name that we first know He is real.

The Name is honoured, praised, its power recognized, in all the world's religions. 'Hallowed be Thy Name' is the first statement of the Lord's Prayer. The 40-page colophon concluding Whitall Perry's magnificent thousand-page Treasury of Traditional Wisdom is devoted exclusively to the Invocation of the Holy Name. In the words of a great contemporary master, FRITHJOF SCHUON:

> Lastly, we must emphasize the fundamental and truly universal significance of the invocation of the Divine Name.... It is in the Divine Name that there takes place the mysterious meeting of the created and the Uncreate, the contingent and the Absolute, the finite and the Infinite. The Divine Name is thus a manifestation of the Supreme Principle, or to speak still more plainly, it is the Supreme Principle manifesting Itself; it is not therefore in the first place a manifestation, but the Principle Itself.

As we read in the Taittiriya Upanishad, '*OM is Brahman.*'

So we adore the Name and acknowledge its independent right to our worship. He has given Himself to us in His Name. Ordinarily, repetition is mental, but there are times when the love of God can become so great, when we simply feel it so intensely, that we know that if we say the Name aloud, if only in a murmur, quietly but audibly, just once, our hearts will melt utterly, an unimaginable 'maximum' of joy will be experienced: some indescribable timeless Event will occur: everything illusory and transient will collapse into the nothingness it always was, leaving only the Real. At that moment, we feel we will be addressing Him directly. Realizing His Complete Presence.

And sometimes we say it, and sometimes we don't.

ON THE ROAD TO YOURSELF

The first gift of God in exchange for our sincerity is our reality. Before God we become real.

In prayer and meditation everything accidental about us—the details of an individual life, everything that makes us appear particular and unique, our 'personality', the person our friends believe they know so well—gradually fades away and we emerge as what we truly and always really are: a human soul here in the universe and present before God. We become essential, generic, universal, representative, archetypal. Given the usual sea of troubles and worries, plaintive anticipations and subterranean apprehensions, in which the illusory individual self is customarily swimming around, this comes as a tremendous relief.

We become humanity. Not yet the Self, but not the self either. Rather something in between, *en route* from the latter to the former: a worshipper, a confession, a candidate, an appeal for Grace. And in this state we know ourselves to be in the same boat with everyone else, indeed identical with all others, for this state is everyone's truth, their potential whether realized or not. We are aware then of God as an over-arching all-pervading loving Presence in which all distinctions disappear. In Him we receive the gift of oneness with all beings, a truth in heaven which becomes a reality on earth when we turn to Him with devotion.

It's important to understand in what sense God makes us real, because our awareness of oneness with all emerges from it; from the intuition of who, or what, we really are which is given to us by God in return for the sincerity of our worship. There is room for misconceptions here.

To present ourselves before Him in sincerity means to discard every layer of our social selves, our 'worldly' selves, to remove the masks we wear in social situations and even, although to a lesser extent, when we are alone. Undiluted honesty. It is definitely not the ego, the psychological self which 'pours its heart out' to a therapist, and for two big reasons. First, because the ego is precisely the 'lower self,' composed of fears and desires, which divine wisdom unanimously declares we are not; second, because this self is always defined by the past, by time—it's actually what we call our 'biography'—and is therefore a mental construct, whereas presentation before God always happens now, in immediacy, in a pure Present sometimes called 'the Eternal Now'. Our true reality is always *now*. The real and the present are metaphysically synonymous. Discourse with God is neither calculated nor restrained.

This unmasking of the soul can occur because God is 'the Absolute'. A metaphysical term meaning totally independent and self-determined, the Absolute is beyond everything relative and contingent; it's the 'feel' behind words like Infinite, Eternal, Everlasting, Truth with a capital T. The Absolute, quite simply, is the invisible Reality behind the visible universe *and within ourselves* because we are 'made in His image.' When we are in touch with our genuine humanity we have an intuition of it, we know there's 'something' beyond all this, whether we call It God or Buddha Nature or Tao or the Good or Love or the Great Spirit.

To long to be real is to long to present ourselves before the Absolute, before God. It's the same longing. Our longing for God is the longing to escape from everything relative and consequently compromised, insubstantial, ephemeral and impure, partial and finite, all of which we are vaguely yet unwaveringly convinced is beneath us, unworthy of us, a flickering seemingly inexhaustible inconsequence, and become, instead, what we really are. The companion promises of the world, that things are what they appear to be and will be durable in our lives, are always broken. This treachery of 'the relative world' is our daily experience; our loss of innocence is recognition of that treachery, as sophistication and worldly wisdom are our adjustment to it.

Our intuition of the Absolute, as a matter of fact, precedes our relationship to a personal deity. We encounter the Absolute, before we call It 'God', as an unwavering and incorruptible surveillance within us before which we have no secrets and wish none, and with which we are at peace. It used to be called, in the derivative sense of 'conscience', 'the angel on your shoulder,' 'the still small voice'. Outwardly, we intuit the Absolute in our awe before Nature, Creation, Existence, in the impulse to revere and adore an invisible transcendent Majesty behind the visible world, to bow down before, worship and in some sense obey an infinite Source or Center, a supreme Authority, beyond the power of our minds to grasp.

In a word, we came to realize, as our lives deepen, that the person we really are is the person who prays. Our other identities are all, in varying degrees and without prejudice, artificial, expedient, ephemeral.

Sometimes I try to imagine the expressions that might appear on my friends' faces if they experienced a spiritual awakening. W's face, peaceful and radiant. B's face, fearless at last. All would know. All would be at rest in the divine wisdom. Everyone whole, therefore at one with one another. We wouldn't have to be ironic anymore.

Those transfigurations, though unlikely in these times, are always possible. Separateness and individual biography are a dream from which devotional meditation, the love of God, is the awakening.

WE SEE BETTER WHEN OUR EYES ARE CLOSED

The love of God is like a light in which the true 'state of affairs' becomes visible. Love illuminates the world.

As we sit in meditation feeling the love of God surging and ebbing within us, rising and subsiding and rising again like the wind, and as we feel ourselves identified with that love, being that love, we find ourselves at the same time learning things, seeing things, acquiring that knowledge which is called spiritual. It is this above all, the idea that one can learn anything about the world while sitting with one's eyes closed, 'doing nothing', that is incomprehensible and unacceptable to the prosaic and scientific intelligence. But it's a fact. In a way, it's the whole thing about meditation, the whole purpose of contemplative practice. Truths about the universe, about who we are, where we are and what we are, which in the ordinary state of consciousness are not even conceivable, literally unthinkable, become obvious, transparently self-evident.

For example:

We realize in meditation—see it as clearly as a fruit held in the palm of the hand, as the familiar Hindu simile goes—that everything is 'within God'. We find ourselves murmuring, in our minds, spontaneously, because we see it, blissfully, because it's joy beyond expression, 'All is within Thee.' In the back of our minds the Gospel words, 'In Him we live and move and have our beings.'

At the same time, in the same insight, with the same certitude, we realize that God is 'within us' and within everything, the Soul of the universe. In the back of our minds now the Gospel words, 'The kingdom of heaven is within you,' as well as the unanimous assurance of all religions on this fundamental point. *Intra te quaere deum.*

But if both assertions are true, that God is both 'without' all and 'within' all, then the distinction between 'without' and 'within' is seen to be illusory. The outer and the inner are one. The so-called objective world and the world in consciousness are one. And now we see clearly why it is truly said that Brahman is Knowledge, the Self is all, and everything is God. The consequences in our lives of such an insight, the reverberations in the future, are incalculable.

In devotional meditation the truths we read in scriptural texts are perceived directly.

Nothing is ever the same again.

Once, when I felt this particular insight deeply enough to write about it without losing it, I wrote these words:

> All is within Thee. Everything is Thy Presence. The crickets I hear now at twilight, the sky dark blue turning to pale azure in the west over King's Peak, the sound of my daughter practicing the piano, the notes drifting across the meadow, the gold glow of the kerosene lamp up here in the loft, my reflection in the window, the past etched on my face, the always unwavering sense of my own existence and the existence of the brilliant vast universe out there . . . all is Thee, all is Thee. From the beginning this was the dispensation. What is there to be concerned about? Where does my mind end and the world begin? Who writes these words?

Thou art within all. We are never alone. I remember Swami Swananda saying those same words, as if to himself, in the kitchen of the Vedanta Center: We are never alone. 'Thou alone art, Thou the Light Imperishable, Adorable—Great Glory is Thy Name.' Who can bear the joy of the miracle that Thou art within us, the joy that floods our hearts in the moment of experiencing it directly, without dissolving in tears? I am one with all those who have known it.

Darkness now. A sea of black pressing against the window pane. I'll see the stars when I go out.

These times of silence with Thee are the whole worth of life.

TWO? ONE? HOW MANY?

Sometimes, in devotional meditation, when the universe appears as nothing but an infinite love which is silence and an infinite silence which is love, we find ourselves mentally murmuring phrases like, 'You are in my heart,' 'You are my very heart,' 'God of my heart'. The faint smile, the inward ocean of bliss.

A loving oneness with God, tranquil and self-assured, is the deep feeling, the conviction, of these affirmations. They're like an oath of fidelity, sworn directly to the Being in Whom our faith is placed, in Whom our lives originate and are sustained, Who is the Source of everything. This is the first or immediate joy when we think these words: the direct offering of our fidelity. And we also feel joy—taking a step back, as it were—in the awareness of the act itself, the act of offering, in the knowledge that 'I am one for whom God is everything,' 'I am one who holds God in his heart.'

The presence of God, 'responding' to the love which is actually God's gift to us, is intimate in an absolute sense. It takes possession of the center of our being, which humanity has been unanimous in calling our Heart, and fills us completely. God's complete possession of us then is experienced as 'our' possession of God. He is 'mine', as in 'Nearer, my God, to Thee'. A sense of mutual possession arising from union, from identity.

But let's examine what is actually happening here. It is this: we only think of ourselves as 'His' and of Him as 'ours' because there aren't really and never were two here, as we experience it and try to express it, but One. There were never two, but always One. That actual Oneness, where there is the illusion of duality, of two, is experienced as a force—it's the supreme Force in the universe, actually, the divine Reality or Truth itself—which we call 'love' drawing the illusory 'two' together. But there never were two, there always was and forever is only One. We call that Oneness Love, we call it God.

❁

GLINTS & GLIMPSES II

DREAMER, DREAMER, ETERNAL DREAMER,
ETERNAL DREAMER, ETERNAL DREAM.

As with many *mantras*, there's a crooning, musing feeling in these words. A lingering feeling, like a drifting into trance, absorbed reverie. Dreamlike, as a matter of fact and appropriately. It's the repetition, the suggestion of an incantation. There are really only two words.

The decisive element is contained in the word 'eternal'. The dimension of timelessness, endlessness, is introduced into the metaphor of the Dream. *Maya* is without beginning and end so long as we project linear temporality into the Eternal Present of the Self; it's never-ending. The only way we'll ever get out of it is by Awakening.

❁

There's a beautiful illuminating analogy, relevant here, I came across in one of Frithjof Schuon's beautiful books. 'God became man that man might become God,' the classic Christian summary attributed to more than one saint, is juxtaposed with 'The Self became the Heart that the Heart might become the Self.' When we dwell upon the stupendous fact that the infinite transcendent unknowable Being or Reality behind the illusory universe actually cares about 'us', actually *loves* 'us', dwell in other words upon what is called 'the miracle of Grace', the tears of love flow readily. We know our status and stature, know the glorious Truth. That Self is the Dreamer Who is alone awake and wills 'our' Awakening, having created us to that end alone, Dreamer and Dream being One.

❁

'But the Dream, the Dream...'

This is a quotation from Buck's great translation of *Ramayana*. Rama says it, towards the end of the story, in a context which leaves its actual import somewhat ambiguous—at least in Buck's translation, which is really more like a re-telling.

An interpretation came immediately to my mind, however. I take it to mean that despite the glory of God, which is the only Reality, despite the Self which is alone real, this world, even while we concede it to be a dream, is too compelling, too marvellous, to renounce absolutely. How can we turn our backs on this incredible story, this miracle, this world? Walk away from this music, the sea and the stars, the Earth and Humanity, acknowledge that it's not our home but a place of exile and bondage? And the impulse is correct, doctrinally correct. For the saint who sees God everywhere, who is one with the immortal Self, there is no world to renounce, no Dream to affirm.

❁

'To remember Thee, to remember Thee'

If we find that—for reasons sometimes painfully obvious and at other times utterly inscrutable, utterly undiscoverable—we cannot feel love for God, we can at least dwell upon the *idea* of it, our memories of it. We can recall what a marvellous thing it is, what an excellent goal, what a priceless gift it is. The mere thought is a consolation, the mere recollection that it is possible. And can happen again.

❁

'It is a Dream of Love.'

The world is both pervaded by and a manifestation of 'His Love' which He is. (And, as I feel enjoined to tirelessly insist, can be directly experienced as such in devotional meditation, we can see it: scientific instruments, even the most up-to-date lasers and optics, cannot detect it, just as an MRI or a CAT-scan cannot reveal the Self.) The Love that is God appears to us as this world, and that appearance includes 'us' as well.

Love is the lesson we are taught by our existence in this Dream. The world is the form, the medium, in which Love is revealed to us. 'It is a Dream of Love' focuses our minds on this moment of insight into the nature of the Dream, the nature of the world. It's a moment that can be prolonged, repeated, re-experienced. An eternal insight. The Dream is motivated by Love. 'I was a hidden treasure, and I wanted to be known, so I created the world.'

'I was a hidden treasure
And I wanted to be known,
So I created the world.'
Picture that engraved in stone:

It's the hadith qudsi—Word of God
Not found in the Koran—we see
Most often, and with good reason.
It's the whole answer, it's the key.

You should know immediately
It has to be true. We know it's true
Because it's true. How so? Why is that?
We have a gift. All of us. You too.

'*Aham eva sarvam*: I am the All'

The world is not different from me.
I used to think it was,
But now I know better.
I am the dream.
I myself am all this.

I love it, as I always have,
But not in the same way.
Before (it's a struggle to remember now)
I was a bit afraid
Of the world I loved—

Because I thought
It was different from me.
And you can't really know, and trust,
Something that's different from you.
You tend to be selective, cautious. You over-react.

My enthusiasm was excessive,
And quickly exhausted. My joy
Was a bit shrill, sometimes forced.
I was in a false position
And didn't know it.

The world seemed so much greater than me.
I felt I had to make a place
For myself in it, and might fail.
It responded to my love
With brilliant indifference,

As if I didn't exist.
I felt that I was nothing
And the world was everything.
Now I know
It's the other way around.

Now my love for the world

Is weightless, effortless, detached.
I am that love,
And the world is a dream,
And I am that dream as well.

What I love is a dream.
There's nothing at stake.
My love is a faint smile,
An infinite tenderness pervading
The bliss of Oneness with the Truth.

'Thou art the Dreamer, Thou art the Dream'

God is the Dreamer, God is the Dream. You see it clearly, enter into it, enter heaven, adore it: the world, no longer the objective 'thing' out there but unveiled in its truth, becomes the Oneness, God.

The feeling may be intimate, personal, the unity of Dreamer and Dream appearing as the living presence of the Beloved. Or it may be celebratory, carrying a sense of awe, the unity now a transcendent impersonal splendor, the Splendor of the Real. Undoubtedly there are still other ways it could come across, other angles, flavors, avenues of entry. Spiritual experience is a symphony of fine distinctions, nuances, subtlety *par excellence*. There's no reason to expect or require spiritual life to be any less textured than our profane adventures. On the contrary: the protagonist is the same, and this is the supreme journey, the supreme experience. You put your whole self into it. Our transactions with divinity can be as exquisitely refined as Asian art, as intricate and multi-layered as the French cinema between 1930 and 1945. Even surpass them!

'Glory of Glories, Eternal God'

Look up from the task, stare into space, and repeat to yourself a *mantra* of praise, a Holy Name. How can you keep from smiling? Here is Reality. Then you return, with one more drop of detachment in your reservoir.

❁

CHUANG TZU'S BUTTERFLY, PROSPERO'S FAREWELL, CALDERON'S EPIGRAM

Often, in meditative reverie, the world we have always identified with 'solid reality' takes on a dream-like quality, and sometimes, in our entranced contemplation of the 'dream', we discover in ourselves an overwhelming love for it, as if in redemptive compensation, or compassion, for its apparent loss of stature. Yes; it was, all along, only a dream—but we love it beyond words.

What is at question here, of course, is the status of the world.

In the literature of the Vedanta, and of Buddhism as well, we are consistently assured that the world is 'not real'. We also hear it said that the world is not absolutely *un*real, but that it is *neither* real nor unreal. And sometimes it is asserted that the world is neither real nor unreal nor both nor neither. The cryptic assertions we come across in these texts, such as 'There is no world' or 'I am the universe' or 'Everything is God', are helpful (in one sense!) in their uncompromising contradiction of everything that appears obvious or logical to us, but they are clearly proof that both the status of the world and the experience that reveals it are beyond anything language can convey. These 'definitions' point at the direct experience of the masters and sages, what they 'realized' in meditation, and the masters and sages always tell us that if we wish confirmation of their claims we must ourselves enter upon the ancient and arduous Path. We must meditate.

But on a verbal level, accepting its limitations, the analogy of the dream has proven useful, and for an obvious reason: 'dreamlike' is precisely our experience of the world in meditative reverie when we approach the 'vision of Reality'. The comparison calls for itself.

Let's examine this analogy. A dream is called 'unreal' because reality is equated with waking experience: the dreamer, not the dream, is real. With respect to waking experience, then, the dream is called unreal. In itself, however, no one denies that it is a real experience: it is a real experience, but it's not this other thing we call reality. And this is precisely what is meant when the Eastern sages claim that the world is unreal: it's a real experience, this world of our physical senses, but it isn't the Reality, a Something which is one level 'above' that waking world in the same way that the waking world is one level 'above' our dreams. In Vedantic terms that Something is the Self, or Brahman Supreme; in the language of theism it is simply God; in the language of metaphysics it is the Absolute. For Buddhists it is the Void which is Suchness, or Buddha-Nature; for Taoists it is the Eternal Tao of Heaven and Earth.

If this world is not the Reality, then what is it?

It is an apparent transformation of that Reality. Or a manifestation of that Reality. It is an appearance within or upon that Reality, totally derivative, totally dependent, and totally illusory in the sense that there is never anything actually 'there' but that Reality, 'appearing' as a world. (Vedantic texts refer to it as 'the world-appearance'.) The rope lying in a dark corner of the room mistakenly perceived as a snake is really a rope and never was anything but a rope. When we realize what it really is it looks exactly the same.

In terms of our analogy, the world we call real is still one step removed from Reality. There is a Dreamer—a Pure Consciousness, an Infinite Consciousness, a Self, or God or Supreme Person—in Whom this world appears, Its 'dream', and that Dreamer is alone real in the fullest sense, or in a 'higher' sense than the dream, because that Dreamer alone endures, remains the same forever, 'from everlasting to everlasting', while everything else merely comes and goes, 'the passing show'. Like the dreams we ourselves dream, this world, called *maya* or *samsara* in Eastern texts, is neither real nor unreal. A truth with consequences of infinite import in our lives. The Self, the Dreamer, is Reality. *And that Reality, that Self, is what 'we' really are.* Who else could we be? Think it through:

> If this is a dream, then our closest proximity to the Dreamer—indeed our identity with the Dreamer—must be within, must be our own consciousness, our awareness of things, our very self: the deep impersonal non-individuated Presence we become aware of and become when the surface mind is completely stilled. Hence 'made in His image', the imago dei. Hence the yoga

> system of Patanjali, the Zen Doctrine of No-Mind, the Remembrance of the Sufis. The kingdom of heaven, which is the Reality, is within us, as we are assured by Christ. 'I am seated in the hearts of all,' says Krishna in the Bhagavad Gita. 'Closer to you than the jugular vein,' as we read in the Koran.

But everything is pretty close here—the Dream, the Dreamer, 'us'. It's all *one*, really. And we love this world, this Dream, because love is 'the feel' of oneness—just as oneness is 'the feel' of love.

COLE PORTER'S QUESTION (FIRST NOTE B-FLAT IN THE KEY OF C!)

'What is this thing called love?' Cole Porter's question.

In meditation we realize, with cast-iron finality and absolute certitude, that the love of God is so infinitely beyond anything we've previously thought of as 'love' that we ought to reserve the word for that alone. Everything becomes One, the universe, our hearts, God: all one infinite Light, one infinite Joy.

But down here on this level, as it were, the level of our daily lives, is a kind of love, neither acquisitive nor misinformed, which might be called 'enlightened love.'

This would be, first of all, love of truth. Truth in any context. Christ, Krishna, the Buddhist Dharma, the Quran: all identify themselves as Truth. The word disappears into the infinite. Then love of whatever is beautiful: from the beauty of nature to the beauty of the virtues, of goodness. Love of nobility, simplicity, depth, wisdom, restraint, humility, meaningfulness. Love of the wholeness of things, the existence of things. Love of humankind. Love could be called enlightened when its object elevates the soul, illumines the soul, and is loved for that very reason. When we experience this kind of love in the heightened awareness of meditation, we realize that these 'objects' of our love, because they awaken us to the sense of something within us and in the universe which is beyond our mundane lives, more 'real' than visible things, point us in the direction of the transcendent, the divine, the eternal: they are, as the phrase goes, 'of God'. You could put it this way: we realize that whatever we love with a pure heart is an invitation from heaven. And since invitations from heaven are simultaneous and ultimately identical with the response within us, they reveal our oneness with God.

Enlightened love has a practical side as well—always keeping in mind that the 'practical/impractical' distinction usually conceals a prejudice against contemplative life. Because, contrary to the prevailing consensus and despite its (secretly alarmed) self-assurance, the world is actually Spirit, the full or final understanding of any human moment or event only occurs on the spiritual level. This is not to deny the dignity or importance of secular contributions to our understanding of human affairs, but simply to point out that the spiritual interpretation is ultimately the true one, the 'final say', because it goes deepest. It breaks through the crust of accidence and relativity and casts light upon the inner structures of human experience where our truth resides. It tells us what's really, decisively, going on in our lives by referring us to the wisdom traditions—the Law or Gospel, the Word, the Tao, the Teaching or Immortal Dharma—which explain us to ourselves, illuminate our experience, because they alone, as 'revealed', know what we are.

This means that whatever we may have thought the issue was at the outset divine wisdom either corroborates or corrects that interpretation and enlightened love, in one form or another, points to the answer, directs us to the heart of the matter. Enlightened love works this way because it's a ray of the divine love which 'conceived' Creation and holds it together by knowing and affirming the fulfillment of all its members—even, sometimes, in ways that don't 'make sense' to us. It's enlightened love that urges us, for example, to 'forgive and forget', 'pocket our losses', 'flow with it', that teaches 'Those who blame don't understand, those who understand don't blame.' The parables of Jesus, of course, come to mind, and the Dhammapada.

Wherever our humanity correctly perceives itself, wherever we rise to our true estate, our whole concern is with the divine Presence that pervades the world. Everything is defined and explained by the truths we are perceiving, right there in the living moment, in the light of that Presence. We see the spiritual dimension which was the heart of the matter all along, the intention embracing and expressing itself, pursuing itself, behind the turbulent facade of human affairs. We bow our heads before the unfailing presence of the Infinite.

EXILE, ILLUSIONS, AND OUR WELL-INTENTIONED FRIENDS

In worship, in meditation, prayer and the contemplation of God, we feel we are in the center of our being, that we have returned from an outer exile of which we were unaware to some kind of 'inner home'. The feeling might be articulated, 'Where I worship Thee, there is my heart.'

One of the supreme gifts of worship is the awakening to this very fact of exile and return. We realize that *this* (of which I was ignorant until I entered upon the Path) is Reality, this is Light, Truth, Love, Joy. Peace, Life Eternal, the heart of the universe and the universe itself, while *that* (the daily mundane existence which I thought was real until I entered upon the Path, *which had me in its clutches*) is ultimately nothing: a dream, an appearance, a passing illusion where all that seems so solid and substantial and compelling to my anxious or enthusiastic engagement is merely a sequence of images that come and go, came and went, totally dependent upon an infinite 'ocean of consciousness' or eternal changeless Witness of all things which is my very Self. We realize, now in direct experience, the Teaching.

I once thought my heart was in poetry, creativity. Art; I thought my heart was in political insurgence, 'the movement', 'the revolution'; I thought my heart was in the cultural revolt, 'the sixties'; I thought my heart was history, the aspiration of humanity, the human drama; I even thought my heart was romance. (*I'll Take Romance!*—Ben Oakland and Oscar Hammerstein II, 1937.) I gave my heart to these sirens; and they, true to themselves and to me, revealed to me, in their apparent betrayal, my error. There was nothing there. No time wasted, no regrets—but the affairs of this world, of our life in this world, are not where it's at.

To be free of the world, through knowing what it is, is to have the strength to regard it impassively, with detachment, and thereby to act within it meaningfully, realistically, effectively, with wisdom and compassion, When we're no longer the slaves of what we want to do, because we want nothing, of who we think we are, because we know who we really are, we're free to choose what's best or wisest, which is the secret of living in peace with ourselves and others. We've realized, in other words, that all that matters is already settled, and has been throughout all eternity. 'All that matters' is, quite simply, our life in God. 'All that matters' is orienting our entire life toward the changeless Reality in our hearts, the Self, the 'fountain of bliss.'

That Reality in its personal aspect, when it reaches out to us in this dream world projected by our innocent folly, is called redemptive grace. Krishna, the Teacher and Avatar of God in the Bhagavad Gita, says to us:

You find yourself in this transient joyless world.
Turn from it, and take your delight in Me.

This delight, which we find in the love of God, is also, as Krishna implies, knowledge of the distinction we've been talking about here: between exile and home, the unreal and the Real, the world and God. You could even say that we experience 'delight' in the worship of God *because* it carries with it the direct and dazzling perception of Reality, of 'That', the divine, which enables us simultaneously to perceive 'the world' for what it is, a dream of transience and mortality from which we may awaken, and in that very awakening learn the secret of fulfilling our responsibilities within it.

Our well-intentioned friends, who love us and whom we love, may suggest to us, or think to themselves, that our life in meditation and contemplation is a flight from reality, 'denial'. But Reality is precisely what we now have entered, giving us the perspective from which to observe with calm compassion their latest excited undertaking, their intense fleeting commitments and short-lived passionate enthusiasms, and to laugh along with them at the increasingly ironic remarks with which they take jabs at their fantasies and growing weariness and acknowledge their growing readiness for something durable to hang their lives on.

But you know, not everybody comes around to it. Some people think the Super Bowl is important right up to the day they die. The liberating potential of disillusionment is powerless before a series of compelling, diabolically orchestrated illusions which has no end. Continually distracted by the blare and dazzle of what might be called, in our society, the 'universal happiness advertisement,' spiritual readiness, sadly enough, is repeatedly seduced back into its inverted image: the worldly hope that methodically, even eagerly, eventually desperately, welcomes one doomed expectation after another.

ONE MORE REASON NOT TO WORRY

Here's the paradox:

On the *one* hand, God is real and the world unreal. The Eternal and the Transient, The Real and the Apparent, the Absolute and the Relative, the Infinite and the Finite, the Dreamer and the Dream, Atma and Maya.

On the *other* hand, God *is* the world, there is nothing *but* God, the Self, the Infinite Consciousness, and Atma and Maya are *One*.

The Sanskrit *mantra* enunciating the first great metaphysical truth is *Brahman satyam, jagan mithya*: Brahman is real, the world is not.

The Sanskrit *mantra* enunciating the second great metaphysical truth is *Sarvam idam brahma*: All this is Brahman.

And we live with this paradox, this and many others. Spiritual knowledge is replete with paradoxes: apparently contradictory truths affirmed in scripture and directly experienced in meditation. Sometimes one, sometimes the other. In the previous entry (and in 'Chuang-Tse's Butterfly, etc.') we talked about the first truth, *Brahman satyam, jagan mithya.* We can also directly experience the second. The world is God.

The feeling is wonderment, inexpressible appreciation, a joy so pure and calm it's almost tangible. The divine Presence is everywhere, all-pervading, all we have to do to become aware of it is love God. And when we love God we always realize immediately that He is everything. It works in reverse as well: to sense the divine Presence in all things is to awaken divine love, to immediately experience the 'collapse' of the ego and the transformation of the entire inner being into infinite love.

This realization, like many others we arrive at in devotional meditation, implies and refers back to the prior unarticulated state of consciousness—the worldly mind, occupied with worldly affairs and believing in their autonomous reality—from which we enter, by God's grace, the meditative state. The meditative life style, as a matter of fact, is characterized by a regular oscillation between these two states, a regular emergence from darkness into light, the unreal into the real, from dream into truth. If this particular state of heightened consciousness were verbalized, it might go: 'I thought everything was just what it appeared to be, the solid everyday world where all moments, objects, events and relationships were just what their names or descriptions proclaimed, but now I see that all along everything was Thee. Thou art all things, Thou art everything.' And this verbalization, like many others, can also be quite real; sometimes the realization is inarticulate, sometimes we actually say it to ourselves, murmur it in our minds, dwell upon the blissful expression of a revealed truth.

And this realization, of course, is liberation—a liberation all the more joyous, and total, because it carries with it the realization that there never was any bondage. If everything is God, and always was God, where is anyone in bondage? Where is 'anyone' at all? As Frithjof Schuon writes, 'When the sun rises, there was never any night.'

True, we will return to that illusory bondage, the inexhaustible divine comedy of mundane consciousness, because *karma* must exhaust itself, our scripts must be read through to the last word, the final scene of the story we are must be enacted. But each time we return from meditation the grip of *karma* is a bit loosened, until finally our *karma* becomes a mere spectacle, the impersonal unfolding of cause and effect which we thought was 'our life.' There are dramas, but no biographies.

God is all things, we realize, all things whatsoever. We didn't know it. All along, throughout all those years, decades, of anticipation and apprehension, we were not actually there, no one was anywhere. Nothing to celebrate, nothing to lament.

A MOMENT OF PEACE: ALWAYS, SOMETIMES OR NEVER?

The love of God is Peace.

In devotional meditation the duality of lover and Beloved, worshipper and God, dissolves into a unity which is experienced as perfect peace, *pax profunda*. Once again and as always, meditation unveils Reality, and peace is the 'real state of affairs', the truth, forever undisturbed beneath and within the apparent turbulence of the universe, like the ocean beneath its waves. Through our love of God—not only as directly experienced in meditation but, gradually and gratefully with the years, in our day-to-day lives—that turbulence fades away, the duality of humanity and God fades away, and peace alone remains. 'For,' in the words of Philalethes, the 17th-century English mystic, 'things find rest only in that which is the end of their being.'

If we examine our experience carefully and honestly, we can see that the disrupter of peace is always a form of self-assertion. To employ a homely simile, the assertion of self—our wants, our preferences, our opinions—is like stroking the fur of a cat in the wrong direction. It leaves a mark, it's uncomfortable and unsightly, it's going against the grain and flow of things and asks to be rectified, restored, healed. It was an error, a misreading. Self-assertion breeds conflict, self-effacement breeds peace, and this is true not because a consequential moralism of self-denial is being imposed upon us from without by divine decree but simply because self-effacement establishes us in harmony with the real nature of things, which is, in Buddhist terms, *anatta*, or selflessness: there really is no separate self.'

Love of God is love of Reality, love of things as they are and as they cannot be other than what they are. It is a heroism of acceptance, contentment and humility. On the plane of daily living it is recognition of the natural tendency toward proportion, symmetry and recovery of balance, restoration of equilibrium: compensation, give-and-take: live and let live. We are reminded here of Taoism,

> the doctrine of universal reversion, of eternal cycles, of every end becoming a beginning, and things reverting to their original state. . . . Taoism . . . is a philosophy of the essential unity of the universe (monism), of reversion, polarization (yin and yang), and eternal cycles, of the levelling of all differences, the relativity of all standards, and the return of all to the Primeval One, the divine intelligence, the source of all things. From this naturally arises the absence of desire for strife and contention and fighting for advantage.
>
> ~ LIN YUTANG

As CHUANG TZU paraphrases Kuan Yin:

> Be illusive, appearing as if not to exist; be still, appearing like clear water. Who accepts things merges with them; who makes things, breaks. Do not ever put yourself forward, but always follow behind.

And this is a hard truth to put into effect, hard advice to follow, because it is direct confrontation with the ego. But the *Tao te Ching* is quietly insistent: 'The universe is ruled by allowing matters to take their course. It cannot be ruled by interfering.' Another 'paradox' well worth pondering.

In meditation, in our love of God, we see the truth of Peace directly, the truth that Peace is the Reality of the universe, disrupted by the self-assertive passions of humanity only, by nothing else. The real challenge is to preserve that vision, act in accordance with it, while we are out in the world, living our lives, instead of merely recalling it, after we've already succumbed, with vaguely irritated nostalgia and a feeling of remorse. The confused intermittent sense of dissatisfaction which often haunts our minds during the day is really the frustration of self-assertion, beating its head against the inveterate intransigence of the world.

The root of self-assertion is the ego. The ego does not exist. The realization of the non-existence of the ego, the permanent triumph over this tenacious illusion, is the most difficult thing of all. But it is the heart of the teaching, and the only path to peace. The self-effacement or self-giving of total and unconditional love is one method, and I suspect that that's the secret of the peace bequeathed to us by Jesus in JOHN 14:27. 'Peace I leave with you, my peace I give unto you: not as the world giveth, give I unto you.' St. Augustine put it this way: 'Thou madest us for Thyself, and our heart is restless until it repose in Thee.'

Devotional meditation reveals in direct experience the peace at the heart of the universe, the impassive tranquillity that is our own true nature. We inhabit Reality. For the vast majority of us this is as far as it goes. We alternate between inhabiting and remembering.

❁

GLINTS & GLIMPSES III

When we meditate upon His greatness—which should be easy enough—we realize that we have, in that very meditation, a secret invulnerability, an infallible recourse, a refuge where no one could ever find us: a power to annul the world. He negates everything, because He is infinite: *anantam Brahma*. He knows what He is, and when we know it too it's like sharing the great truth which, if they ever discovered it, if ever we or anyone else could get it across to them, would save our friends and loved ones, save everyone, from the gradual inevitable terrifying darkening of their hope.

❁

'Brahman Supreme': the pinnacle, the ultimate Reality, of the Vedanta. Brahman, the Absolute Divine Reality behind the stupendous breath-taking unsurpassable spectacle of Its Manifestation, is what the religion of India is all about. To glimpse It, or simply address It in the dark, is like turning a bend in the trail and suddenly seeing before you, disappearing into the clouds, the majestic snow-capped mountain for which the area is named. There It is and always was and always will be, world without end, silent, unmistakable, unanswerable. 'Thou alone art: Great Glory is Thy Name.'

'Brahman Supreme', as a Holy Name, evokes the religion itself, the fullness of the Vedanta, *sanatana dharma*. We are in the presence of, and pervaded, embraced, enveloped by the religion we practice, the Truth by which we were found and saved from death.

❁

Sometimes it feels as if we're seeing the Truth, the Reality, God, and yet not *really* seeing it, not *grasping* it. We're seeing a shadow, a reflection, an aura, an image or silhouette of Something incomprehensible, Something too big to fit into a human mind—the 'little mind', that is, that Suzuki Roshi urged us to abandon (but never with a gaining intention!) in favor of Big Mind. We're feeling a presence: the presence of a Conscious Presence, or the presence of an infinite disembodied Consciousness. A vast reality or entity or Person always just beyond the margins of intelligibility, Something about which we can never really say 'I know what It is.' We know It's there, Something is there (wherever 'there' is), never any doubt about that, but It's indefinable. It simply *is*, 'I am that I am.' We feel, in this meditation, that the only thing we can say about God with certainty, the only thing we know for sure (and not only 'about God' but in this world), the one *attribute* of God we can affirm without the slightest doubt, is that God *is*.

Now this simply reflects the Teaching. That the Self alone is real, the Self alone exists, and that the Self cannot be grasped by the senses nor known by the mind are two fundamental points reiterated throughout the Upanishads. So when we have this experience we know we're on the right track. It's not a blind alley, it's the main road.

❁

The three 'L's': Light, Love and Life. *Jñana, Bhakti, Karma*: the head, the heart, the will: Consciousness, Bliss, Existence: *Satchidananda*. The perennial Trio. Who is Krishna? 'The essence of *Satchidananda* personified into a human form.' (Swami Tapasyananda) Krishna is within you: your very Self, your Heart.

❁

It's possible to repeat the word 'Truth' over and over again to yourself and get an effect simply from that. Just repeat the word, lose yourself in the rapture of dwelling upon it, loving it, worshiping it.

And what is this 'it'? The word, or what the word refers to?

The presence of the word on our lips, in our minds, is the presence of the reality it stands for. This is the miracle of *mantra*. The same thing can happen with the word 'God.'

But you have to really be sincere. 'Sincere' derives from a Latin word whose root meaning is *one*. You have to mean business. You have to know it's a matter of life or death. *Nothing else is there but the mantra.*

❁

It's a good idea to remind ourselves, from time to time, in meditation, that the divine 'state of affairs' we experience directly there is actually the state of affairs all the time, not only when we perceive or realize it. 'I am always the Self.' We are confessing and apologizing for our forgetfulness—as if we want to make sure that God knows that we know He is always within us.

❁

'The Universe is a Person, and I am that Person'

This is far out. Theistic Self-Realization. A metaphysical explication would look something like this:

The Personal God, Supreme Person, *Param Purusam*, is the Self: the Self is everything, all things are contained within It, the universe is Self-Manifestation: and I AM (is) the Self, I AM (is) Pure Consciousness. Therefore in meditation we may experience Reality in the manner epitomized.

The Self is All, and I am the Self.
The Self is All, and Thou art the Self.
We are One.
I am my Beloved.
I am Krishna.

It's the eclipse of the ego, of course, but in a particular angle of vision. The vision of those in whose emptiness that Person has appeared before, and Who now speaks.

❁

HEAVEN: 'WHEN WE'RE CLOSE TOGETHER DANCING CHEEK TO CHEEK'? NOT QUITE

'Heaven' is a word we use often in figures of speech: This is heaven! I was in heaven! It was pure heaven! But never seriously, as if it referred to a real location of some kind—which would sound crazy or 'fundamentalist'—to indicate a state of pure happiness and uninterrupted peace, free from the care and sorrow, trouble and suffering and potential for unpleasant surprise and disquieting revelation which plague without respite our earthly existence. In its implication of complete and eternal satisfaction, fulfillment and absence of all want, relocation to 'heaven' is generally conceived as a post-mortem reward, if not for saintly virtue at least for enduring our frustrated expectations, if not actual misery, with resignation, humility and patient faith. The obvious incompatibility of such a 'place' with earthly reality compels us to situate it beyond the grave, where the one thing of which we may be certain is that we are no longer here.

In its deeper sense, the concept of heaven expresses our profound and ineradicable suspicion that happiness—actually perfection: it goes that far—is our natural state, our birthright, and that evil is some kind of accidental calamity that befell and befalls us, insulting and outrageous, and inconsistent with the true intended nature of things. The intuition of the Fall, of punishment for a primordial transgression, is implicit in our very consciousness. Understood as liberation, fleeting or permanent, from that mysterious cosmic sentence, 'heaven' then symbolizes the goal of life, the reattainment of the state originally intended for us, the retrieval of the great and pure joy whose indestructible and tantalizing presence beneath the mottled surface of human affairs we so often sense with anxiety, confused remorse and desperate longing.

In the temporal dimension of our minds, and as an aspect of our intuition of the Fall from Grace, we tend to locate this joy in the past: the longing for heaven becomes a nostalgia for paradise. We remember, with a pain so brilliant that we are mercifully blinded by it and forced to look away, the expulsion from Eden, whose crystallization on the earthly plane we are presently experiencing, with an equivalent inability to 'look it in the face', as the destruction of Nature: environmental degradation, extinction of species, pollution and deforestation, the entire constellation of ecological calamities. 'Heaven' is a powerful word, a powerful concept. Whether interpreted as *fana* (the Sufic 'extinction of the ego'), Buddhist *nirvana*, Hindu *moksha* or Christian salvation, 'heaven', the state of beatitude for which we believe we are (or were) intended, is a central, inescapable and indispensable category in our understanding of the human condition, implicit in our daily aspiration and explicit in the revealed doctrines.

In meditation we can enter heaven. In meditation we see that heaven, metaphorically a place or state, is actually God, the being of God. All that has ever been associated with the word, and infinitely more, is present within us—within, always within, 'the kingdom of heaven is within thee,' 'I am seated in the hearts of all'—as the indwelling Spirit, as God the Beloved, the Lord of Love and Grace. This radiant Presence is Heaven. This incredible Person we meet in the silence of our hearts, in our minds which have been emptied of all worldly thoughts, all identification with a biography, is Heaven. The mere utterance of His Name: that's Heaven.

We say a Name of God, or simply the word 'God', and the Silence that follows, infinite, depthless, eternal, is still His Name. That Silence, the wordless Name in which the whole world and all that has ever happened is revealed as a vanishing dream, is Heaven.

DO WE GET WHAT WE DESERVE? DO WE DESERVE WHAT WE GET? WHAT *DO* WE GET? WHO *ARE* WE?

At certain times in our lives, as in reviewing, with confused compunction, the sequence of flickering shapes, brilliantly colored by mutually exclusive emotions, our imagined auto-biography can assume in the course of a single day, even a single hour, *five minutes*, we feel a need to pray or petition for a refuge, for worthiness, worthiness of spiritual illumination, of Grace. We feel we have to be deserving before we receive, and we know we haven't the power to make ourselves deserving by any effort of our own will. The feeling arises spontaneously, not at all necessarily following upon some lapse of rectitude, and lingers until we've 'purged' ourselves, as it were, by actual prayer.

Three questions of interpretation may come to mind as we reflect upon the implications of our request. And since the plea for worthiness, ascending as it does from the depths of our hearts and appearing throughout canonical prayer in the theistic traditions, is divinely sanctioned, the questions have answers, and the logic of the response serves to deepen our understanding.

In the first place, it is axiomatic that Grace—understood here as a vision of God or divine truths, or the Mahayana 'Thought of Enlightenment', or, in general, any divine intimation or progress of the soul toward heaven—cannot be coerced. There is nothing we can do, no effort or attainment on our part, no sacrifice, austerity or traditional practice—no 'worthiness', in other words—that can guarantee or determine a divine response. 'I can of mine own self do nothing.' (St. John of the Cross) 'The Vision of God is possible only through His Grace.' (Ananda Moyi)

We are never the active agent in our relationship to God. As Bayazid al-Bistami put it so well: 'For thirty years I went in search of God, and when I opened my eyes at the end of this time, I discovered that it was really He who sought for me.' Cause and effect, then, a future grace granted in reward for a present 'worthiness', is out of the question. This can't be the rationale of our petition. We may pray, out of a misplaced response of our self-respect (the kind of self-respect that prompts us to refuse payment for a job we didn't do well, or to be determined to 'carry our part of the load', or 'hold up our end'), to be worthy of a grace that will be freely bestowed; and we may pray that *by* grace we may be *made* worthy. But we cannot assume that there is some kind of worthiness, whether achieved or bestowed freely, that can assure a response from heaven.

Why, then, do we experience this spiritual want? Why is it codified in tradition? What do we learn from it, where does it take us?

The lesson, the answer, is implicit in the plea. We become definitively aware of our own powerlessness. We become aware of the Omnipotence, the infinite Sovereignty, in which we are contained. We understand, and experience, our permanent relationship to Mercy, we understand what humanity is, what it means to be human.

Second question. The question of scale.

There is clearly no common measure between our finite merits, however great they may be and at whatever cost they may have been acquired, and the infinity that is God's Grace. How can we be 'worthy' of the Vision of God, the bliss of the divine Presence? 'Let nobody presume upon his own powers for such exaltation or uplifting of the heart or ascribe it to his own merits. For it is certain that this comes not from human deserving but is a divine gift.' (RICHARD OF SAINT-VICTOR) Do we feel 'worthy' of the gift of life, of our own existence, of this universe, of Existence itself, all of which must be regarded as God's grace freely showered upon us, or do we simply feel a measureless and uncomprehending gratitude? Where is worthiness? How can we deserve all this?

Given this discontinuity, this incommensurability, our plea becomes symbolic. By focusing attention upon our utter dependence, our metaphysical negligibility, it forces us to become aware, once again, of our true status in the scheme of things. Before Him we are nothing. Our truth, our proper attitude, is what the saints have been insisting upon, and exemplifying, forever: humility. We recall the response from the whirlwind. Being what we are, we *ought* to feel unworthy from time to time, and want to be worthy, and know that, on our own, we cannot be—the sum of which is a 'classic' spiritual state extolled by the divine wisdom we inherit: Self-Surrender.

> Fill your heart and mind with Me, adore me, make all your acts an offering to Me, bow down to Me in self-surrender. If you set your heart upon Me thus, and take Me for your ideal above all others, you will come into My Being.
> ~ BHAGAVAD GITA

> Verily religion with Allah is submission.
> ~ KORAN

So once again, by compelling us to examine more closely our relationship to God, the plea for worthiness, on the surface an inescapable error or misunderstanding decreed for us by the divine economy, nevertheless points us toward deeper insight. Repeated in one form or another in all revelations and rooted in our mistaken identification with the ego, the lower self, this plea is a response to the prompting of the Heart-Intellect, that divine center of our being: we want to be worthy, totally and with all our soul, because worthiness is conformity to the Divine Will: Self-Surrender. 'Thy Will be done'. And 'Be ye perfect....' We are haunted by the specter of unworthiness, of dissipation, defection from an intended excellence, spiritual failure. We know that, although God may never turn away from us, we may certainly turn away from God, and we have no doubt that the consequences are immediate.

Third question, Metaphysical.

A paradox (again!) arises when we regard our plea in the context of non-dual realization. Who's asking Whom for What? If there is only the One, only God, the Ocean of Consciousness, the Self—and this is the highest wisdom we are taught—who is there to pray for anything, to be worthy or unworthy, to be denied or awarded Grace? What is Grace itself when there are no recipients, or when the Donor and the recipient are One? When 'we' realize this supreme Final Truth, that 'we' do not exist as separate entities, there is no worthiness or unworthiness, no approval or disapproval, no giver and no receiver: no subject, no object. There is only the blissful Atman, the Light, Brahman Supreme, the One Spirit beyond all attributes and predicates which is yet all things.

However: so long as we are fated to return from the state of beatitude in which this Final Truth is realized, and we can all be comfortably or uncomfortably certain of that fate, the plea for worthiness has not became meaningless or obsolete. Its content has merely been given a new, and ultimate, definition.

We will know now that the ultimate Grace, which is the ultimate bliss, the true Ananda, is our own non-existence, the extinction of the ego: the celebrated *fana* of Sufism. This, the gift incomparable, is our truth, and the Grace for which we pray to be worthy. Our insights gained by examining the petition for worthiness in its intrinsic dualist mode—revealing our powerlessness and dependence, and their consequence in humility and self-surrender—were signposts pointing in this direction.

His Grace is everything and everything is Him. We become worthy when we become no one, which is what, by His Grace, and to our unutterable joy when we realize it, we already are.

MACBETH WAS WRONG ABOUT LIFE (ACT V, SCENE 5)

In meditation we *see*. Meditation is a way of seeing the realities beneath the visible world which appear, to our physical eyes, *as* the physical world. Something like the way the mind sees heroism or generosity or patience beneath the mere physical acts visible to the eye. The 'eye of the heart' sees the spiritual reality within what is seen by the eyes of the head. It sees, in other words, truths, essences, realities: coming fully into its own, it sees the Truth, the supreme divine Reality at the heart of all things.

Recall Plato's Allegory of the Cave. The 'prisoners' see only the shadows cast on the wall before them. The enlightened, the 'philosophers', see the realities that cast them—and the Light itself: above all the Light.

One of the great divine realities that become visible to us in devotional meditation is *life*. We become vividly aware, in direct spiritual perception, of *what life is*—not in the mind, as a concept, the meaning of a word, but as a reality. We can directly feel and perceive the reality to which we have given the name 'life', and we can clearly see and feel that that reality is an infinite holiness, a great 'truth of the universe'. A glorious Spirit pervading the Cosmos. Life becomes a Presence, and we realize immediately that it is *the* Presence: it is God. There is a simultaneous perception that God is Life and real-ization that Life is God. The intuition of God and the intuition of Life merge into one. We experience a great fullness of joy that is at the same time completely calm, motionless: a serene adoration of God or the

Self in their aspect as eternal Life. A shining stillness fills our heart, and we became what we adore, and always were.

Life can appear then as a kind of triumph. Not over death—which we feel as something that is preceded by and befalls life—but over a primordial aboriginal absence of sentience. We imagine a vast soundless landscape of dimly illuminated bare rock, the black silent reaches of intergalactic space, the interior of ice: scenarios of, and alternatives to, life's victory.

And we realize, with deeper insight, sinking deeper into the meditation, that such alternatives never existed. There was always Life, there *is* always Life, in the eternal Now that is God—the eternal Now that is called, in the Indian tradition, for example, 'Krishna the Changeless'. We perceive—seated there in the calm bliss of the shrine, our eyes closed, lips faintly smiling, faintly aware of the fragrance of the incense—that Life is an eternal reality, inseparable from the eternal being of God, and that we are immersed in it, pervaded by it, a part of it, an expression of its inexhaustible fecundity. The biblical phrase, Life Eternal, becomes a direct experience, the promise of immortality. The 'well of water springing up into everlasting life' (JOHN 4:14) becomes intelligible, because visible.

The sense of triumph, however, seems inherent in the meditation on Life, and we soon realize why. The infinite Life in whose tranquil eternity we are immersed, and which we acknowledge as a focus of worship, is actually and originally a 'divine conception', an 'Idea' of God's whose 'victorious' physical manifestation 'here below' carries with it a permanent sense of triumph, as indeed it *is* a permanent triumph, a continuous victory or testimony: the Sovereign Good cannot but radiate. We see Life as an Idea in the mind of God ('What an utterly incredible idea' we marvel to ourselves, smiling at the simultaneous aptness and absurdity of the figure of speech), and this world of life as the triumph, the eternal birth, of that Idea.

And we see furthermore that the Idea and the world are one and the same. This is always the case with divine categories, for there is only the divine Self, the immortal Atman, the Dreamer, One without a Second. God's 'vision' or Idea of things is our manifested universe, the Great Dream. Atman and Maya, Nirvana and Samsara, are eternally One.

We inhabit the Idea of Life. And that Idea, as meditation convincingly demonstrates, is also within us. We are projections or reflections—made in His image—of the Being in Whom the world exists, in Whom Life was, in both senses of the word, conceived. Shiva (the absolute Consciousness) and *jiva* (the individual soul) are one.

I am the sacred smell of the earth,
The light of the fire,
Life of all lives...
Know Me, eternal seed
Of everything that grows.
(GITA, Book VII)

And we go still deeper.

As we meditate, the distinction between life and awareness, in their earthly forms, starts to become fluid. Are the two equivalent or merely inseparable? Is life the *joy* within awareness, the joy *of* awareness, the bliss of consciousness, of being the Light in which a world appears? We see awareness as the joy of life and life as the joy of awareness. We gain an intuition, a vision, of Hinduism's *Satchidananda*: the Existence-Consciousness-Bliss Absolute. The inseparability of consciousness, life and joy appears as the reflection of a prototype *in divinis*, an Archetype, a Face of God. Again, the contemplation of Life culminates in a vision of God.

In the spiritual world, *satyaloka*, in God, *sub specie aeternitatis*, there are Life and Joy, divine Qualities, Quranic 'Names of God'. In the manifested world, where 'we' are bodies and biographies, these archetypes are depicted and enacted in the dramas of *samsara*. Because Life and Joy, as we perceive in meditation, are inseparable in heaven, they must also be so on earth. Therefore marriage and sexual union are Life's heralds, birth its appearance or arrival, morning and springtime its awaited resumption, ardor and vitality its material expression. Its manifestations are joyous occasions. Its destruction or suppression is sorrowful, grievous or tragic. We call it sacred. Here, in the Dream, life is welcomed, celebrated, solemnized.

And above all, loved. We love life. It is our standard, our measure. We say, 'I love that child more than my own life.' 'A matter of life and death' takes precedence over all other priorities. We watch anxiously for 'signs of life', we lament and deplore the 'loss of life', we hold on 'for dear life'. We applaud someone's *joie de vivre*. We speak with approval and a sense of vindication—even as if, on some level, this was all that mattered—of a departed person's 'great love of life': again, there is a feeling of triumph. To have managed to love life, right through to the end, despite all its misfortune and disillusion, despite death itself, is regarded as a victory of the spirit, a measure of success, the passing of a test we all must face. We are inspired.

Life is God and God is Life Eternal. In devotional meditation we are able to apprehend and love Life directly, as a divine Essence, an immanent Presence of God. 'Thou art Life', we murmur in smiling rapture. In our normal day-to-day consciousness that infinite Life, translated by the magic of *maya*, appears as our own fragile existence, priceless and irreplaceable, as the contents of ever-unfolding Time, which we call the river of life, and as Earth, the Great Mother, Gaia Tellus, upon whose boundless breast burgeons a flowering of life so inexhaustible in its beauty, grandeur and variety that our hearts are choked, and we are humbled by the worthlessness of praise. Such is His gift, His gift of Himself. To worship God as Life is a great worship, a great experience of love.

Having attained to Brahman,
a sage declared:
I am Life.
My glory is like the mountain peak.
~ Taittiriya Upanishad

X-RAYS, CAT-SCAN, MRI, EVEN SURGERY: THEY ALL DRAW A BLANK ON THIS ONE

There are episodes in devotional meditation where the focus is exclusively upon what seems then to be without doubt the supreme miracle of spiritual life, the whole and sufficient rationale for any 'sacrifice' undergone on the Path, the whole point of it all, a spiritual experience compared with which no other is even worth mentioning: the realization, the direct unmistakable awareness, that God is within us. Actually within us, just as the world's scriptures have always claimed.

And this knowledge that God is within us is our enduring haven, our great recourse.

It's like a magic wand we can draw at any time to render the world weightless, to blow away our worries and burdens like dust in the wind. If the infinite and eternal Spirit is within us, the Lord, what else can really matter? How can the trivial contingency of daily life have any real power over us? The recollection of this single great fact, the indwelling of God, drives all other thoughts from the mind. Everything we'd thought was important, urgent, threatening, all the issues that have been gnawing away in our stream of consciousness, are seen now as inconsequential details of an inconsequential circumstance, our own biographies, some of them to be tended to at the proper time with detached competence, others to be forgotten altogether.

This Presence within us is utterly independent of external conditions, events and affairs. Unassailable, indestructible, absolute. Our attention is diverted immediately. The faint inward-looking smile of joy appears on our faces. The awareness of the divine Reality, the ineffable Glory behind all visible things, surges again into consciousness, like the apparent resumption of music which had never really ceased, but from which we had been temporarily distracted. We remember the Truth, the Grace, which is God. We know that we can never be abandoned. A supreme infinite Being, Who in some incredible way 'loves us'—as we are forced to express it in the hopelessly, even ridiculously incommensurable medium of human speech—Whom we love and Who is Love itself, is within us, the joy in our hearts and in the heart of the universe.

In our knowledge that God, the infinite Person, is within us, the world of time, space and causality, the entire world of forms, is shattered like glass struck by a hammer. We perceive the truth of our condition, the miracle of human birth. Whatever will be required of us originates here, whatever knowledge, virtue or fulfillment that may be ours originate here, in the fact of this Presence within us.

Here is our true concern, everything derives from it. Here we are born, determined and annihilated at once. Here we find peace, temporal and eternal, and salvation.

And also something painful and eloquent. The fact is, in the noise and agitation of our busy daily lives we never experience the indwelling Presence. Rarely even pause to recall it, even though it is 'our enduring haven, our great recourse,' our truth and our joy. This consideration, eventually, can motivate decisions about how we might want to live our lives, changes we might make, patterns we might decide to break.

A SEQUENCE ON IDENTITY

The disciple listened attentively to the words of his teacher. He learned the supreme truth of Brahman. He then withdraw his senses from the objective world and concentrated his mind upon the Atman. His body appeared as immovable as a rock. His mind was completely absorbed in Brahman. After awhile he returned to normal consciousness. Then, out of the fullness of his joy, he spoke:

The ego has disappeared. I have realized my identity with Brahman. . . .
Now, finally and clearly, I know that I am the Atman, whose nature is eternal joy. I see nothing, I hear nothing, I know nothing that is separate from me. . . .
Nothing binds me to this world. I no longer identify myself with the physical body or the mind. I am one with the Atman, the undying. I am the Atman, infinite, pure, eternal, at peace forever. . . .
I am beyond action and am changeless. My nature is pure consciousness. I am absolute reality, eternal goodness. . . .
I am That which makes all objects manifest. . . .
I am reality, without beginning, without equal. I have no part in the illusion of 'I' and 'you', 'this' and 'that'. I am Brahman, one without a second, bliss without end, the eternal, unchanging Truth. . . .
Now I know that I am All. . . .
I am that Brahman, one without a second, the ground of all existences. I make all things manifest. . . .
I am the soul of the universe. I am all things, and above all things. I am one without a second. I am pure consciousness, single and universal. I am joy. I am life everlasting.
~ From *Viveka Chudamani, Crest-Jewel of Discrimination*, by SHANKARA

> Constantly search for 'I', the source of the ego. Find out 'Who am I?' The pure 'I' is the reality, the Absolute Existence-Consciousness-Bliss. . . . Of all the japas, 'Who am I?' is the best.
> ~ Sri Ramana Maharshi

> In Sri Ramana Maharshi one meets again ancient and eternal India. The Vedantic truth—the truth of the Upanishads—is brought back to its simplest expression but without any kind of betrayal. . . . The great question 'Who am I?' appears, with him, as a concrete expression of a reality that is 'lived', if one may so put it, and this authenticity gives to each word of the sage a flavour of inimitable freshness. . . . The whole Vedanta is contained in the Maharshi's question 'Who am I?' The answer is the Inexpressible.
> ~ Frithjof Schuon

The tone is not interrogatory. Uttering the Maharshi's question as a *mantra*, we are initially simply marvelling over the fact, now completely and joyfully accepted, that we are not the ego with which we have identified all our lives: to admit the question as cogent is already a taste of the bliss of the answer. The tone is of lingering wonder, ascending (when we say it twice) in the first voicing, then descending. We smile at the incredible truth, contemplating with speechless appreciation the flawless symmetry and irreducible economy of the question, and the paradox of asking it. In a sense, leaving the question unanswered is the perfect answer. Rest in the suspension of identity, in the space vacated by the ego, in the simple wonder. Allow the amazement to unroll, to level out, into contentless peace, emptiness, pure joy.

❁

Two things immediately now, to set the stage for reading the sequence on Identity.

First, the entries in this section deal with the direct experience of *jñana*, the Path of Knowledge. The Path of Knowledge aims, through the acquisition of spiritual knowledge in which the illusion of the individual ego is destroyed, through the realization of 'pure consciousness', at a pre-existing eternal *identity* with the *impersonal* presentation or aspect of the Reality, the Truth: in the language of Vedanta, with the Atman, the Brahman, the Self. It can be conceived of as the 'I-Consciousness of the Universe.' Or the 'I AMness' celebrated by Nisargadatta Maharaj. We might say 'I AM the Self-Awareness of the Universe which *is* the Universe'. This approach is contrasted, as the serious reader will immediately recall from the Introduction, with *bhakti*, or *union* through a pre-existing eternal *love* with the *personal* dimension of the Reality. The two paths intertwine, alternate, dance together, as it were, and lead to the same supreme goal, the *summum bonum*, and are distinguished only by the emphasis of the practitioner.

Second, the frequent use of the word 'is' in parentheses is a syntactical stratagem which seeks to indicate that there are always two meanings in the phrases in which this construction appears, one where the word is articulated and one where it is not. Where the word is articulated we are thinking of the infinite consciousness, the infinite I AM, the Brahman of Vedanta. When we delete the word 'is' in our minds the reference is to the Atman, or Brahman understood as 'lodged' in the individual person as our true Self. (Imagine, for example, the bliss, the unqualified infinite emancipation, of realizing 'I AM (is) everyone'.) In the first case I AM is being regarded as an objective reality, in the second case it is being experienced as a subjective reality. But Atman and Brahman are One. This is fundamental, the 'name of the game', as it were. *Ayam atma brahma*: this Self is Brahman. One of the four *mahavakyas*, or 'great utterances', of Vedanta.

Now let us examine some of the countless ways in which this great Truth, this infinite Bliss — for Bliss is Brahman – offers itself to our indestructible resolve; understanding, of course, that both the offer and the resolve are Grace, for there is only the One: *Kham Brahman*: All is Brahman.

❁

The Self shines, the Self is everything, the Self has many masks—what do you ever see but those masks?—and each mask is still the Self. The Self is One. The Self is the All.

> The universe . . . is both One and Many
> ~ DIONYSIUS

> There must first be one from which the many arise. This one is competent to lend itself to all yet remain one, because while it penetrates all things it cannot itself be sundered; this is identity in variety.
> ~ PLOTINUS

Think of a mountain. A mountain changes in appearance continuously with the time of day, the weather and the seasons, and their combinations, yet it is always familiar, reappearing in its great diurnal moments exactly as we've seen it before, the same grand presence, the same name. We see it in the morning light, the glare of midday and the glow of sunset, through the filters of wind, rain and snow, silvered in moonlight and starlight, red, green, brown, gold and white as the months pass across it, and it's always the same mountain. The Self is like that, ever-changing and ever One, infinite in Its transformations yet One and changeless forever in Itself. In Its changing It is the Universe. In Its changelessness It is You.

Mountains, real or metaphorical, and all Creation including the egos we think we are, are appearances in Consciousness, lightning flashes in that same eternal Self. The Self is All, the Self is One. The Sufic formula reads 'Unity is in multiplicity and multiplicity in Unity.'

The 'oneness' of things, this oneness you always hear about, is the oneness you are.

❁

The Self appears to the Self as Its great moments, Its moments as God, the Avatar or the Universe, as Revelation and Humanity, as Light, Love, Truth and Bliss, the 'special manifestations', and It appears to Itself as the human mental states in which the great moments are discovered and reflected, yet It remains always One, the great moments and their reflections are never anything but the Self: always One, always untouched, always distinct from Its own appearances, always identical with them: unthinkable, unutterable, beyond predication, Absolute Unity: One without a second. There is nothing but the Self, and the Self is everything.

But like the oceans and the mountains and the sky, like the stars and the rivers and the flight of the hawk, like the grass in the wind and the single wildflower sprouting from the granite, It has Its great moments.

> The Self is Brahma, the Self is Vishnu, the Self is Indra, the Self is Shiva; the Self is all this universe. Nothing exists except the Self.
> ~ Sri Sankaracharya

❁

As the illusion, as the illusory 'personal' identity, the ego which has no real existence, how would I identify 'myself'? Like this:

I am made of the universe, made of the contents of the world. That's all. I am not some ghost-like self *behind* this content, there is no such thing, but rather the sum total of everything that has ever flowed by (through what? through noumenon, phenomenal absence, Big Mind, the Knower, Pure consciousness, the Self, the Atman, the I AM: *That*: what can never be known, never be an object of cognition, pure subjectivity) from the apparently time-bound dawn of 'my' consciousness to the present moment: I am the total content of the stream of experience, and nothing more. I am nobody!

I am not somewhere or something separate from the universe, I am not a discrete *part* of the universe, I am rather a particular infinitesimal fraction of the countless ever-flowing moments whose continuous appearance and dizzying transformations within countless apparently separate minds, including 'mine', make up the infinite universe as it unfolds in Time. I am *constructed*, from haphazard 'pieces' of the universe, a chance assemblage extracted and temporarily preserved (by those countless minds, including 'mine') from the universal transience and then arbitrarily assigned or declared an identity, an 'I', and given the name to which 'I' answer.

I am made of the universe, with nothing else 'left over'. The universe is my being, my substance, beginning at the crudest level with this body I call 'mine' and ultimately incorporating the total content of 'my' experience, and that's all: there is no 'person' comprised of the elements of this totality, no 'I'. Which explains the smile on the face of the Buddha. There's just the universe, a continuously unfolding appearance in consciousness upon which innumerable non-existent 'I's' have been projected, among them the precious 'me', fleeting imaginary containers of a share allotted to them from the ceaseless infinite simultaneous blossoming and disappearing called Creation.

Now when you *realize* all this in meditation, when you *see* it, something very wonderful happens. A jump.

The 'personal' I, which realized it was 'made of' the universe and felt within itself its share of the universe, its biography, as its very being and sole reality, perceives immediately that this is not, and couldn't be, the whole story. The personal 'I' is not replaced by a personal 'share'. It's replaced by the infinite I AM, the Self, of which it was an illusory reflection. It fades away not into the universe but into the Self which *is* the universe.

When I 'drown' in the universe, realizing that 'I' do not exist, I discover my true identity, and that is the Self. I AM (is) the world, but I AM (is) not of this world. The realization that the personal I is 'made of the universe' delivers yet another vision of that blissful intimacy of union which is our human fulfillment and our reality all along, another sudden realization of Oneness, another angle of perception revealing the eternal identity of subject and object. I don't have to be 'me', I AM (is) really 'all this'. 'The entire man is in his being the three worlds'. (JACOB BOEHME) 'Man is an image which comprises everything'. (The ZOHAR) 'All things in heaven above, and Earth beneath, meet in the Constitution of each Individual'. (Peter Sterry) And furthermore, in the trenchant words of 'the terrible Wei Wu-Wei': 'The Buddha forbore to specify: as long as there is any "one" to suffer—he will.' Discovering your true identity is what it's all about.

✲

'I AM (is) the universe' is a metaphysical equation implicit in (the Vedantic concept of) the Self.

> That which is the finest essence—this whole world has that as its Self. That is Reality. That is Atman. That art Thou, Svetaketu.
> ~ Chandogya Upanishad

> He (the Yogi delivered in this life, jivan-mukta) knows that all contingent things are not different from Atma (in their principle), and that apart from Atma there is nothing.
> ~ Sri Shankaracharya

When we realize 'I am the existence of the universe,' or 'I am the presence of the World,' aspects of that metaphysical truth are being made explicit. The existence and presence of the universe are both dependent upon the Pure Consciousness (that) I AM; or I AM (is) the invisible Conscious Presence in which the world is suspended, through which the world streams, and which alone truly exists because It alone is changeless and eternal. I AM (is) Existence and I AM (is) Presence. The existence and presence of Manifestation is a function of the Self, of God. I AM (as) Existence and Presence can be directly experienced in meditation. The feeling is not sublimity, but infinite humility deriving from our realization that this incredible state of affairs is of the nature of a Gift, a Grace, a Blessing, of which, since we know full well 'we' are not the Giver, we can only be the receiver.

'I am the Soul of the World.' The Atman is the indwelling life, animating principle, the loving self-awareness of the universe which is independent of its physical nature—what the Maharshi calls the Heart.

> The universe is composed of a part that is material and a part that is incorporeal; and inasmuch as its body is made with a soul in it, the universe is a living creature.
> ~ Hermes

I AM (is) that living creature. I AM (is) its life: I AM (is) the knowledge of what it needs and merits, how to care for it and love it and live in it. All this is my very Self. I AM (is) the world, and I AM (is) the Soul of the World as well, like the heart in the body.

> You never enjoy the world aright, till the Sea itself floweth in your veins, till you are clothed with the heavens, and crowned with the stars. . . . Till your spirit filleth the whole world, and the stars are your jewels: till you are as familiar with the ways of God in all Ages as with your walk and table: till you are intimately acquainted with that shady nothing out of which the world was made: till you love men so as to desire their happiness, with a thirst equal to the zeal of your own: till you delight in God for being good to all: you never enjoy the world.
> ~ THOMAS TRAHERNE

❁

TIME. LINEAR TEMPORALITY. THE CLOCK.

If we could see through that Trick! We would be released.

And we do see through it, in meditation, we do penetrate the shimmering opaque veil of this supreme legerdemain, and from more than one direction as well, in a variety of insights. It's not impossible. St Augustine, Eckhart, Clement of Alexandria, Rumi, Boethius, and many others, have testified to the Truth, to the Timeless Present, the Eternal Now, behind the smokescreen of linear temporality.

Probably everyone has enjoyed the taste of timelessness at least once—walking down the beach or simply sitting there lost in the spell of the waves (it takes a preoccupation of clinical proportions to withstand the spell of the waves), in the suspension of duration that seems to accompany silence, filtered sunlight and solitude in the wilderness, in reverie and absorption in a task, or in a purely intellectual experience, as for example in the intuition that nostalgia is insipid not because it's weakening but because it's a disingenuous evasion of the hard, and refreshing, truth that the only reality we have is Now.

See through that Trick, and hold on to what we see. It's a strange thing, this returning from meditation to daily life, from Reality to illusion, Nirvana to samsara, every day, day after day, knowing what's happening and not being able to do anything about it. We fall into Time: an aspect of the Fall from Grace. Nothing seems more real—because it is reality by definition, of course—than the illusion when we are living in it: this zone, reappearing with implacable regularity like a chronic illness, in which I locate myself by noting the date on the newspaper masthead and looking about twenty times a day at my wristwatch (the fine tuning), this zone in which one of the few things we better know for sure and all agree upon is the day of the week. I recall a Dostoievsky novel in which a witness' ignorance of what year it was, under cross-examination at a trial, was clear proof of mental incompetence.

But what's the issue here? To complain about linear temporality in our earthly existence is as pointless as haranguing against *maya*, and really amounts to the same thing. Why bother to talk about it?

Time is pain: that's the issue.

> Time is an unwholesome physician, for it deceives the patient daily with the expectation of the future, and before expelling the old pains, it adds new ones to the old and accumulates daily so many evils that through the fallacious hope of life it leads to death. We must live today; he who lives tomorrow never lives. If you want to live today, live for God, in whom yesterday and tomorrow are naught but today.
>
> ~ MARSILIO FICINO

Time is pain. Not as the 'river of mortality', of course—we were not born, we do not die—but simply in daily experience, in our entrapment within an erroneous self-conception made up of nothing more than mere thoughts, some referred to a 'past', called 'memories', and often experienced as melancholy resignation, nagging regret or, at best, imperiled satisfaction, others referred to a 'future', called 'plans' (schemes, strategies, subterfuges, gambits), and often experienced as restless anticipation, inner conflict, dread, or the apprehensive eagerness that invariably precedes disappointment and a feeling of emptiness. The illusion of the temporal continuum does not derive from anything objective, from the universe or from our social situation and responsibilities, nor does our competence in worldly affairs require uninterrupted complicity with it; the illusion originates in our own minds, and it would be nice if we could turn it off whenever our departure from the world of clock-time would cause no confusion for the dream-characters who inhabit it. Time is pain because it's a function of the ego, its very precondition, its substance, and the ego, as we know very well, is more than an error: it's the intrinsic disgrace, the barrier to spiritual awakening, the essence of the sin of pride.

How fortunate we are that it isn't real!

The 'past' is a memory,
The 'future' is a supposition,
The 'present' is passed before we can apprehend it.
The only 'present' therefore is presence and must necessarily be what we are. Such presence, then, is inevitably outside time and must be 'intemporality'.
The 'future' is a dream. The 'past' is recollection of a dream. The 'present' is an unlikely hypothesis.
What, then, is left? Must I say it? Why, Intemporality, of course!
It never was any 'where' or at any time but Here and Now, and Here and Now it will be forever.

~ WEI WU WEI, from *Posthumous Pieces*

But it's true; this discussion is of the nature of rattling our chains. Bravado. The Fall into Time that recurs whenever we return from deep meditation is merely an echo or reenactment of the original Fall into Time, or into Beginningless Ignorance, that inaugurated our present state of separation, disequilibrium or, in the Islamic point of view, rebellion. No one, *qua* individual, escapes the conditioning of time and space. 'The man who has found reality, as well as the man who is still in the coils of the phenomenal, is like one travelling over a flooded road.' (HONEN) We long for Eden, for recovery of Truth and our true nature, for timelessness in the Eternal Now of heaven, in the ancient Tao, in the Pure Land of the

Buddhas. We know, in our identification with the cardiac intelligence within us, that our exile, real enough in our experience, is actually an illusion. All this is Brahman, and I am always the Self. So we rattle our chains.

Penetrating the illusion of linear temporality is always accompanied by extinction of the false identity, the ego, the biography, because that identity is the source of the illusion and the illusion is its substance. In my false identity I am the origin of Time: but in my true identity, the Atman, I AM (one with) the origin of timelessness, the Truth. I AM (is) Now, I AM (is) eternal, I AM (is) not of this world of time and space. And I AM (is) always in Eternity, never here, in this dream of Time, never here, where there are days, months and years, birth, decay and death. I have no history: I was never born, I've had no 'life', and I will not die. I AM (is) timeless.

The feeling is bliss, the bliss of emancipation. The Truth is Nirvana. The chains which were never real are broken.

The past is already past.
The future is not yet here.
The present never abides.
Things are constantly changing,
with nothing on which to depend:
So many names and words confusingly self-created—
What is the use of wasting your life thus idly all day?
~ RYOKWAN

The disciples said to Jesus: Tell us how our end will be.
Jesus said:
Have you discovered the beginning so that you inquire about the end? For where the beginning is, there shall be the end. Blessed is he who shall stand at the beginning, and he shall know the end and he shall not taste death.
~ THE GOSPEL ACCORDING TO THOMAS

❁

From texts whose origins are lost in the mists of pre-history I learn today, in the twentieth century, the century we call home, who I am. I learn the eternal Truth. Apparently an American guy topped with a rainbow-colored stocking cap sitting here in Clwyd County, North Wales, listening to *Les Scenes Historique* of Sibelius, the Composer of the Week on BBC, I am actually the infinite immortal Self celebrated in the Upanishads of ancient India, and everything defining this 'me', and everything 'other' than 'me', actually exists only within the infinite Awareness (that) I AM.

I understand this and I believe it. It's why I smile when you'd think I'd grit my teeth.

Meditate. There's no other way you'll ever know it's true. I mean know *for sure*.

✲

Direct experience of the Self, the one I AM, is contentless, 'mindless', 'nobody home'. No thoughts, no words, no conceptions hopping around in there, no one thinking anything: no one aware of 'contemplating the Self'. Beyond the *pranava*—which is OM, the supreme symbol of the Atman, the supreme 'support', the supreme *mantra*, the syllable that is God—lies, we are told, the 'unvoiced' pranava. Absorption in OM, or any non-dual *mantra*, is a threshold, a foretaste, a vision: on the practical level, a constant reminder. On the level of the will, a dedication. And, on a deeper level still, repeatedly concluding a survey of what we have called our 'life', a non-dual *mantra* is a joyous farewell. Goodbye to all that! I AM (is) no one!

✲

'I am immortal love.' Directly realized. As clear as a fruit in the palm of your hand, as they say, so I am informed, in the subcontinent.

Self-Realization in meditation is something like the progressive dropping away of all false identities, the cause of all our suffering, until nothing remains but the true Identity which was always there.

It is invariably experienced as infinite and immortal: sometimes personal, sometimes impersonal. As we have seen, and shall continue to see, in Its impersonal mode It appears under many aspects, Its 'great moments', the many views of the mountain, while remaining always One: the unity in variety and variety in unity attested by the masters and traditions.

One of these aspects, of course, is Love.

I AM (is) Love, the immortal divine Love in which all things are held in Oneness. I AM (is) the ocean of Love from which all things draw their existence, the Love which manifests as the universe. To taste our identity with infinite impersonal Love is to recognize immediately the simultaneous legitimacy and absurdity of all earthly loves, Its faint, distorted and misinformed reflections, which have brought such (precarious) joy and wreaked such (instructive) havoc in our lives. We become habituated, not without a certain mingled amusement and dispassionate submission, to the unvoiced reservations or qualifications, muttered or sighed in our minds, which now accompany the pronouncement of those crucial, stupendously consequential three little words whose heartfelt utterance has precipitated such unexpected wretchedness, desolation, bewilderment and bitter cynicism into our innocent generosity, and so repeatedly. Everyone over about the age of fourteen for girls and sixteen for boys has their poignant story to tell here.

Yet Love pervades the world. It lends validity to those magic words, purifies them, provided that we love things and people in God—which means, quite concretely, that when we say those words we are thinking of Him, of His Reality and our derivative status with the comportment it charges, of His Presence in every heart. The finite and temporal are manifestations of the infinite and eternal, and must be loved as such. We are enjoined by our Saviour to love one another: but this injunction, the Second Great Commandment, derives from the First. The immortal Love (that) I AM—which is, from another perspective, 'my' love of God—preceded 'my' appearance here and will survive 'my' departure. This is not true of Its reflections in the relative world, because they are personal and It is not. Hence, perhaps, the cultural association of romantic love with folly, disillusion and death.

For the *bhakta*, the love of God in the bliss of union transcends dualism: it is *advaita*, Oneness. 'We love God with His own love; awareness of it deifies us.' (Eckhart) The impersonal Love into which the *jnani* merges, through 'discrimination between the unreal and the Real,' is realized as 'my' true Identity, Reality, the Self, the Truth (that) I AM: It *is* God. 'God is love, and he that has learnt to live in the Spirit of love has learnt to live and dwell in God.' (William Law) These experiences, that of the *bhakta* and that of the *jñana*, are ultimately identical. In their wake the word 'love' takes on a new meaning, a 'fulfilled' meaning, that makes all previous usages seem merely anticipatory. We feel compassion, in the thought that they will probably never know anything else, never discover what they are actually seeking, longing for, pining for, dreaming of, for those of our friends who are more 'in love with love' than the others. Their dim apprehension of its incompleteness, its fatal finitude, can be detected in a certain defensive sorrow, mingled with fear, in their eyes.

Our transactions with God—which are really 'transactions' *within* God, for He is One without a second—and our realizations of true Identity in the great formless moments of the Self are what life is all about. Where it's at. These alone, because they are eternal, are real. The rest is not. It's impossible not to love this transience, because it's so beautiful, such a miracle, *of* God and therefore divine: but what we seek and cannot help seeking, what we're made for, is behind and within it, within our Self.

✿

The One is all things and no one of them.
~ PLOTINUS

Whatever happens, in any form or at any time or place, is but a variation of the One Self-Existent Reality.
~ YOGA-VASISHTHA

There is one realization, there are many realizations, the One appears as many, the many are always the One. You may experience the Nameless as something or someone that can be named, knowing that your words can only describe how It appears to us but never what It is, you may perceive features in the featureless Infinity into which everything disappears in the final moment which is the Eternal Now of their transtemporal appearance as well, you may see the lineaments of a Face which does not exist. You may hear the sound of Kabir's Unstruck Music. But who are you?

The two birds. One, the ego, we know to be unreal: that leaves only the other one, the Self. You are That.

Ultimate Reality is always experienced as Identity.

> *Before all beginnings, after all endings—I AM. All has its being in me, in the I AM that shines in every living being.*
> ~ Nisargadatta Maharaj

❁

The cables of *karma*, the massive, writhing, intricately woven network of objectified memories and definitions in which I feel myself so tightly entrapped, so inescapably identified, is always maya, the world-appearance, never (what) I AM. I AM (is) free, eternally and uninterruptedly emancipated. The Self is ever-realized as the Maharshi patiently, and frequently, pointed out.

I AM always the Self: retrospective redemption, present-tense disengagement.

I AM always the Self: not what I see in the mirror. Not the image in the photograph. Not what is pointed at by 'my name'. Not the character in the imaginations of my friends. Nor in my own.

> *When the mind is quiet, we come to know ourselves as the pure witness. We withdraw from the experience and its experiencer and stand apart in pure awareness. . . . The personality, based on self-identification, on imagining oneself to be something: 'I am this, I am that', continues, but only as a part of the objective world. Its identification with the witness snaps.*
> ~ Nisargadatta Maharaj

❁

The present moment is always really weightless.

Look at 'yourself'! How quickly one thought replaces the other! What could be more slippery and insubstantial than the mercurial transformations of the mental world and the stream of sensory impressions we memorize and regard as a 'biography'? Memorize, regard, flounder about in, protest against, fret about, make plans for, entertain hopes for, celebrate, regret. This story is written on water.

We look up, not from the task alone but from the entire spectacle, the whole dream-world, and think 'I AM the Self,' and the gentle distant smile returns to our faces. Tears come to our eyes. What words could describe the over-whelming love we suddenly feel, the love in which this gratuitous beatitude originates, this radiant divine largesse, this gift of infinite Presence given by no one to no one which is Reality? What words could describe this joy?

Personality is an unspeakable burden. An inconsolable sorrow. A wrenchingly pathetic disgrace, the ultimate error. If you ever feel as if you can't go on, can't face another day, it's your knees buckling under that weight.

❁

'I am Peace.' Go deep enough and that's what you find.

There's an air of finality in this matter-of-fact insight, an end-of-the-Path feeling. It's as if there are only two orders of being: the ceaseless feverish change, activity and dynamism of this world, and the silent, changeless radiance of heaven, empty of all event, which has been called 'the peace that surpasseth understanding': the Peace that is God, which He gave, and gives eternally, saying 'not as the world giveth, give I unto you.' And I AM (is) that Peace. That pure Identity, devoid of content, utterly untouched by the world, is my very Self.

I AM (is) Peace.

I realize that all this *karma* of mine, this turbulence, restlessness and agitation that assails me, these plans and anticipations with which I mistakenly, and ruefully, identify myself, and the world's *karma* as well, history and 'the story of mankind', are actually nothing but thoughts passing through the transpersonal Serenity (that) I AM: the Self. They come and they go. My very ego now appears to me as 'that thought', and nothing more. It doesn't make sense to call it anything else. That's all it is.

Detachment, in other words, although on one level very definitely a goal to be striven for, is actually our true nature all along, our true identity. We are already and forever 'in the world but not of it.' The expression 'finding inner peace', which usually refers to the fruit of a readjustment of attitude or redistribution of priorities, and therefore to a created or causally determined state, is far more literal than its general usage implies, where, furthermore, it often means little more than the absence of worry. (Not to be sneezed at, however!) Infinite Peace is found within us in meditation, already there, and not as 'our' state or the simple absence of anxiety, not as anything 'personal' whatsoever, but as the Real Presence, or *Shekinah*, of the Divinity, the silent background of Pure Consciousness in which the universe, in its 'waking state', reliably appears. Its translation in our daily life is unruffled equanimity of spirit, desirelessness and contentment, abiding in the Will of God: oneness with the ancient everflowing Tao, or with *wei wu-wei*, the 'Non-acting Activity' of the Spirit. The peace we seek and find in Nature, where 'everything gets done without anyone intending anything,' is Self-Awareness.

I AM (is) Peace, infinite tranquillity. We smile with joy as we meditate. This is the Peace of the Earth—of still waters, halcyon shorelines, cumulus clouds, intermittent bird calls on motionless afternoons. Immanent Peace. We experience something like an infinite indifference, an absolute dispassion whose self-awareness is itself dispassionate. We feel a kind of 'cold strength', immovable and intangible at once, deriving from the untouchable glacial remoteness of this Peace. This is Transcendent Peace, not of this world. The Peace prior to Creation, which returns whenever universes are reabsorbed into their Source at the end of the cycle, and which can be known by human beings Now.

When a man has restrained the turbulent passions of his breast by the power of right judgment, and has spread the garment of soft compassion and sweet content over his heart and mind, let him then worship divine serenity within himself.
—Yoga-Vasishtha

Everyone thirsts for peace, but few people understand perfect peace cannot be obtained so long as the inner soul is not filled with the presence of God . . . this God who is always present in all the fibres of your body and who nonetheless prefers to remain hidden. When through appropriate and assiduous exercises the blackness of your soul is effaced, God reveals Himself, and it is absolute peace.
—Ananda Moyi

Devotees: We are pacifists. We want to bring about Peace.
Maharshi: Peace is always present. Get rid of the disturbances to peace. This Peace is the Self.
—Sri Ramana Maharshi

✿

Light is the perfect symbol of the Self, the Pure Consciousness. The Light (that) I AM is pure Subjectivity, forever unknowable because It can never be an object of cognition ('How shall the Knower be known?'), never be a 'thing', the infinite all-pervading Awareness in which everything 'objective' exists.

It's not like physical light, however, and here It departs from Its symbol, in the sense that physical light merely illuminates and makes visible objects which are already there. There is nothing 'already there'. Objective reality exists only in 'that unborn Light', utterly dependent upon It, in the same way that a dream exists in the mind of the dreamer: Subject and Object are One. The world and I, the world and I AM, flow along together, as One.

The world is an appearance in Consciousness, a cosmic Consciousness, Atman, the Self, whose refraction in innumerable apparently separate consciousnesses, human and non-human, guarantees the coherence and consistency of a shared world. That was the 'plan', as it were, for this particular Manifestation. In naïve 'original' perception we assume there's an autonomous world 'out there', objective and independent of awareness, which we observe as passive witnesses. The Vedantic Revelation teaches, and the teaching is confirmed by direct experience in meditation, that dualism is an illusion, that subject and object, apparently separated, are actually united in that paradigmatic divine intimacy which is Supreme Identity. (The good Bishop Berkeley almost had it!) I AM (is) that unborn Light, and that Light is the world. Atman and *maya* are One. There is only the Self.

To know this as Truth is to understand what Jesus meant—among many other things, of course—when He, 'light of the world', said 'I have conquered the world.' Who died on the Cross? Who lives in our hearts?

Our nature as the Light is first suspected (the Path to Enlightenment often begins with a suspicion) when we consider the dependence of the world, or Being, upon Consciousness. It's as blindingly obvious when you see it as it is logically self-evident when you think about it.

Two consequences then become immediately inescapable: first, that I AM (that) Awareness, and second, the transcendent and eternal nature of this Awareness (that) I AM. What ensues or supervenes at this 'point of insight' is a matter of Grace. Insights, no matter how profound, can only set the stage,

I AM (is) His Light, not the ego's *karma*. Realizing (what) I AM is the key to the prison, liberation from *karma*.

Far below me, as if seen from a cloud, or deep within me, as if situated in another dimension, the play is enacted within the Light (that) I AM. The player with 'my name' seems to be the central character, but only because he summons up the memories—the handful that survive, and therefore grow increasingly vivid, from among the millions he's forgotten—with which he feverishly, methodically, vindictively (he has an agenda), cunningly and with wild inconsistence (there's really nobody here at all) weaves and re-weaves the endless sequence of mental images, ranging from exact copies to startling originals created on the spot, which he calls 'me.'

But I AM (is) His Light. This is the teaching. The Truth. To be realized.

❁

Only that yogi
Whose joy is inward,
Inward his peace,
And his vision inward,
Shall came to Brahman
And know Nirvana.

And I AM (is) Nirvana.

The word 'Nirvana' may be employed not only as a specific of Buddhist doctrine but in its general 'poetic' sense, common to both Hinduism and Buddhism, in which it refers to extinction in the infinite Bliss which is ultimate Reality or the Self. That beyond which there is nothing. The goal, the end of the Path, the Absolute, in which the individual as such disappears, the twin illusions of bondage and the ego are dispelled, and nothing remains but the impersonal pure Bliss which is eternal Reality: Brahman. I AM (is) that Reality, I AM (is) that Bliss. I AM (is) Nirvana,

Nirvana, once known, there is nothing further to pursue. We experience a dreamy detachment from earthly affairs, an inwardness of focus, the features of the world recede and fade: all along, I was *this*. *Everything* is this. I AM (is) Nirvana because Reality is Nirvana—which in no way contradicts the fact that *within* the dream, *within* the illusion, *within* Samsara, in the world of embodied beings, suffering is real and we are most assuredly responsible for relieving it where we can. I have heard that when a group of Buddhists was asked how they can extol compassion at the same time as they deny the existence of its recipients, as well as its donors, they simply smiled. The truths we see in meditation and the facts we live with in daily life are often reconciled by submission to the latter—with a smile that knows what it knows.

I perceive that my innermost Self, the changeless and eternal Witness of transience, untouched by the world, is pure Bliss. I know immediately that that Bliss is the Reality, the Truth in which the entities and events we call the world appear and disappear. But Bliss suggests an experience, an enjoyer of Bliss, and since there is none, this ultimate impersonal 'state of affairs', this impersonal Bliss that is Reality, is given its own name—Nirvana. But I AM also (is) Reality, and I AM also (is) no one. So I AM (is) Nirvana as well.

> That which is Bliss is verily the Self. Bliss and the Self are not distinct and separate but are one and identical. And That alone is real.
>
> ~ Sri Ramana Maharshi

❁

Bhakti and Self-Enquiry are one and the same. The Self of the Advaitins is the God of the bhaktas.

~ Sri Ramana Maharshi

How does it happen?

The fulfillment of love, Love Supreme, divine love, is love of God: we know it when it happens, with a certitude that makes every 'certitude' we had formerly experienced seem, in comparison, like a cursory and somewhat precarious surmise. God transcendent, utterly distinct from His Manifestation, or God immanent, one with the world ('All this is Brahman'), either way or both, the love of this Infinity fills us completely, obliterates the petty self we thought we were, and we enter Reality.

And when this divine love is experienced we realize immediately that it was always there, our true Self, beneath the lower self which is now seen to have been but a tattered illusion, a caprice of the mind so arbitrary and haphazard that only continually repeated projection could give it any semblance of reality. And we realize further, in calm and blissful acquiescence to what is immediately self-evident, that this divine love is itself God. My true Self, which is Love, is God. We have loved God throughout all eternity, and that is known in direct experience.

He is within us as the Love with which we love Him and in which we discover Him, for knowing Him and loving Him are one. 'To love is to know Me, my innermost nature, the Truth which I am.' I AM (is) this Love. Lover, Love and Beloved, they are all One in the Self.

> Blessed indeed are those who meditate on the Lord of Love as the Self within, for they are free from the bondage of ignorance and from enslavement to karma.
> ~ SRIMAD BHAGAVATAM

'WHO AM I BUT THOU?'

If I were to quote authorities here, the saints and sages of the world's traditions, there would be no end to it. Let Eckhart suffice: 'The soul is not like God, she is identical with him.' (But have we heard yet from Clement of Alexandria in these pages? No? 'If a man knows himself, He shall know God.') Theomorphism is the Message. Self-Realization and God-Realization are the same. The Self of the *jnani* and the God of the *bhakta* are the same. I AM (is) God.

There's a tinge of difference, however, in the view from our side of the river, between theistic realization of I AM and the *jnani's* Self-Realization. God-Realization feels something like two-in-one and one-in-two: a faint exquisite aura of duality surrounds the unity, like backlight behind a portrait. We contemplate in marvelling adoration, in a rapt glowing silence that fills the universe, the blissful Being we know now to be our very Self. And we can't tear ourselves away. Can't do it. A trace of ego remains: we can't bring ourselves to completely relinquish the infinite joy of loving Him. A part of us would still rather love Him than merge with Him and thereby lose Him. The *bhaktas* have made their choice, and God holds them to it: their request, and God grants it. As the traditional Hindu saying goes, 'I would rather taste honey than be honey.' (But who is it that makes this choice?)

❁

All realizations or intimations of our identity with Something other than the ego have as their precondition and consequence a dissociation to some degree from that ego. We drift through such dissociations, experiencing them in varying depths and flavors, whenever we 'forget ourselves', meaning whenever we contemplate anything without opinions, preferences or purposes, in pure detached awareness, what Krishnamurti called 'choiceless awareness'. In these moments we know peace even if we don't know we are knowing it. Who's knowing what, when the ego's gone?

One way to help induce this detached state is to try to imagine ourselves on our deathbed, looking back at all this, all this hope and fear and anxious urgency that seem so vivid and real right now. We project ourselves into a future perspective from which our entire life is past tense, over and done with, an object of contemplation rather than a present 'situation' demanding attitudes and responses.

To enter this retrospective appraisal is a step toward dissociation from the ego. We may then be able to see, and say, 'I *was* all that. "I" was not localized *here*, in this body, but "I" was diffused throughout all that, that whole world called "my life", that whole world "I" thought "I" was "living in" and perceiving and entertaining opinions about and reacting to but which was actually my Self, suspended before and within "me" now like a dream in an infinite Mind, a cloud in the infinite sky. And this "I" was actually utterly beyond the "me"; it was not identified anymore with one part of "all that" than with another.'

We can re-read this appraisal in the present tense. What will be seen as true then, on the deathbed, is true now.

❁

God became man, that man might become God.
~ ST. ATHANASIUS, ST. AUGUSTINE, ST. CYRIL OF ALEXANDRIA, ECKHART, BOEHME, and others)

I am Humanity.

From 'I am a human being,' one of a class, to 'I am Humanity,' a universal of which my individuality is merely a local expression, is but a short step for any thoughtful person suddenly seized by a moment of thoughtfulness.

This short step, however, as the focus of a meditation, can be a giant step toward Self-Realization. It enables us to discard the attributes of the individual ego as accidental and to seek, and identify with, the attributes of humanity as such; and since it is these latter attributes, not the former, which reflect our theomorphic nature, realization of our humanity merges, in its highest stages, with realization of the immortal Self.

The essential insight here, attained in meditation, is precisely that 'humanity' is a *consciousness*, not a material being, individual or collective, not an historical evolution, and indeed the central consciousness of this Manifestation—which is why Adam named the creatures and why language, unique to humans, is divine, both in itself and as the vehicle of the Word. Humanity, in other words, is a reflection of the Divine Consciousness that is the Self of the universe. The human presence is the Divine Presence.

The richness of our identification with Humanity truly overflows without end. And what we feel, in our contemplation of this incredible being, this incredible presence, this miracle that we are, is love: it couldn't be otherwise. (As well as, of course, dismay, pity, cynicism and bemused despair: richness in all senses here.) 'Humanity' is something like a focus or perspective enabling us to meditate on everything: Nature and the Earth, everything and everyone we have ever loved, all the moments and dramas, the inexhaustible content of the human adventure whose proper interpretation and 'handling' is our *raison d'être* in this world and in the universe that springs into existence around this being, the universe now seen to be human. The whole trip. And each of us, individually, *is* 'the whole trip': *aham eva sarvam*, I myself am All. This fragile, infinitely precious spark of light, apparently lost in the Cosmos, is actually, and simultaneously, the foundation of that Cosmos, in its every detail, the central consciousness in which all the attributes of the Earth and the universe originate: we are deiform, we are the Center—or rather the Center, which is God, has manifested as us: as Humanity.

Love of Humanity and love of the Universe are one love, because the two are identical. More precisely, love of the Universe, and the consciousness, which *is* Humanity, in which the Universe is suspended, are now also seen to be identical. The Universe exists in a Consciousness whose nature is Love, and in the experience of that Love the Self is intuited before It is named, before It is identified by Revelation and Grace. (This insight is often the inarticulate content of a certain spontaneous rapture people experience in Nature, although it can really be felt anywhere when the mind is temporarily derailed from the commonplace.) Love of Humanity merges into Self-Realization, because Humanity is the Self and to love the Self is to know It. And vice versa. 'To love is to know Me, my innermost nature, the Truth that I am'. The words of Sri Krishna. The Scriptures constantly insist upon the preciousness of human birth, the infinite opportunity it offers and the catastrophe of failing to realize its potential, its implicit intention. To meditate on Humanity is to understand why.

The greater our prior love of Humanity, no matter what the reason for it, what ideology or sentimentalism may have inspired it, the more we are offered by the meditative focus, or *mantra*, 'I am Humanity.' We can draw upon all our experience. All the deep feelings we have ever known, all the droll or rending insights, all the deep moments of intimacy with earthly things, the images, dramas and revelations we can never forget, the always vanishing joys and sorrows, the faces of old people and of children, the sacrifices, the compassion for human beings in their folly, mortality and inescapable grandeur, all can be poured into our contemplation of this *mantra*. The life we lived prior to spiritual awakening is redeemed and fulfilled: God was always present.

I AM (is) Humanity. I AM (is) my own blessing, my salvation.

Man, is not he Creation's last appeal,
The light of Wisdom's eye? Behold the wheel
Of universal life as 'twere a ring,
But Man the superscription and the seal.
~ OMAR KHAYYAM

Human birth . . . reflects My image.
~ SRIMAD BHAGAVATAM

Realize thy Simple Self,
Embrace thy Original Nature.
~ Tao Te Ching

❁

A Supreme Person pervades and sustains the universe, and I AM (is) that Person.

We may imagine an immense smiling figure whose outlines are traced by stars, like a single constellation filling the whole breadth and depth of the heavens. Infinite Beauty, Beauty Itself, the Beauty which makes all things beautiful. In devotional meditation this immense figure is suddenly perceived in our hearts.

The Self of the universe is my Self. I AM (is) the Person in my Heart.

> It is a great truth, which you should seriously consider, that there is nothing in heaven or upon the earth which does not also exist in Man, and God who is in heaven exists also in Man, and the two are but One.
> ~ Paracelsus

> Thou art but an atom, He, the great whole; but if for a few days thou meditate with care on the whole, thou becomest one with it.
> ~ Jami

❁

When I AM the universe
I know I AM,
and I AM what I know.
The content is like fireworks
and I AM the vault of heaven,
radiant emptiness, radiant night.

A greater abyss between the way things appear to be and the way they actually are is unimaginable. Trying to describe the Reality from within the dream is not merely futile, it's ruled out *a priori* as if the only designation we can assign to the Reality within the dream is The Incomprehensible.

But we can remember It. Though we can't describe It, we can remember It, and immerse ourselves, for fleeting moments, in the joy of knowing that what we knew and saw in meditation is true forever. This biography and body are not only not 'me', they are no one at all. My salvation was ordained, and accomplished, before the beginning of time. I AM (is) the Witness: I AM (is) the Self-Awareness of the universe which *is* the universe.

I am the wind that breathes on the sea
I am the wave of the ocean
I am the murmur of the waves
I am the ox of seven combats
I am the eagle on the rocks
I am the beam of the sun
I am the fairness of plants
I am the valor of the wild boar
I am the salmon leaping
I am the stillness of the lake
I am the word of science
I am the lance-point of battle
I am the divinity who created in the head the fire.
Who throws light on the meeting in the mountains?
Who tells the ages of the moon?
Who teaches where sets the sun?
Who, if not I?

~ ORTHA NAN GAIDHEAL [*Songs of the Gaels*]

I AM (is) the universe.

Basic Vedanta. *Aham eva sarvam* in Sanskrit.

We often recall this great truth in the flat prosaic light of our daily lives, when nothing could seem more distant from our present strait-jacket reality, more contrary, more inconceivable. But you might want to give it a try.

You really have to stop everything, withdraw someplace and meditate for awhile to get a taste of it again. And you have to be more or less at peace with yourself and the world at the time. If there are any hard little knots of preoccupation lingering in your soul, or if weariness has motivated a sudden evasion of responsibility masquerading as piety, or if you are nervously reacting to a fear of 'losing ground' in your *sadhana*, it won't work. The circumstances in which Grace is withheld become familiar—although, in accordance with the teaching 'the Spirit bloweth where it listeth,' He is never predictable.

I wrote a little poem:

Everything that has ever happened
really happens Now in the Self.
The living and the dead mingle,
and the blue wildflower tremoring against the sky
in the cold clear air of the Sierras
blooms forever, in the Self.

❁

Son, when thou art quiet and silent, then art thou as God was before nature and creature: thou art that which God then was . . . then thou hearest and seest even with that wherewith God himself saw and heard in thee, before even thine own willing or thine own seeing began.

~ BOEHME

He (the American Indian) believes profoundly in silence—the sign of a perfect equilibrium. Silence is the absolute poise or balance of body, mind, and spirit. The man who preserves his selfhood ever calm and unshaken by the storms of existence—not a leaf, as it were, astir on the tree: not a ripple upon the surface of shining pool—his, in the mind of the unlettered sage, is the ideal attitude and conduct of life. If you ask him: 'What is silence?' he will answer: 'It is the Great Mystery! The holy silence is His voice!'

~ OHIYESA

Silence is the language of God; it is also the language of the heart.
~ Swami Sivananda

The point is made. I AM (is) Silence. As Dogen said, 'Think the not-thought.' Listen to the Silence that you are. It is also Peace. I AM (is) Peace. And Peace is Bliss, the Peace that surpasses understanding. I AM (is) Bliss.

Think this and believe it and see it and know it: *The Silence within alone is real.*

In other words: *This Eternal Silence is the Truth.*

❁

'I am the Glory of the Vedas'

Our appeal in spiritual life is to the Absolute, the formless Principle. To God. But this appeal always passes through the mediating symbols, doctrines and categories of a particular tradition which is a crystallization of that Principle, a 'form of the Formless', a religion. In this book, although I have endeavored throughout to suggest the 'transcendent unity' (Schuon's phrase) of the various formal traditions, that religion is the Vedanta, the religion of India, whose Wisdom is discovered in the revelation of the Vedas, and it is to the Vedanta that I am indebted for my hope of salvation.

'I am the Glory of the Vedas.' This final mantra on identity refers to the identification with the Truth of the tradition that fills our hearts with gratitude when we turn towards it, and meditate upon it, in an attitude of loving worship and total self-surrender.

The *sanatana dharma*, Eternal Wisdom, is God: He is One with His Word. And since the Vedantic doctrine, the doctrine of Atman and Brahman, is the doctrine of identity *par excellence*, Self-Realization can be experienced as the realization or fulfillment of the Vedic Truth within us. Indeed, the realization of the Vedic Truth in its actualization, can have no other meaning. The heart of that Truth is the Self.

Indeed the term Vedas, as used by the orthodox, not only names a large body of texts handed down by generation after generation, but in another sense stands for nothing less than the inexpressible truth of which all scriptures are of necessity a pale reflection. Regarded in this second aspect, the Vedas are infinite and eternal. They are that perfect knowledge which is God.
—Swami Prabhavananda, from his introduction to the Upanishads

I AM (is) the Glory of the Vedas.

PART TWO

COCK THE EAR OF YOUR HEART: HEAR IT? ('HEARD MELODIES ARE SWEET, BUT THOSE UNHEARD...')

To the eye of the heart—or, which is the same thing, to the power of vision liberated in devotional meditation—Creation sometimes appears to be a song become visible, a congealed hosanna. In its familiar features, the flora and fauna, the terrain and weathers, it remains in bondage to gravity and multiplicity. But as music it is one song, and it ascends. No longer circumscribed within terrestrial occasions, Creation stands unveiled as a living being, looking upward in eager and joyous adoration, singing. The stars become a choir, an orison of light, their radiance a longing and reaching out for union with God.

This is not 'a way of seeing things'. On the contrary, the vision of the physical eyes is merely a way of seeing things. And it casts a veil over the dazzling truth visible to the eye of the heart.

The emphasis in this perception is on the magnetic centrality of God. We realize that every created thing, merely by being itself, which means carrying out the divine intention, conforming to the will of God, praises and celebrates the Creator. We love what we call 'nature' because there the celebration is ubiquitous, unanimous and uninterrupted: that's why we call nature *pure*. For the same reason—perfect conformity to the divine will which is consequently a mode of praise—nature is beautiful, innocent and synonymous with peace. Humanity alone, as well we know, can deviate from conformity—therefore the Law—just as humanity alone can, through worship, consciously and deliberately celebrate the Creator. We can literally, as well as spiritually, through that apparent submission which is really freedom, sing the Name. And melt into the Oneness, the universal hosanna. We can see clearly, see with a knowledge that is the joy in our hearts, inseparable from that joy: *The whole world sings Thy Name.* The words come to our lips.

EITHER WAY YOU LOOK AT IT...

Devotional rapture is sometimes initiated or provoked by a keen awareness of the transience of all created things. By the sudden and indisputable realization that there is absolutely nothing to hold on to here, that all earthly things are ephemeral, devoid of durable substance or significance, especially and above all ourselves.

When this is the spiritual 'structure' of the meditational event, the recollection, as of a great truth once again forgotten, of the ineffable and indestructible beatitude pervading the fleeting insubstantiality of the visible universe then flashes immediately to mind, experienced as overwhelming love of the eternal Spirit beyond all change: love of God. It's a corollary, as it were, of the humble sincerity of our appraisal, a reward for honesty. We have indirectly confessed our longing for God, acknowledged that 'Everything is perishing save His Face.'

And, contrariwise, the love of God is also initiated or provoked by an opposite perception. How so?

Because the things of this world, although legitimately regarded as transient, are from another point of view, equally legitimate and despite that transience, quite breathtakingly glorious. In this aspect we love the world, love transience itself as the poignant essence of every moment's pricelessness, love the whole incredible scene, with a helpless and grateful amazement. We find ourselves in love with the universe, head over heels, transported by the sheer bliss of existence in it, and this love of Creation overflows, as it were, with irresistible precipitance, into love of the Creator. We have realized that 'He is veiled in His own glory.'

Either way, and in innumerable other ways as well, the world implies God. Earth implies Heaven. Creation implies Creator. Transience implies Eternity. The Relative implies the Absolute. *This* implies *That.*

GLINTS & GLIMPSES IV

'Love of God' is a concept, a spiritual category, something you can think about, mull over. We can place it in front of us, like putting an art object on the table, and examine it from all angles, or place it on an altar and adore it. We can isolate it from the rest of the world fairly easily and appreciate it at its true worth, without distraction. We can focus our minds on it, get into it. Dwell upon it, imagine it, think of all the reasons for it. Simply say the words over and over again: *The Love of God.* What is temporarily inaccessible to direct experience can be contemplated instead, to 'tide us over'. It's one of the countless ways we can practice 'remembrance of God', the heart of all practice.

❁

The truth of our lives unfolds in our dialogue with God, discontinuous, of greatly varying intensity and duration, elicited by actual events or decisions or by nothing at all apparent. How could it be otherwise? And since God alone exists, the dialogue is actually a monologue, and can be enriched, deepened, by conceiving it as such. This communion within the Self, in an Eternal Now, is alone real, and *known* in the priceless lived moment to be alone real, while the 'individual biography' in that same moment is *known* to be simply nothing at all, a fetish, a spasmodic discontinuous blather of ridiculous imaginings. Stubborn in its invariable return, but always fading, always a little less vivid, less insistent, increasingly an object of compassion, an object of impersonal love.

❁

When we finally realize that there's no essential difference between a crowd that's rioting in the streets and a crowd that's dancing in the streets we have arrived at *param dama*, the Supreme Abode, the Abode of Peace. This realization is not politically correct. Nor, for that matter, are any others.

❁

'Our God'

Ours, instead of mine.The collective possessive pronoun unites us with all others, all other human beings, and also with our impersonal identity as humanity. We are all manifestations of the one being, Humanity, each an embodiment, and He is the God, the Heart, of that All-as-One.

Our worshipping identity is expanded, universalized, in this *mantra*. We identify more with the spiritual definitions of the human norm than with any individual departures from, or 'specializations' of that norm with which we may be currently deluding ourselves.

We love Him, in this *mantra*, but with a love that has a different quality, a different flavor, from the ecstatic personal love of the *bhakta*. There's a solemnity, a restraint, paradoxically coupled with a very strong feeling of secure possessiveness, as if we are welded to Him collectively, in our collective identity, with an even stronger bond than individually—probably because the individual bond, on the level of experience, is by no means guaranteed: we know, from vivid memory, that we can feel the pain of separation from Him, whereas the collective impersonal bond is independent of our individual successes and failures on the Path. It seems more secure. The distinction is false, however, because the sense of separation is always illusory. Powerful, but illusory. He is always within us.

❁

'Thou alone art, Thou the Light imperishable, adorable: Great Glory is Thy Name.' *Svetasvatara Upanishad.*

All that we feel or 'know' about God, every spiritual truth or state we have ever known, the whole *sadhana*, accumulates in the Holy Name: everything is packed into the Name, concentrated there in an intensity, which can be infinite, directly proportional to the inten-sity of our love, the intensity and reality in direct experience of the divine Presence in the moment of utterance. Each statement about or praising God or the divine Reality containing a Holy Name—Christ, Krishna, Shiva, Rama, Allah, Buddha—adds something more to the Name, each one contributes to its infinite richness and power. The content is swallowed up in the Name and transformed into its substance, its taste, its shape in our minds, on our lips, its reverberations in our hearts. If the affirmation in these statements, the spiritual truth, were compared to an arrow, the Holy Name is where the arrow strikes the target. Or, in another metaphor, every spiritual truth is another harmonic vibration in the music of the Name. Less figuratively, experientially, each truth becomes a part of the love for Him that expresses itself in the pronouncement of His Name. The Name sanctifies the statement, the statement glorifies the Name.

'The scriptures enjoin that man's supreme duty (Dharma) consists in cultivating devotion through hearing and repeating His Names and through other devotional practices.'
~ SRIMAD BHAGAVATAM, 6.3.22

'THOU ART THE JOY IN MY HEART'

There's a pure joy that doesn't depend upon external circumstances, utterly independent of them. Divine joy, the joy we *are*, the joy of the Self, is something like divine love: in each case we realize that we didn't really know what the word meant, or could mean, until we experienced it in the spirit, in meditation and in the rare moments when the meditative state is successfully recaptured, or briefly surfaces of its own accord, in the midst of the daily ambivalence whose tenacious 'pairs of opposites' torment our lives so reliably. Suddenly there He is, smiling, so far beyond us, so deep within us.

❁

There are moments of nostalgia in our spiritual lives, of wistfulness, vague sorrow, when we suddenly recall, in the midst of the racket, and are forced to concede, that our spirituality in that moment doesn't exist as a present experience but rather as a rather perfunctory objective or remembered truth, a poignant recollection. But we know, and affirm to ourselves, that the joy is still there, always there, within us, because we cannot be separated from Him. We know that whatever we have ever experienced of Spirit, or ever will, is a gift of Grace, 'out of our hands'. Which knowledge is itself tranquillity, and even a kind of comforting certitude.

❁

'BUT IF THE WHILE I THINK ON THEE...' (SONNET 30; 116 ALSO, OF COURSE)

'Thou beloved One of my heart'

This canonical encomium, seen so often in liturgical texts, arises spontaneously, in its feeling if not in the actual words, when devotional meditation approaches the silence of union.

There are no competitors, no rivals. In the blazing radiance of His unique reality no one and nothing else even exists. He is the invisible eternal Friend and the impersonal Absolute as well, Brahman Supreme. He is the universe and He is the Self of all: our immortality. He is the Light of awareness in which we perceive all things and beings as contemporary with each other and with 'me', simultaneous in an Eternal Now which is His own eternal Presence within us as the Self. The spirit or style or flavor or essence of this sublime Presence, this realized Truth, is what we call love, and in the path of devotion, *bhakti,* it is experienced as 'my love for God.' In reality, there is no one beside God. 'My love for God' is a metaphor for His Self-Awareness. When the ego is annihilated the world is God, and God is Love. And, God knows, the ego was never real in the first place!

Beloved One of my heart. The address carries a feeling of 'declaring our love', confessing it, making it explicit—as if the love had been kept hidden for a very long time, secretly confirmed in innumerable moments of silent adoration, cherished and elaborated through years of solitary rapture, and now, certain of itself and no longer able to resist expression, can embrace the joy of revealing itself to the Beloved. There is then an air of quiet finality. Nothing is to follow, no request or plea, no praise, no prayer. The state in which we love God is a terminus, a home-coming, the end of the road. No need to present reasons, no more to ask. This was the purpose of our human birth. It will seem as if we return to the world, to the Dream, to *maya*, but actually this is forever.

A single atom of the love of God in a heart is worth more than a hundred thousand paradises.
~ BAYAZID AL-BISTAMI

We love God with His own love; awareness of it deifies us.
~ ECKHART

ASK THE TEACHER

In our life in the spirit we have to keep reading. Not every day, necessarily, not even every other day, but at least regularly, consistently. Always a book we're opening from time to time, pondering.

Scriptural texts first of all. (And for some of us nothing more.) We need to study, explore, constantly and throughout our lives, the sacred texts of our chosen tradition, its 'bibles', what is called Holy Writ, the revealed Word of God. The words in which a divine saving Truth first blazed from heaven into this world. Nothing else 'sounds' like those words. They are the bedrock upon which the entire Revelation is erected.

Next, the inspired commentaries, the commentaries on the commentaries, the wisdom of the saints and the sages, the transcripts of their statements, sermons, interviews. And also the many excellent books and essays written by sincere practitioners in our own times. These, because they are close to our concrete daily lives, our lives as they are actually lived these days, can be extremely helpful.

Some of our reading will be informative and some devotional. We will discover that the speakers in this library can become something like familiar friends, whose style or orientation of reli-gious experience gradually becomes visible to us as we learn to interpret the tenor and nuances of their texts. The traditional guru relationship is not available to the overwhelming majority of householders, but because we are literate in a literate civilization we have access to an enormous bibliography. The form changes, but something of the substance can be salvaged—a very great deal, as a matter of fact, if we are sincere and tenacious. I can remember Swami Swananda saying to me, in the library of the Vedanta Center, 'Why do you think we read these as if they were written with our own blood?' I knew why.

And finally, there's a very basic social, historical reason why we have to be always reading in the tradition we have chosen—or which has chosen us. If we don't remain in contact with voices which assume and know there's a divine Reality—a God, if you will—the only voices we'll hear are those which don't. And they can slowly, almost invisibly, grind you down, make you forget, drag you back. Our knowledge that this is happening, our awareness of a choreographed unintentional defection, and our feeling of self-betrayal, of failure in His eyes, our wretchedness and shuddering grief, even anger, are induced by Him, inevitable responses of the Truth that we are: manifestations of the eternal Grace. These are militantly secular times. And it's very doubtful that we'll be able to hold on to the truth in a beleaguered isolation. Books, in other words, in our times, are equivalent to that 'society of the holy' which tradition is unanimous in declaring indispensable.

So reading is necessary.

But not sufficient. Which is the point I've been leading up to.

We need to go directly to the Teacher. To the Source. And in devotional meditation, that's Who we are going to: the Teacher. He is within us, and He alone can definitively, so we'll never doubt it again, impart the Truth, the Truth which He is. He can reveal the Truth because He is the Truth. 'I am the Teacher of all teachers,' says Krishna in the *Bhagavatam*. The books we read—I use the classic image—are fingers pointing at Him.

The divine Presence, as we discover in meditation, is Illumination, God teaches us merely by being present to us. God *is* the Teaching. This is why Jesus can claim 'I am the Way and the Truth and the Life' and Krishna can claim 'I am the Truth and the Joy forever' and the Prophet can claim 'He who has seen me has seen the Truth.' When we murmur to ourselves, dissolved in love, as we are moved to when our meditation on this theme is rewarded, 'Thou art my Teacher,' we are also saying 'Thou art my salvation,' the Answer to my life's question, to the question implicit in my human existence, my intelligence.

The Teacher is the Truth, and since we were made for the Truth, as the *imago dei*, since knowing and realizing the Truth is the purpose and fulfillment of our lives, the relationship to God in its form as disciple to Teacher is very fundamental, very holy. In acknowledging God as our Teacher we are affirming that He is more important to us than anything else—which was precisely the essence of the traditional guru-disciple relationship. We are, in a sense, honoring Him as the divine Wisdom in which we, and the entire universe, are suspended. He is the Knowledge—the Christian Logos, the Infinite Mind, the 'universe-in-consciousness', the Shining Void, the Tao—which is Creation *in divinis*, what we and everything else actually are, but which, by the mysterious obscuration of *avidya*, or Ignorance, is inaccessible to us except by His Grace. In His wordless Presence during meditation the veil is lifted and we behold the Truth of things, the Reality, the 'actual state of affairs.' 'Thou art my Teacher' is one of the many ways of saying 'Thou art my everything.' His role as Teacher is not incidental: it is essential.

The feeling beneath the words or thought, 'Thou art my Teacher,' is one of absolute security. To be in the presence of the Teacher, in the state of receiving instruction from Him, enlightenment, is peace. It is one of the forms of 'spiritual drowning', or loss of self in God, described in much of the world's religious literature, testified to by so many saints. Simply to realize that we have at last *found* the Teacher is bliss. This Teacher Will never abandon us. His Self-Presentation as Teacher and His manifestation of the world around us, and including us, are simultaneous and mutual. He comes to us to teach us because we were put here by Him to learn, and we can learn because we are made in His image. The Teacher and the taught are a simultaneous Reality, a simultaneous Presence, a mutual implication, 'two sides of the same coin'. What could be more reassuring? Who else could we truly love? What else could love be?

There's no way to 'confirm' all this except by beginning the practice of regular meditation. The Teacher is always there, in our hearts, waiting for us, but we have to present ourselves before Him. And He reveals the Truth, when all is said and done, only to those who can't live without it, or, to be more precise, to those who know, somehow really *know*, that life without Truth is a waste of human birth, a calamity.

MEMORIES OF EDEN, PRE-EMPTIVE RELATIVISM, RECOGNIZING 'HIS SIGNATURE'

'Beauty is the splendor of the True.' (Or of the Real—I can't recall or recover the source of this quotation—I've been told that no one can!—but either way we get the idea.) And therefore in meditation we find ourselves exclaiming, with or without the actual words, something like 'O Beautiful Truth'. Because we've seen It. Truth, Reality, Nirvana.

The Truth, when we finally find it, or It finds us, is infinitely beyond anything we could have imagined earlier in our quest. There was no way to foresee this glory, and there is no way to convey it in words once it has been seen. It shines before us, silent, changeless, eternal, complete, ineffable radiance, the Oneness of all things in God. Behind the veil, behind the illusion, behind the fleeting, ambiguous, tantalizing, spell-binding drama in which we suffer so reliably and rejoice so innocently, the Reality that appears to our earthly eyes as the universe stands revealed to the eye of the heart as infinite Bliss, ineffable Perfection.

We behold It in meditation. And at the center of what we behold, wonder of wonders, is a Person, an infinite Person, *Paramatman*, the Supreme Self. The word 'truth' suggests impersonality, the discovery by a purely intellectual intuition of something akin to itself. But the Truth we perceive in meditation is personal as well: the 'personal-impersonal' ultimate Reality revealed to the *rishis* of ancient India and evoked most powerfully, evoked with irresistibly convincing finality, in the depiction and 'personality' of Krishna in the *Bhagavad-Gita*.

This vision doesn't emerge from a vacuum.

The stage is set by our intuition of the perfection of the world before some kind of protracted catastrophe (yes: the Fall) obliterated it, before humankind's violation of what Native Americans called 'the Original Instructions', the remnants of which are occasionally glimpsed behind the massive interventions we witness today. Primeval Nature, the untouched Earth. It is intuitively obvious, in other words, if you really think about it—and this is true even for an 'atheistic' apprehension—that there cannot be anything 'wrong', fundamentally and down to the last detail, with a universe, a creation. The Truth behind the material world, of which Nature has already supplied us with countless intimations, must also be Perfection, and must appear to our inward eye as absolute Beauty: *shyama sunduram*.

How could the Agency in which all this originated be intellectually, morally or aesthetically 'less' than our own achievements or conceptions? How could it be anything but infinite in all respects? How could Creation, of which we are a part, fall short of 'our standards'? The aboriginal perfection of Creation is metaphysically self-evident. (One of those statements where acquiescence or dissent divides the human race into the two great camps—actually one very large, enjoying a temporary victory, and one very small, destined for final triumph, for *vincit omnia veritas*—that confront each other the twilight of the cosmic cycle.) The only errors in the universe, the only flaws, are our own. The ineffable beauty of the Truth, in other words, of 'the Perfection of the Origin', is anticipated by anyone capable of serious reflection—anyone with eyes to see and a brain in his or her head, I am tempted to say. The Truth we perceive in meditation confirms the anticipation we already harbor, based upon our intuition of the Origin, and in a sense depends upon it. We are unlikely to discover anything whose existence we deny in advance.

I always knew, never doubted, that there was, 'somewhere', such a thing as Truth with an upper-case 'T', but I didn't know what it was. I simply knew that it had to be. And I knew that this Truth, by that very fact, was Perfection. I also always knew (and how many would immediately realize that they share this confession if they could only stop to think about it!) that every moment or instance of beauty, no matter how fleeting or fragile, how 'subjective' or 'personal', testified to an infinite and eternal Beauty behind it—and not just because I'd read Plato—which was the creative Source of these finite and temporal expressions, these materializations, crystallizations, and I knew that this Beauty and Truth and Perfection were the invisible realities behind the visible world, and that somehow they were implicit in my own essential nature, in my Humanity. It wasn't a matter of faith, still less of hope: it was certitude—the certitude, as

I later learned, that accompanies all cognitions of the Intellect, 'cardiac intelligence', the metaphysical intuition that literally defines our humanity and which corresponds on the microcosmic level to Revelation on the macrocosmic.

Entering upon the Path to emancipation, then, presupposes the certitude—or belief or faith, or hope, even suspicion, if that's as far as it goes, if it's enough to motivate—that there is such a thing as the Truth. Accepting this proposition, on whatever level, spontaneously as a function of character type or in despair as a response to life's remorseless disappointments, is absolutely fundamental, a *sine qua non*. It's precisely this hurdle, believing that there's such a thing as the Truth, *wanting* to believe it, that prevents very many people in these times from anything more than a wishy-washy commitment to spiritual engagement, anything more than a fashionable, vaguely exotic variant of 'the pursuit of happiness' which is always spearheaded by the ego in its blindness to anything beyond its own gratification. (Truth implies authority and authority obedience, and nobody's going to tell *me* what to do! That's the heart of the matter.) In a way it's a question of getting beyond relativism, the 'different strokes for different folks' version of the universe, the alternative to which always seems, to certain people, to be some form of tyranny—which indeed it would be, if there were no such thing as the Truth! Consequently, imprisoned in a relativist perspective, unaware that the repudiation of relativism is of the very essence of spiritual life, they can't put their whole hearts into it. The thing can't be done the way it has to be done, we can't become single-minded, or 'one-pointed', to use the traditional term, we'll never be able to persevere without at least a provisional commitment to the idea that there is a Truth accessible to us and that we are in search of it. This means, in these times, swimming against the current, because we live in a world where we are relentlessly, even fiendishly, distracted from experiences which might awaken and reinforce our intuition of the Absolute, which we sometimes call Truth, sometimes God, sometimes the Real.

This intuition is recovered, or at least glimpsed, in the presence of beauty. The Absolute, or Truth, is like a halo or aura surrounding all objects and moments of beauty. Beauty characterizes the aboriginal being, the purity of being, as it was, and eternally is, breathed forth from That which we call God. It is the style of the Absolute: 'His signature is the beauty of things,' as Robinson Jeffers put it so memorably. We can't help but feel that the beauty of the universe, of creation, the perfection of beauty we find in simple natural things, leaves, shells, stars, waves, garden snakes, shiny beetles, dewdrops, twilights, shadows on the grass, in their innocent invulnerable presence, is proof of Something, evidence of Something. Beauty testifies to It as smoke testifies to fire. If there is Beauty there is Truth.

Find out what that Something is, that Something that appears to us as Beauty, or behind Beauty, or within Beauty, or simply perceive It, with the eye of the heart, and don't worry about giving It a name. Let It be nameless, a nameless Presence—which is what It really is, after all. We call It the Reality, the Truth, we call It God. Buddhists call it *prajna*, a word very variously translated. We give It names. But in the holy *Upanishads* It's often referred to simply as That. No name: simply That. And the *mahavakya*, or Great Saying, of the *Upanishad* affirms: That art Thou. You, you yourself, are the nameless Presence. The nameless Presence behind Beauty, the nameless Presence to which the constellation Orion, Half Dome at sunrise, and every snowflake, every call of a bird, bear witness.

SOME PREFER TO ACCENTUATE THE NEGATIVE (DESPITE JOHNNY MERCER AND HAROLD ARLEN'S DISSENTING OPINION IN *HERE COME THE WAVES*)

In our devotional meditation we sometimes feel we are looking into an infinite emptiness or absence, a nothingness: a gulf, a bottomless abyss. This is a classic perception, and is richly testified in all spiritual traditions, both in their scriptures and in the experience of the saints and the sages.

In our rapt contemplation of this abyss, feeling ourselves sink into its silent tranquil depths, we are treading the apophatic path, we are apprehending, 'knowing' God in His unknowability, which here appears to us as an undifferentiated internal infinity devoid of attributes. The Mystery, *Mysterium Magnum*, goal of the *via negativa, die ganze anderer* or 'wholly other', the utterly transcendent. The Godhead. 'The Tao that can be named is not the eternal Tao.'

Second dimension:

The abyss is also, however, the Knower, the one Knower. It is the Pure Consciousness of Vedanta, the Self, the Atman, Brahman Supreme. The infinite Awareness in which the mirage of a world is suspended. What we have already encountered as the Mind of the Dreamer.

Third:

It is also the *avyaktam* or Unmanifest, the utterly absent (from manifestation) Source of all phenomenal manifestation. The Void which is also the noumenal Reality: the domain of the eternal Archetypes—the divine ideas of all moments and things—which appears as, becomes, when objectified, when cast forth into time and space, the *samsara*, the world. This is where the world originates, the power, the infinite potential, the conceiving of all things. The infinite Mind of the Creator.

Fourth:

The abyss is the static motionless Peace upon which the world-appearance is projected like a film on a screen. Beneath the restless activity of our minds, It is the detached true Mind, always there, indestructible, transecting the flickering insubstantial myriad drama, ceaselessly changing, never the same from instant to instant, that we call daily life: indestructible, changeless, utterly serene. *Pax Profunda.*

The abyss is deep, and deep within us. It is our refuge. It is the Reality. The Great Silence.

It is the end of the Path, there is nothing beyond It. Anything which can be said to 'be', to 'exist', anything positive, emerges from It and returns to It. It is victory over the world, on the plane of action, and, on the plane of contemplation, the world's secure and compassionate foundation.

Let's call it 'the Abyss of God', pausing slightly after the word 'abyss'. The Abyss . . . of God. Pause slightly, then focus with undiluted one-pointedness on the word 'God'. When you say it this way, the word 'Abyss' is, as it were, gathered up into the word 'God', *cast* into the word 'God', which then contains the sense and feel of the word 'Abyss' within it. The Abyss . . . of God. Try it. God resonates: infinite emptiness, infinite fullness. The negation of all things in which all things are nonetheless contained.

> A man may in this life reach the point at which he understands himself to be one with that which is nothing as compared with all the things that one can imagine or express in words. By common agreement, men call this Nothing 'God', and it is itself a most essential Something.
>
> ~ Henry Suso

> It is only a few more days, in this world, and each shall return to its own fountain; the blood-drop to the abysmal heart, the water to the river, the river to the shining sea; and the dewdrop which fell from heaven shall rise to heaven again, shaking off the dust grains which weighed it down, thawed from the earth frost which chained it here to herb and sward, upward and upward ever through stars and suns, through gods, and through the parents of the gods, purer and purer through successive lives, until it enters the Nothing, which is the All, and finds its home at last.
>
> ~ Hypatia

> Everything depends on this: a fathomless sinking into a fathomless nothingness.
>
> ~ Tauler

Stop creating the world with your mind. Stop sustaining it all by the self-deception called 'remembering', and you'll see that there's really nothing but the perpetual explosion, like fireworks, of an illusory past, present and future, an illusory 'world', in an eternal Now *which you are.* The plenitude we love so deeply, so passionately, and with such good reason—for He saw that it was good—floats like a glorious mirage, a miracle, quite securely unsurpassable, in the Abyss of God. *Which you are.*

✿

GLINTS & GLIMPSES V

'Thou art the joy of the Universe'

Joy is impersonal, or transpersonal; we think it's our own, but it isn't. God is the treasure of every consciousness. He is the Self, the Pure Consciousness of which each individual consciousness is a manifestation, the Light in which everything exists, the Bliss which is Reality. Knowledge of His existence, the existence of God, is already Joy.

And although 'knowledge of His existence' and 'experience of His Presence' are not identical, they are so close that the transition is more like a deepening than a change from one thing to another. Truth and Presence: these are the saving manifestations of the Absolute.

❁

'I pray for my salvation'

This is one of the 'torn-from-the-heart' moments. We realize our absolute dependence, and to the depths of our being, not just intellectually. There's a feeling of purity, or safety, or release from tension, in this prayer. We know we've gotten down to the solid rock bottom of our human condition. Our truth. This feeling of genuineness, this recognition of desolation, this plea, this humility—it's all real. No way it could be called a posture. I am the being who needs to be saved from my own condition: this is fundamental.

❁

'I am before God'

It's sometimes a good idea to make this affirmation, if your mind has been more agitated than usual by the day's unpleasant surprises or unexpected explosions, if your cheerful equanimity has been shattered once again by some sudden outburst of passion from a son or daughter, a husband or wife, before beginning to meditate. You want to push the world out of your mind, with gentle but firm insistence, and establish yourself in the new and infinitely happier setting. You might enjoy a pungent realization of how truly hideous and shameful your degradation was during the day, and a rending feeling within as you humbly and dumbly observe yourself being slowly disengaged from the wretched clinging identification with the lower self in which your misery was rooted. Maybe you'll even sob briefly with remorse, and bitterness, in your sudden awareness of how low you sank, and how much of your life is spent at that depth. It's a good idea to wallow for awhile in this feeling. Get into it. Then pray for forgiveness and strength in the future. Hopefully you won't be driven too often to this extremity; but there are times when cleansing is the best, maybe the only way to begin a meditation.

At the other end of the spectrum 'I am before God' can be an expression of the purest joy. Where else should you be but before God? When else is life perfect?

❁

The easiest, most natural way to 'talk' to God is to praise His attributes. It's that simple.

This praise is never subservient. It's jubilant, celebratory. Actually triumphant. Our praise is His Presence.

Thou are the joy of the universe. Thou art the One, the All, the Truth. Thou art Life, Love, Light, Joy and Peace. Thou art the beloved one of us all. And so on, forever. Our praise is His Presence.

❁

'My Creator'

Not only a humble awareness of absolute dependence, but a chastened feeling as well, the feeling of having been put in one's place. (It's good to be put in your place. You feel right, and precisely because you're in your place!) On the one side, then, humility, and on the other loving devotion: the rapt adoration we breathe into the words 'My Creator', which should be uttered as a direct address. 'Creator' is experienced not as a remote power but in a quite literal sense as immediate fashioner, maker; we are suddenly aware of ourselves as created beings, sculpted 'clay', incapable of making the slightest personal claim.

This is a very deep intuition of God. Creator is one of His great Names. It's a divine hypostasis that reveals one layer, or dimension, or vision, or version (there are others) of the Cosmic Reality. To become aware of ourselves in relation to that Name is to know ourselves *in divinis*, as we exist in the infinite being of God. To know ourselves as we really are, in our Truth.

All knowledge of God is knowledge of ourselves, both as we receive it in doctrine and in the living moment of meditative intuition. We feel, in making this address from the heart, as if we have finally discovered something we desperately needed and have always been searching for, or finally arrived back on our doorstep after a long exhausting journey, or finally remembered something vitally important and immediately efficacious.

✲

'I'D WALK A MILLION MILES FOR ONE OF THOSE SMILES!'

Resolutely withdrawing the senses from their objects by an effort of will, he should, with the help of the discriminating intellect, concentrate the mind on My form and on every several feature of it. Then withdrawing it from all other parts of the body, he should steadily focus it on one—the smiling face and nothing else. Then, meditate on Me as the Supreme Cause, in whom the whole universe exists and from whom the whole universe evolves. Last of all, meditate on the oneness of the Self with God, the one blissful existence, the one I AM. With the mind thus absorbed, he sees Me alone in himself and sees himself in Me, the Self of all—light joined to Light. A yogi, thus practicing meditation regularly, with intense devotion, soon rises above all limitations and realizes the one all-pervading Reality.

~ SRIMAD BHAGAVATAM, XI.14

These are instructions in devotional meditation—straight from the lips of God, as far as a Hindu *bhakta* is concerned. They can be interpreted, generalized beyond their specific content, and serve as inspiration in our spiritual practice. What we're most interested in is the significance of their two emphases: the smile and the Light.

Initially, it's the sheer pricelessness of the passage that strikes us: *this is how to do it.* We're reminded of the first question of the disciples of Christ: how shall we pray? We perceive, in the insightful genius of the technique, that both aspects of God, the personal and the impersonal, are evoked, the former as a stepping stone to the latter, the latter as the inner truth of the former. Krishna smiling (it's the Hindu Avatar, Krishna, Who is speaking here) is the God Who loves us, the Person to Whom we pray, redeeming Grace. Krishna as Light is the Pure Awareness, the Atman, the Self of all. These two are the One, and beyond this Oneness words are left behind.

From the smile to the Light. Let's take the smile first.

In the *Bhagavad-Gita*, the actual beginning of Krishna's instructions to Arjuna is introduced by Sanjaya with the words: 'Then to him who thus sorrowed between the two armies, the ruler of the senses spoke, smiling.'

Again the smile. A smile on the face of God. God smiles at us. It expresses, first of all, the fond, sympathetic and even slightly amused understanding with which mothers and fathers patiently regard the limited grasp of their children. We can read in that smile a guarantee of guidance; it's promising, a good omen, an unmistakable reassurance. Our inability to penetrate to the truth of things—the true interpretation, the right path, the sense of our own presence—is being recognized by a being Who is Wisdom itself. What can follow but teaching? His smile is the assurance of salva-tion, of actual immortality, Life Eternal. Errors will be corrected, questions will be answered, where there was darkness there will be light, where there was doubt there will be certitude. So Arjuna says, at the end of the last chapter of the Gita, 'By your grace. O Lord, my delusions have been dispelled. My mind stands firm. Its doubts are ended.'

And the smile, of course, expresses love. The warmth of love. (The passage as a whole depicts what are called the solar qualities: the warmth of love, the light of knowledge.) He is forgiving, He is indulgent, He will not abandon us. This God Who understands us in our frailties and limitations is devoted to us, 'our refuge and our hope,' the source of a love in the absence of which, we realize, we would not even exist. His loving smile announces that all this, the world and our presence, is good, that behind the daily ambiguity, the seemingly ineradicable objectless troubled concern, is not only a God Who loves all of us but an infinite Perfection, inviolable and absolute, the Sovereign Good. The Teacher Who loves us is also the Reality, 'in whom the whole universe exists and from whom the whole universe evolves.' In other words, the universe manifests an infinite Benevolence, where suffering is traceable to errors we have the power to identify and correct.

The smile also expresses, finally, His absolute transcendence. Infinitely detached, He is the Spectator of everything, utterly beyond all this, utterly untouched by it, forever disengaged from the stream of events in which we imprison ourselves by our mistaken conviction that it is final: the smile tells us that there is no finality here. The smile is one of detached compassion, remote and intimate at once, as He is transcendent and immanent at once.

The transition to the Light carries a feeling of fulfillment, completion, actual relief. It's reassuring to know, by direct experience, that the human originates in the superhuman transcendent, that the personal is also impersonal, dispassionate, forever, solely and unwaveringly Its eternal Self. The smiling face of a personal God originating in the impassive inscrutable grace of the impersonal Brahman is something like a concession to limitations imposed by that very Brahman. The return to impersonality, on all levels of our lives, and when mature experience has finally driven home the increasingly obvious liabilities and painful consequences of commitment to a personal identity, is as comforting in its time and place as the return to the personal God in our seasons of that need. We oscillate back and forth. Even Shankara, even the great *jnani*, Ramana Maharshi, returned repeatedly to the welcoming ineffaceable reality of the Supreme Person.

When we meditate on this passage from the *Srimad Bhagavatam*, and whenever we manage to glimpse and become that eternal love for God which is the very Self within us, the supreme Oneness, His smile, in all its dimensions, appears on our own faces. We are the theomorphic beings in this universe. Made in His image. We are the Infinite Consciousness in which the universe is suspended. Supreme Person, *param purusam*, and Brahman Supreme. The Smile and the Light.

INCIDENT ON UPPER BRYN COCH LANE AND A METAPHYSICAL PARALLEL

We learn the Truth in meditation. Then we're out in the world, having experiences, 'chalking things up to experience', thinking about things, making snap judgments or mulling it over, living the life. What is essential, and so very difficult, is that we carry, or at least try to carry, that Truth out into the world—seeing things through Its eyes, as it were. Or, more precisely, what is essential is that the 'we' who perceived the Truth in meditation doesn't promptly disappear when the body It inhabits emerges from the meditation session but rather manages to survive the rudely disorienting transition. This entails the 'transformation' of appearances into the Reality they actually were all along, or the recognition that there is nothing but the Oneness, the Self—which we are. *Sarvam idam Brahma*: All this is Brahman.

I present two illustrations. The first describes a 'moment of truth' that came my way in Wales some years ago; the second addresses an almost universally unexamined assumption about who and where we are.

❁

Here I am in Wales. Not through any initiative of my own—'the sage takes no initiatives,' we are taught, a proscription I find increasingly easier to observe as I grow older and the futility of worldly maneuvers becomes increasingly and gratefully apparent—but as a passenger, cheerful and industrious, on the vessel of other people's plans.

I'm returning from the second-hand bookstore where I picked up a copy of Richard Llewellyn's *How Green Was My Valley* for my daughters, thinking they might enrich their experience in Wales through reading the great saga of love, courage, resignation and pride in which Llewellyn records how the Welsh responded to the invasion of twentieth-century industrial mining. I read it about thirty years ago and found, when the bookseller handed it to me, that I still remembered correctly the last line of the novel. 'How green was my valley then, and the valley of them that are gone.' How it must have moved me when I was twenty, to have been held in my memory for three decades.

It's a beautiful day in late August as I return with the book in my backpack. I'm walking on Upper Bryn Coch Lane only a few minutes away, down Ruthin Road, from those same Welsh valleys Llewellyn loved so well; I was just hiking through them yesterday. Reflecting upon the book, I imagine the coal mines and slag heaps ravaging the heather, the destruction, the calamity, and admire once again the human spirit's miraculous ability to record its insults, protest them and commemorate its defiance, and ultimately prove its superiority by accepting them without loss of dignity, and in this way prevail. 'It's still very popular,' the bookseller had told me, and the poignancy of her matter-of-factness suddenly strikes my heart. Tears spring to my eyes.

Then I remember, and I recover. I say the Holy Name.

The sentiment I had been feeling, originating in love and solidarity, was permissible and appropriate. It's right and good to have generous feelings. But through a lapse of memory on a level far deeper than my recollection of the last line, that classic 'forgetfulness of God' to which we are permanently prone, and owing also to the depth of the emotion, I had allowed myself to fall into illusion. I had accepted *maya*, the world-appearance—time, space, history, the stream of events—as reality. Fallen completely into it. This forgetfulness defines the greater part of our daily lives, and in our mundane impetuous affairs need not be contested; it's obviously inescapable. But where opportunities to return to Reality arise of their own accord, spontaneously, and especially when our emotive state has become profound, when we're feeling something about life deeply and truly, the return, because it is an occasion for God-Realization, is a gift of Grace, a command and a responsibility—if we want to think of ourselves as serious anyway. The moment has to be redeemed, the time seized.

There are intervals in our daily stream of consciousness, moments of expansion or heightened insight, which are auspicious precisely because of their proximity to spiritual states, because they contain a potential for divine illumination, and they should be identified and grasped, the offer accepted. Developing this sensitivity to invitations is an important aspect of our spiritual engagement. These moments are occasions for 'the practice of the presence of God,' in Brother Lawrence's familiar phrase.

So I uttered the Holy Name, and recalled that 'All this is Brahman.' This moment of profound love was a moment in the being of God. Llewellyn, Llewellyn's book, the last line, my memory of it, the booksellers remark, my hope for my daughters, the tears in my eyes,

Upper Bryn Coch Lane, Wales and Welsh history, the green valleys and the collieries and the blue August sky, every element of the experience without exception—all were a moment in the being of God, all woven together in the Eternal Now that is the Self. This love I was feeling was the Love that manifests and fills the universe, and it was utterly impersonal. It was the changeless infinitely repeated Self-Awareness of God, His instruction to me and His gift of Himself. The moment is one of Plato's *anamnesis*, the cancellation of amnesia: remembrance, recollection, recovery.

❁

We think of the earth, the environment, as hospitable and appropriate, both materially and aesthetically, and explain this happy conjunction in the language of Darwinian evolution: we evolved here. Like the other creatures, we have our niche in the ecosystem, the earth is our natural habitat, and that's why everything is just right for us—why we can breathe the air, drink the water, eat the fruits, admire the rainbows and move in metabolic harmony with the alternation of night and day.

This way of thinking, however, although valid on its level, like all thought circumscribed by the categories of the relative world, is ultimately a misreading—like the episode in Wales. It assumes duality: ourselves on the one hand, the earth on the other. More significantly, it assumes mechanism.

Actually, and as always, there is only One: a living, right-there-in-the-living-moment, always-present One. The earth appears hospitable to us, suitable for us, through identity. *We are* the earth, *we are* that hospitality—not as egos, of course, but as the Atman, the Self. As we read in the *Shiva Sutras: The Yoga of Supreme Identity*, '*Ahameva sarvam*': I myself am All.

Whenever possible we should recall to ourselves that the real world is not 'out there' as it appears to be, but is rather within us, within the Infinite Consciousness we are, and what we locate 'out there' is its dispersed and fragmentary projection into, and as, time and space—this is how God 'creates a universe'. This is how there's a

Manifestation, Creation, anything and everything, this is what's always happening—rendered intelligible, and compelling and lovable and spell-binding and meaningful, only by continuous reference back to the originating archetype within us, within the Self. We are 'out there', and 'out there' is in us.

This great central metaphysical Truth could be expressed by the phrase, the wonderful *mantra*, 'Thou art the world in our hearts.' Because the Self in which the world resides, through which it streams, is of the nature of *Ananda*, a Sanskrit word translated as both Bliss and Love, the world is better located, symbolically speaking, in our hearts than in our minds, where we customarily situate consciousness, and that world-in-our-hearts, the world *in divinis*, is God, the Dreamer and the Dream at once. The Blissful Atman, One without a Second.

The hospitality of the earth, then, its quality as *our home*, as well as the earth itself, are not 'out there' but exist only in consciousness, and we are that Consciousness in which they exist. The Dream is coherent and consistent, intelligible and inherently harmonious, because the Mind of the Dreamer is One, *because we are dreaming it that way*. We belong Here-and-Now because-Here-and-Now originates in us. The habitat is suitable to the inhabitants, and cherished by them, and fulfilling for them, because it exists within them, their dream of themselves in their world—or of humans, or simply beings, in a world: because it *is* them. *We are the whole thing*. Always, ever and again, there is only the One, only the Self. And this, as much as anything else, can claim to be the Final Truth of religion, of the Divine Wisdom.

Once this sacred Truth, so difficult to grasp or believe, has been realized in meditation we can resort to it repeatedly. (And we will want to, of course, with a fervent longing making all worldly desires seen trivial, because to perceive the world this way, in its Truth, is to experience the fulfillment of human birth: Nirvana.) It serves as a corrective to the dualist and mechanistic scientific world-view which, without malice and by its very nature, is literally a death sentence because it incarcerates us in the lower self (unanimously accepted within that world-view as the *real* self, a fact whose significance can scarcely be overstated) and the *samsara*, the round of birth-and-death, the 'transmigratory travail', the world of matter, and in this way effects a tragic exile from our divine nature, *imago dei*, and deprives us, because for all intents and purposes we are fated to become what we think we are, of that Life Eternal we inherit with our human estate.

But even that catastrophe is still only derivative. What is fundamental, and intolerable, is the separation from truth: the truth about the world and ourselves, what we are, where we are, why we are here, what we must do. To be alienated from our true nature is to be alienated from Truth itself, which is God, and from the Oneness which is Reality. It is the fall from grace into death. The Self is the Truth and the Self is immortal. The 'animal in its habitat' vanishes in that Truth and Its Realization by the slandered being reborn into its eternal legacy, the Self.

I'M SUPPOSED TO LOVE *EVERYONE?*

God and the world. These two are everything. To love either is to love the other, and this love of both as one is an affirmation of the divine unity, that Unity which is the heart of the Islamic Word. Love, in other words—this love of either which is really love of both—awakens direct experience of the divine Unity, the Oneness, the identity of God and the world, *Atma* and *maya*. The love we experience in devotional meditation is an awakening love, illuminating, enlightening, unveiling, and one of the great spiritual truths to which our minds are awakened is the truth of Unity.

We are embraced by the sensation of immersion in and identity with an all-encompassing ocean of love. That's what the whole world is revealed as, feels like, becomes for us: it becomes what it was all along. On the one hand the unity of Creator and Creation, on the other the love of which that unity is an expression and in which it subsists. At the center, the human soul in its true state, the state of worship, the state in which the truth of things becomes visible and is realized.

We rejoice in the perfection of it all, the beauty and perfection of the structure of things, of what Ananda Coomaraswamy called the 'Entirety'. This is just as it should be, we feel, it makes sense and it's sublime: love of God and love of the world are one love. This coincidence is what we had hoped for without knowing it, this is what we expected or suspected, it strikes a chord of joyful recognition. The structure of a divine universe is imprinted on the Intellect, and its confirmation in meditation is experienced as bliss.

❁

We're supposed to love everyone. Or at least have compassion. And sometimes in devotional meditation, when our attention is in that direction, we realize that our love of God does encompass everyone. We perceive that the love of God enjoins, commands, and actually generates, if only temporarily, a love of all people, all humanity, and we perceive, as well, that a love of humanity reflects back, as it were, and generates a love of God. There's a mutual implication here. We recall the two Great Commandments of Jesus.

But we are also put on the spot.

We think of all the people, from historical characters to our immediate circle of acquaintance, from the nameless ones, briefly glimpsed or narrowly observed days and even years ago, to the various repellent types we have encountered and summarily or reluctantly disqualified, we recall the faces of our relatives and neighbors, and we ask ourselves: 'Do I really love that one?'

Divine love is impartial and universal, so we have heard and are compelled to believe, and we are obliged to inquire into the nature of such a love. From what direction do I manage to find within me a love for Hitler, Goring, Goebbels and Himmler, or Pinochet, the contemporary ethnic-cleansers, or the leaders of the Khmer Rouge or Jack the Ripper or the guy who blew up the building in Oklahoma or Basil II (*bulgaronocus*, 'Bulgar-slayer') who had fifteen thousand prisoners blinded with every hundredth man blinded in only one eye so these could lead the others home, or the men who bayonetted pregnant women and tortured children in front of their parents, the torturers of all times and places, the man who raped and mutilated my daughter, or that man or woman who has thrust so much misery and resentment into my life or the 'step-Dad' who beat the girl in my class? The issue seems naive or scholastic, even sophomoric, in the context of worldly life, of that gruff or cheerful resignation to the imperfections of earthly existence which characterizes our maturity after the Fall, but when we are before God it becomes quite real, a real problem. How do we advance beyond *libido*, *philia* and *eros* to *agape*, or *caritas*, which 'affirms the other unconditionally, accepts the other in spite of resistance, suffers and forgives'? (PAUL TILLICH) Can I locate a universal compassion within me? Were detestation, hatred and contempt merely passing fevers, or are they still palely glowing within me, ready to flare again into lurid brilliance at any one of the numerous provocations with which I am sufficiently familiar? The meditational insight demands self-examination, because we know it has to be true.

The answer or resolution is contained, I think, in the insight itself. If the world is God, and the multiplicity is really a unity, then there are no actual individuals—no autonomous independent 'self-nature' of anything, as the Buddhists would say—and the distinction between good and evil, and all discriminations between people, are seen to be a function within *maya*, real enough on their own level but ultimately illusory. What we condemn rightfully from a moral perspective (or unworthily, insofar as we have allowed ourselves to become playthings of egoistic self-serving passions—passions which, in retrospective contrition, are themselves appropriately condemned) we simply accept, in those all-too-brief intervals we spend at the summit of our hierarchy of selves, as moments in the Cosmic Dream, moments in the infinite unchallengeable being of God. We see from that eminence, in our true identity as the Self, the impersonal Witness, that all are merely playing their roles, all are puppets, ourselves included, all are threads in the divine tapestry: everything is what it 'is' only through interaction with everything else and by virtue of its situation in the whole. No one, as we are taught, is an agent, and emancipation from the illusion and vivid sense of agency, as we are also taught, is Enlightenment.

By loving the whole, which is easy, we can accept the parts.

> However ugly the parts appear the whole remains beautiful.... Love that, not man apart from that, or else you will share man's pitiful confusions, or drown in despair when his days darken.
> ~ ROBINSON JEFFERS

Because we love God we can be at peace with any sort of human presence, regarding all with an equal eye. If we can love God, if we are given that love by His grace, then we will be unable to hate or condemn. In a word, 'to love all' means self-surrender: surrender or extinction of the ego, which will never relinquish the preferences which are its very definition, never be able to love all, and identity with the immortal *Atman*, the one I AM, which is Love itself and sees no distinctions because It is Itself everything, One without a second.

> When we see the One Self in all things, equal-mindedness, freedom from selfish desires, surrender of our whole nature to the Indwelling Spirit and love for all arise. When these qualities are manifested, our devotion is perfect and we are God's arm.
> ~ RADHAKRISHNAN, commentary on XII.20 of *Bhagavad-Gita*

'The end of all otherness,' as Coomaraswamy put it.

The challenge of the insight doesn't aim at some resolute, and almost certainly hypocritical adjustment of attitude in conformity with that suave or unctuous pretense of 'universal tolerance' or compassion with which insincerity seeks to flatter its evasion of depth. It aims at, and demands, nothing less than Self-Realization: that love of God which, in the purity of its self-surrender, leads to union. When the world is resolved into the Self there is no one to be loved and no one to be hated, no one who loves and no one who hates. And this is the final truth. 'The beginning is *Atman*, the middle is *Atman*, and the end is *Atman*. What appears other than *Atman* is mere illusion.' The *Yoga-Vasishtha* is succinct. As was Christ: 'Thy Will be done.' To have achieved this state, realized this truth in direct and continuous experience, is rare.

❁

All things and beings are loved, in the deepest sense and whether we experience it in that sense or not, simply because they exist. There are 'layers' of love, as it were, above this one, of course. But if we manage to look down through these layers, we discover that beneath it all, most fundamentally, gratefully and even ecstatically, we love things and beings—a tree or landscape, a son or daughter, a friend—for their simple existence, for that quality alone, regardless of particularities. Which opens another avenue toward all-embracing love.

Whatever has arisen into shape and presence against the backdrop of infinite nothingness, whatever drifts by, appearing and disappearing, arising and subsiding, whatever the magician conjures into being, the least speck of dust suspended in the void that surrounds us, has its legitimate claim to be loved: it is a triumph. The world is good because it is there. In loving the world, the drama, the things and beings and all the people we admire or who fall short of some 'mark' by which we pass judgment and which would certainly merit scrutiny, we are loving the miracle of Manifestation—which is, incidentally, one of the ways of 'seeing God everywhere'—with an infinite and appropriate gratitude that far outweighs our episodes of reservation. 'I was a hidden treasure and I wanted to be known, so I created the world' (*Hadith qudsi* of the Prophet, Peace upon him and his family).

❁

The existence of things, in other words, is God.

'In Him we live and move and have our being.' God is Existence itself. *Mahatattva*, *Parabrahman*: the Supreme Reality. Not only the things that exist in visibility and tangibility, from bacteria to galaxies, but the invisible principle of *presence* which contains and projects them. This principle is God, the Self, the blissful *Atman*, infinite and eternal. It is the secret of Consciousness. It is what we are.

❁

Meditational insights submit only grudgingly, always under protest and never completely, to the efforts and devices of language, no matter how strenuous or ingenious. They are attained, the vision is granted, only in the wordless states of consciousness induced by meditative focus. In these states we enter the realm of love and vision within the trio, as it were, like the three sides of a triangle, of God, the world and the *jiva*, or individual soul, *atmajagatjiva*, which is the Heart of the universe and our very Heart. That realm of Light, entered in the silent hours of meditation, is the 'classroom' in which we begin to learn the divine truths, all of which begin in paradox and terminate in Oneness.

The four insights we have been exploring, concerning love of the world, love of people, love of God and the equation of God with Existence, as well as the relationships among the consequences they imply, are arrows pointing toward that Oneness in which all insights, assertions and thought itself vanish with the illusion that entertained them.

Love and pity and wish well to every soul in the world;
dwell in love, and then you dwell in God; hate nothing
but the evil that stirs in your own heart.
~ WILLIAM LAW

Lo, verily, not for love of all is all dear,
but for love of the Self is all dear.
~ BRIHAD-ARANYAKA UPANISHAD

TIME'S UP!

There's a phrase, THIS-HERE-NOW, which appears occasionally in essays by 'the terrible Wei Wu-Wei,' as he calls himself—English-speaking, probably British, fluent in French, mainly Buddhist, publishes in the Hong Kong University Press, and certainly among the most brilliant expounders of the 'negative way' tradition. It emphasizes that Reality is always *present*, it's always NOW. We have never known anything but NOW, and anytime we know anything it's

NOW. The 'past' and the 'future' are always known NOW, which means they *are* always NOW. THIS, right in front of you, HERE, in this 'place', NOW, is all there ever *is*. Nothing can appear in consciousness (be 'present' to consciousness), which is the only place anything ever appears, meaning ever *exists*, except NOW. The Self, the one blissful I AM, is Pure Consciousness, and everything exists in It NOW.

ECKHART describes it in theistic language:

> The now wherein God made the first man and the now wherein the last man disappears and the now I speak in, all are the same in God where there is but the now.

NICHOLAS OF CUSA:

> Whatever is seen by us in time, thou, Lord God, didst not preconceive, as it is. For in the eternity in which Thou dost conceive, all temporal succession coincides in one and the same Eternal Now.

And IBN AL-FARID:

> Before it there is no 'before' and after it there is no 'after': the beginning of the centuries is the seal of its existence.

To know or believe this with the mind is one thing. To experience directly, to inhabit the Eternal Now and be conscious of It as such, is another. ('We' are really always 'there' of course!) It's a back and forth affair for the meditator, until the final unimaginable irreversible illumination.

We have to focus on it. Dwell deeply in our meditation on the absolute immediacy implied in each word of the three-word phrase. THIS... HERE... NOW. Or, alternatively, we can simply utter THIS-HERE-NOW, mentally and somewhat abruptly, snatching everything, from the historical to the personal, into the living present moment: NOW. The effect, or at least the goal, the hope, is to drag, pluck or cajole the mind out of the imprisoning illusion of the temporal sequence into the ecstasy of Reality, the Timeless Present.

If we're successful, we experience a blissful sense of liberation and expansion, a joyful certitude of now seeing things as they really are, of true vision. (And of relief, a word I've used often in these pages; worldly existence is a state of pain—of compression, unidentifiable expectation, contentless nostalgia—to which we have grown so accustomed that we are not aware of it: in spiritual experience, the only negation of worldly existence, that existence—the sense of exile, incompleteness, inconclusiveness, ambiguity, temporariness, separation from Something—suddenly becomes visible, we see it for what it is because we have stepped outside of it, and we become aware of the pain in the flashing instant of its immediate relief.) And then, invariably, we snap back, as if on a rubber band, into the iron corridor of hours, weeks, years and centuries.

Time is tenacious: confident, implacable and tirelessly tenacious. The habit of attaching temporal definitions and assignments to the thoughts arising in our minds is as deeply rooted as the habit of imputing an ego behind the impersonal stream of events we call 'our lives'. Again and again, so long as we are actively involved in the world, so long as any *karma* remains to be burned, until we have fulfilled the responsibilities we inherit as a result of past decisions and so long as we pursue personal goals, we will fall back into the treadmill of time and the ego. (The issue is contested: there are other, more affirmative definitions of 'final liberation', in which, it is claimed, the *karma* unfolds but is no longer experienced. We attain identity with the Self, the eternal impersonal Witness.)

But we remember the truth we've seen, we remember the joy. We become increasingly detached. Gradually, more and more frequently, we capture glimpses in daily life of what we saw so clearly in meditation. Timelessness is the Reality, time is an illusion, and the Reality, by that very fact—and due, on the deepest level, to the necessary radiation of Beatitude, the 'desire' of the Good to be present everywhere: in a word, due to a Grace which can be directly experienced—is always shining behind the veil, a still changeless Conscious Presence impassively observing the ever-flowing 'current of forms' within it or withdrawing their existence by 'turning away' into Its own eternal infinite Peace... always shining behind the veil, always seeking to make itself known.

In Nature, where we find stillness and tranquillity, where change is cyclic and wherever the cyclic can be discerned, where we contemplate the eternal return (MIRCEA ELIADE's memorable phrase) of waves, mornings, blossoms and snow, the simple unutterably beautiful changelessness of every aspect of the natural world, always joyously proclaiming 'I am what I always am!' we can glimpse, even more than glimpse, the Eternal Now which is our God. And after all: every birth is the one Birth, every child is the one Child, every man and every woman the one Man, the one Woman, every death the one Death. Isn't that so? The Ideas in the Mind of God, the archetypes. They are everywhere we turn, alone real, and they are timeless, ageless: the unchanging inhabitants of the Eternal Now. Time is annulled in the eternal repetition and return of the great Forms which loom like clouds behind the shifting time-bound patterns and dramas of their innumerable incarnations. Why should we say 'What I felt then I feel now,' when what I feel now and felt then are simultaneous in my present awareness?

The meditation on time is very important. Temporality is an essential support of the illusion of the ego, as Wei Wu-Wei emphasizes, and that illusion is the fundamental one from which Enlightenment seeks to deliver us, epitomized in the Upanishadic petition, 'Lead me from death to immortality.' *No time, no ego.* To perceive the presence of everything, the whole world, in THIS-HERE-NOW is a powerful antidote to Ignorance as well as a source of strength. It enables us to see 'our lives' as a perpetual mechanical projection into time of what are merely present thoughts and actions, indiscriminately, habitually and interminably duplicated, arising without our volition or examination. It enables us to see that we ourselves constantly construct and sustain, remodel and elaborate, stories which we then experience as our 'biographies' and in which we then 'discover' ourselves to be entrapped—an entrapment suspended only in those generally spontaneous moments of what we call, significantly enough, self-forgetfulness, which we always recall, again significantly, as 'timeless'. 'I was so happy—or moved or absorbed or at peace or entranced—that I forgot myself.' No one is 'bound' or 'liberated', as the Eastern doctrines delight in announcing, because there isn't anyone.

The false self originates in our own imaginations, weaving a web of entities and relationships which have no existence independent of that industrious weaving, and then casting that web into the linear temporality those imaginations simultaneously project. In a word, the false self originates in present thoughts which we label 'memories'. (But it's all really THIS-HERE-NOW.) These thoughts either arise of their own accord in the field of consciousness, or they are summoned with a sometimes ferocious urgency—an imperious ego-creating command of the ego!—and from their combinations biographies are incessantly manufactured. Since everyone does it in endlessly overlapping patterns of collective creativity, a common world is generated. And since there is no objective reality behind that world (or anywhere else), since the 'past' to which these biographies appeal does not exist, there arises that generalized 'clashing' of experience, that spectacular and spell-binding encounter of interpretations, that universal controversy, that music ranging from cacophony to ethereal, which is nothing less than the whole of our lives: we are the novelists, we are the characters. It is Humanity, the tapestry of innumerable biographies—the Humanity we love so irrevocably, as Our Saviour instructed us to love it: the ever-unfolding Drama. All along, however, we are really the Self, the Witness, utterly detached, utterly free and utterly independent of 'time.'

The story unfolds within us, but we are motionless. The scenes change, but it's always NOW. Time is mutation, God is the Immutable. THIS-HERE-NOW, the collapse of time, is a leap into the Self, the Immortal Atman.

> The pure one is plunged in the Light of the Glorious; he is not the son of anyone, free from 'times' and 'states.'
>
> —RUMI

> Things that are not immutable, are not at all.
>
> —ST. AUGUSTINE

TAKING ADVANTAGE OF A VERB TENSE

There's an invocational 'trick' we can try involving the use of the past tense. It can be surprisingly effective.

We're familiar by now with the meditative technique of repeating *mantra* phrases to ourselves, mentally or in a murmur, in order to focus the mind on a spiritual truth and eventually, hopefully, realize that truth. The idea here is to state these phrases in the past instead of present tense. 'There was Light' instead of 'There is only the Light.' 'There was only God' instead of 'There is only God' or 'Everything is God.' 'Once there was a Dream' instead of 'All this is a Dream'.

To what end?

The effect of the past tense is either to suggest the *supremacy* of whatever is being affirmed, its paramount nature, and the irrelevance or subordination of everything else; or the exclusive *existence* of whatever is being affirmed and the non-existence of everything else. It's just the way the language works, the feel or 'spirit' of the past tense in certain contexts. It implies, and we now realize, that we made a mistake: that all along things were really different from what we thought. Everything *was*—and of course, as we now see clearly, *is*—Light. Everything *was*—and of course, as we now see clearly, *is*—God. What we thought was real is now seen to have been a dream; we loved it then as reality, and we still love it now, because it is altogether marvellous, indeed unsurpassable—but it *was*, and as we now see clearly *is*, a Dream. We have awakened.

Secondly, and equally important, the past tense establishes a sense of distance. We are 'looking back' (but only linguistically, as we shall see), and from the vantage point of this detachment, this 'superiority', are selecting out the essential from the accidental, the saving grace, the one aspect that redeemed an ambiguous or confusing totality, the one thing that really mattered from all the rest that appeared to matter but didn't, the one thing of which we are *certain*: the Truth. We are looking back in the feeling of grateful recovery that pervades such phrases as: 'when all is said and done,' 'the one thing I know for sure,' 'after it was all over,' 'when I was finally able to gain perspective on it all,' 'when I grew up,' 'when I saw things clearly at last,' 'when I came to my senses,' 'when I finally realized what had been going on all along,' 'when I recovered my wits,' 'when I was finally able to sort it all out.' We are no longer 'there', caught up in it all, buffeted by a thousand impressions and sensations, and by that very fact—detachment, perspective, distance—can now see the truth of things. All the distortions and delusions 'formerly' generated by a time-bound individuated consciousness vanish. No longer seeing things through the eyes of the lower self, we view the world in an impersonal retrospective. In other words, the past tense, as a spiritual technique, is a verbal concretization of or metaphor for Self-Realization: disidentification with the ego. The future from which we are looking back is post-mortem.

Finally, although we are employing the past tense verbally, we are looking back not into the past but at our *present* state from an imaginary *future*. The truth we are seeing from that perspective refers to our present reality, as we meditate, right there in the room. This is why we feel joy and tranquillity. In these victorious affirmations the imaginary projection into the future enables us to see the truth about the present, and to inhabit that vision. There's a feeling of ascending into a blissful peace, we float above the vast panorama of the world like a cloud, detached, serene, wise at last. The disengagement from the present, the 'disorientation', has enabled us to *see*. All along, it was Light: it was God: it was a Dream. And it is so right now. *This* is God: *this* is Light: *this* is a glorious unsurpassable absolutely sublime Dream.

Can you really believe that this works? That this supreme realization can be achieved by a device as artificial, abstract, forced, pedantic, shallow and *cheap*—a 'cheap trick'!—as the manipulation of a verb tense?

It's a gradual matter. There are moments of 'instant illumination' on the Path, moments of vision momentarily granted, and there is the long and arduous Path itself. Usually a sincere commitment to the latter is the precondition for the former, as in the tantalizing promise of Zen *satori* that tormented so many seekers in Suzuki's heyday, but exceptions are conceded. 'The Spirit bloweth where it listeneth.' Actually, this technique, because it takes advantage of an automatic and deeply-ingrained pattern of association, is among the easiest to practice. The passage of time really does reward us with perspective. The feeling of the past tense, embodying a 'memory' of that universal experience, really does encourage a sense of detachment.

Sit in a quiet place. Close your eyes. Be silent in your mind for a few minutes, be calm. Repeat, mentally, 'Once there was a dream, Once there was a dream. . . .' Is a faint smile, not unlike the Buddha's, appearing on your face?

❁

GLINTS & GLIMPSES VI

The God we love is eternal, and it's comforting to know that, comforting to know that the object of our love is eternal. It feels right, this is the way things ought to be, this is something we were meant for, built into us. We become immediately aware, when we *experience* this eternity in devotional meditation, that nothing less could satisfy us, we know why nothing less *has* satisfied us (everything we have *ever* known, in every context, has been a disappointment, an eventual betrayal, a foolishness, for this reason: fleeting, ephemeral, transient: another lesson, this insight another reward), that it was for an eternal Beloved that our power to love was intended, in which it is fulfilled. We discover, in short, after so many dashed hopes, so many failed expectations, the great truth, the culminating truth that the love of God is alone love, alone worthy the name. When our love for God fills our hearts completely, when we literally shed tears of love—'the gift of tears,' as the Sufis call it—we feel and know we are united with His Eternity: we realize, in direct experience, that we have loved Him forever.

And sometimes the balance seems slightly tipped in favor of His love for us rather than vice versa. He has chosen to be there.

❁

You sit there and smile, sometimes actually laugh out loud. You say to yourself, 'It really seemed as if there was someone, didn't it? Confess! A "you", a "person", "that guy"! And now you see there wasn't. And not only that! Now you see there isn't anybody else either!'

That's the Good News in the East. The Good News in the West was that a Saviour was born, a Redeemer, a Redemptive Incarnation. The Good News in the East is that there isn't anybody. Paul had the intuition. 'I live, yet not I, but Christ lives within me.'

✽

'O Thou Great Dreamer!' It comes to our lips, and we smile.

This world is a Dream, God is the Dreamer.

Or this is *like* a dream, if that's more comfortable. Dreamer and Dream are metaphorical for *Atma*, the Self, and *maya*, the world-appearance. A felicitous analogy, apparently indispensable; ubiquitous too, in both sacred and secular wisdom.

When we address Him as the Dreamer we are marvelling at His unreachable transcendence, at the sheer incredible *magic* of His relationship to His creation, and, indirectly, we are praising the glory of the world, since we only know of His greatness as a Dreamer from the greatness of the world He dreams. (Again, and always, *hadith qudsi*: 'I was a hidden treasure, and I wanted to be known, so I created the world.') He dreams this infinite universe, this cosmos. (Infinite within us, I might point out, infinite within and as the Self, not the numerical infinity of the astronomers.) He dreams our marvelling at His greatness as Dreamer. To say that we are 'dependent' upon Him seems laughable in its understatement, its metaphysical inaccuracy.

'O Thou Great Dreamer!' is a *mantra* of love and self-extinction. And humor: we smile at the innocent absurdity of human pretention.

✽

'This Dream, this Dream, this Dream.' Slowly shaking your head, smiling with bliss, overwhelmed by the miracle beyond all imagining.

Love of the world, love of the Dream: love of the world as a Dream. And love, above all, of the Dreamer. Inexpressible love. We dwell, in dumb-struck serene adoration, upon the infinite greatness of the Dream, and of the Dreamer. Enter the moment of this Grace. Depart, as you must, when the time is up, in joy. Remember it. It's an unfailing source of strength.

❁

It seems unlikely to many observers—scientists are dragging their feet here, failing to provide hard data one way or another, even ignoring the question altogether—that ours is the only universe being dreamt.

You could say, of course, that each of the innumerable reflected consciousnesses is surrounded by its own universe, and myriads of such universes are appearing and disappearing in every instant (Buddhists relish this vision) with the birth and death, the vicissitudes of mood and mind, even the sleeping and waking, of living beings, including plant life if the criterion is sentience. Even in each individual consciousness there is a successive infinity of universes, because each one's universe is in continual dynamic transformation through the channel of time. But even the cosmic Dream, the shared world, which is one for all of us in this universe, may be only one among an infinity of such dreams.

Who knows? The speculation arises in our minds when we contemplate, in staggered rapture, the vision of His Infinity which He has unveiled before us. And then we know the answer is affirmative. To restrict in any way the creativity of the Sovereign Good contradicts Its necessarily infinite radiation. Krishna assures us, 'In every instant I body forth countless universes.' *Anantam brahma*: Brahman is infinite.

❁

JE SOIS? YO SOY? DU BIST? WHO?

The Self is known to everyone but not clearly. You always exist. The Be-ing is the Self. 'I AM' is the name of God. Of all the definitions of God, none is indeed so well put as the Biblical statement 'I AM THAT I AM' in Exodus. There are other statements, but none is so direct as the name JEHOVAH = I AM. The Absolute Being is what is—It is the Self. It is God. Knowing the Self, God is known. In fact God is none other than the Self.... The Self is all-comprising. In fact Self is All. There is nothing besides the Self.
~ Ramana Maharshi

Before all beginnings, after all endings—I AM. All has its being in me, in the 'I AM' that shines in every living being.... Refuse all thoughts except one: the thought 'I AM'.... Go within, enquiring 'What am I?' or focus your mind on 'I AM', which is pure and simple being.... When you can see everything as it is, you will also see yourself as you are. It is like cleansing a mirror. The same mirror that shows you the world as it is will also show you your own face. The thought 'I AM' is the polishing cloth. Use it.
~ Nisargadatta Maharaj

Then, last of all, meditate on the oneness of the Self with God, the one blissful existence, the one I AM.
~ Srimad Bhagavatam

Referring to the Self, to God, as the 'I AM' may be the clearest and most perfect way to describe it, the closest we can get to it in words, even closer than the assimilation to light. I AM goes about as far as possible to make the sense of the Atman accessible to us in our actual practice, right there in the room where we're trying to get the *feel* of an all-encompassing all-embracing divine Reality which is translated from the Sanskrit as 'the Self.' It's pithy advice. The infinite truth of the Atman, whose communication, evocation and celebration is the whole burden of the Holy Upanishads, is contained in the inner meaning—so subtle to extract—of those two words: I AM.

And this compression, precision and finality tends to make us feel put on the spot. Left with no excuse. (As it should, of course. How could our relationship to the divine Reality, to God, to the whole truth of being human, being blessed with human birth, not put us on the spot?) It's as if someone were saying, 'OK, this is all that can be done for you, it can't be made any clearer: if you don't get it now you never will.'

The I AM:

You see it coming, you see it approaching, you realize it was always there and that you just now noticed it. You see it with a fascinated concentration so acute, so intense, that it almost has an element of fear in it—not quite alarm, but more like apprehension with a trace of shock. Riveted, a riveted gaze, as if at the approach of Something whose very existence is a demand for total attention, for your whole being. ('With all thy heart, with all thy soul, and with all thy mind. . . ,' 'Give Me your whole heart, love and adore Me, worship Me always. . . .') Hypnotized. What is the fear? Fear of losing it? Fear that you're not equal to it? Cards on the table? Or is it simply awe?

It's looking at you. It's aware of you. It's within you.

You can see immediately and feel to the very depths of your being, depths you never knew were there, that it's infinite Peace, infinite Bliss. But incredibly enough, the demand it addresses to you, the challenge, *the fact of the implicit proposal here*, outweighs even that promise. It's giving you a chance. The thought of failure is insupportable.

Its like an eye that isn't there, pure disembodied *seeing*. Within you.

It's nothing. Absolute Absence. It's not even the *presence* of Absence, which would be *something*: it's the Absence of the Presence of Absence, in the remorselessly exact language of 'the terrible Wei Wu-Wei'. And it's *you*.

It's the nothing you have always been in a noplace where there's really no 'always' because there isn't any when. It's everything, it's what everything became, and where everything still is and always was, which is nowhere and forever. We see it, according to the Buddhists, with the wisdom that realizes emptiness: wisdom-realizing-emptiness: our own disappearance: *fana*, the Sufi extinction of the ego. The I AM.

It's 'you'? It's 'aware of you'? It's 'within you'? But there is no 'you'. As it approaches, you fade away. As it fades, you appear again. When you look at it, or *think* you look at it, it disappears, because you have asserted yourself. Realizing this, you think to yourself, 'I'll look away, I'll pretend I don't notice it,' or 'I'll just wait and see what happens,' or 'I'll think about nothing' . . . but by that time its gone completely, so great has your self-assertion swelled in the endeavor to suppress it, and there's nothing there but you, the old familiar you: massive, inert, and unreal. Baffled once again, disappointed, rueful. You turn to the personal God, abashed, praying for mercy and forgiveness, seeking a consolation you aren't sure you deserve. At least you know enough to do that. But what if you're never offered another chance? Impossible. He is infinite Mercy, His Grace is boundless: to that all Scripture attests. Pray for a pure heart. You can always pray for a pure heart. For strength.

Well. At least you had a glimpse of it. A glimpse! How many ever get a glimpse! The I AM, the Nothing that is Everything, The Pure Self-Awareness: the Self-Awareness of the universe, containing all, that is simultaneously the universe itself, that *is* the universe, the All. Your Self, the Ultimate Truth, Liberation.

Think I AM, dream into it, drift into it. Try to imagine what it could be, what the words could mean. I AM. The supreme statement of the Vedanta. Realization. Its already accomplished, and you just don't know it, already there, and you just don't see it. The treasure is yours, you are the treasure, I AM is the Brahman. You are Eternal Bliss.

Don't just wait for it. Time is running out. Look for it. Look for it every day, stop in the middle of everything and try to feel it, feel the *presence* of everything in a *Mind*, a *Self*, an *infinite impersonal Awareness*. Let it know you're in the running, a candidate. Tell it you'll die before you'll give up. And realize that it's not your choice, that you have no choice in this matter, you can't be accused of presumption or selfishness. What did I say earlier? *Something whose very existence is a demand for your whole being*. You have no choice, once you know, or believe, or hope.

Pursuing the secret of existence is the whole joy of life. The invisible eternal Divine Intention, the meaning of being human. Have compassion for the people staring anxiously out the windows of the 707 for the first sight of the beaches in Hawaii, or the runway at Heathrow.

OVERLAPPING CIRCLES, WINDMILLS IN THE MIND

To experience love for God. Love, worship, adoration, that inexpressible joy, peace. What more is there to ask for? It's *reality*. It's not *one* thing among others, it's *the* one thing that really *is*. Truth. *Freedom*.

Sometimes, but rarely, when my mind, my 'lower self', responding with happy alacrity to a lapse of vigilance, skips off into the 'future', I picture myself enjoying uneventful twilight years close to the earth, right up here on this hill, in which my children's love for me has at last matured into appreciation of how this life of mine has been lived, or at least into something approximating a traditional filial deference. Not premature ancestor worship, not veneration—just a little deference, a little decorum, a little respect for my grey hair instead of running their hands through it affectionately and saying, with mock alarm, 'You're getting grey, Dad! Time to start dyeing your hair!' And other hopes, some ancient, some fresh, some panoramic and some unbelievably trivial, may haunt or pester my practice of contentment.

But I recover my senses. I know better than to entertain expectations of this world. And what would it matter, anyway? I can see the sharp line limiting the advantage of all earthly things as clearly as I see now the line where the rug ends and the floor begins. The one thing I have known in this world which I can be certain is real, and that means eternal, is the love of God. Which is to know who I am and what humanity is: *I am* the love of God.

Other things have elicited my love, or what I thought of as 'love'. The common ones, nothing unusual. Music, nature, children, the human presence—but they live only in their fleeting finite moment. (What did the poet say? Kiss the 'something' as it flies? Was it the joy? I forget the line.) Moments that flare and fade. The point is simple, stark: there is no earthly experience of which we do not tire, which doesn't cloy, none exempt from eventual weariness or dissatisfaction. Nature can be a blank, music a surfeit, children exhausting: the human presence the target of a quick cynical glance or a knowing smile.

On the one hand love, flowing from the illumined heart, on the other hand worship, prerogative of the illuminated intelligence. And embracing them both, adoration. Adoration: the thought of God.

What does the face of someone thinking of God look like? Absorbed, remote; sometimes sad, sometimes radiant; defenceless: fearless. All our lives we are like two overlapping circles: the circle of things as they are and the circle of things as we think they should be, or want them to be, or hope they'll become. We never feel things are quite right, there's always something that could be done, some adjustment that could be made, some area in which to exercise diligence or foresight or initiative, some improvement, some wrinkle that could be ironed out, always some nagging absence or defect, often not even identifiable: that perpetual subterranean uneasiness whose import can be correctly interpreted only by the Word. But in love of God, in worship and adoration, the two circles become one. Only then.

How does one come to love God? Hard question to answer.

You could say that we love Him in the moment and whenever we realize that He exists, when we realize His Existence. To be aware of His Presence and to love Him are synonymous. So you want to try very, very hard to imagine His existence. (But before that, picture a startled scientist being unhorsed in a joust with lances: by which I mean only to make the point—light-heartedly here, since any attempt at the appropriate tone in what is merely a parenthetical remark would only insult the infinite gravity of what is, after all, a tragedy without parallel, indeed terminal—and yet, withal, providential: the point that the scientific worldview, scientism, is the great enemy of your quest for God, and must be recognized as such, identified, exposed and destroyed within yourself, at the outset, or else it will be poisoning your Path every step of the way without your knowing it. Your computer is not 'friendly': it's your personal assassin.) And probably the best way to do that is to address Him: to pray. Even if you have to begin with the famous 'atheist's prayer,' 'God, if you exist, save my soul, if I have one!' This is a great prayer, if it comes from the heart. Can't fail to be heard, can't fail to be answered. Not by words, of course, nor by intervention: by Presence. But it has to come from the heart, from the depths of the heart. It has to be total. God is deaf to people harboring reservations.

To love, worship and adore Him *forever* is our only real hope, because it's the only hope that is rooted in, consistent with and fulfills our true potential and the purpose of our existence—eternal life in union with God. Let me be very clear here. The word 'forever' is to be taken literally. In the love of God, because He is eternal and we partake of His eternity, 'rays' of His eternity, we step outside of time, and we know it: we experience Eternity directly. We find ourselves realizing, in blissful recognition of what seems simultaneously stunning and obvious, that we have *always* loved Him. I have loved God forever, and will 'continue' to love Him forever, because the love of God takes place in Eternity, 'establishes' me in the Eternity I had inhabited all along without knowing it. It is an 'eternal event', just as, in Christian metaphysics, we may refer to the 'eternal birth' of Jesus in our hearts.

There is nothing beyond the love of God. It has the nature of an end, and therefore of peace. Infinite Peace. When the joy of that love 'settles down', as it were, when it becomes 'mindless' in the Buddhist sense—when 'we' become *it*—we drown in it, we disappear into it, and find ourselves 'at peace in the being of God.'

> For things find rest only in that which is the end of their being.
> —PHILALETHES

IS ALL THIS A GIFT OR ISN'T IT?

You want to be able to experience Existence, the world, the universe, ALL THIS, as a miracle: absolutely miraculous, stunning, stupefying, spellbinding, marvelous and wonderful a million miles beyond words. There could have been nothing.

Not 'without interruption', of course; but from time to time. It's a theme of meditation. You do it or make yourself available to it, receptive, in meditation. Experiencing the world this way is intrinsic to our humanity. If it never happens in your life, you missed the boat.

So: on the one hand reverential wonder, on the other a universe. On the one hand infinite undeserving, on the other infinite munificence. How can it all be explained by anything other than love?

We meditate upon the miracle and that love. Meditate on it, meaning *realize* it. Perceive it as a reality, a truth. And as we meditate we become aware that we have to add a qualifying adjective... motiveless. The Love in which the miracle of the universe originates is motiveless. It has no purpose. It simply exists. The agency is undivided. It produces the miracle without intention, as a function of Its existence.

The initial state of response, of course, is gratitude. We drift in rapt silence through a calm sea of helpless infinite gratitude, we *become* gratitude, just as before God's infinite glory we *become* praise.

But then, sometimes almost immediately, gratitude starts to fade out: we have become aware of its ridiculous insignificance, its absurd disproportion to the magnitude of the gift. In the face of this disproportion our gratitude seems presumptuous or impertinent, facile, even hypocritical.

And ultimately simply mistaken. Gratitude is a response to generosity, to a statement or initiative, but, as we have realized, this love is motiveless. There is no generosity here, not even any awareness of a beneficiary. In the absence of generosity, then, and since what God is not aware of does not exist—existence *is* His Awareness—our gratitude, and we ourselves, dissolve into a featureless contemplation which is pure bliss. We disappear. This boundless love in which the miracle of Manifestation originates is nothing other than the Absolute, One without a second, the Self. The Self which we are. Gratitude implies two: but there's only One.

Eventually, sometimes after only a few seconds, we emerge, but only partly. The Oneness is now analyzed into three, three interlocking heavens: 'There is a world,' 'I am here in it,' 'Behind everything is God.' (I AM: THIS IS: THOU ART.) A great mantra. Still a miracle, but now we're one step closer to our 'lives', our *karma*. One step closer to re-entry.

When we have completely emerged the memory of what we have seen survives as a question. 'What must I do? How am I supposed to live now, knowing what I know, how am I supposed to go through each day?' Specifically, as we now see quite clearly, 'What is His will for me? How can I serve Him, obey Him?'

Awareness of residence in a miracle is the definitive departure from childhood, the assumption of our full dignity. The implications are inescapable. It imposes the moral dimension, that recognition of responsibility which is one extension of the miracle into our daily lives. We can no longer be comfortable simply pursuing personal goals, we feel ourselves answerable for our lives. 'A man will reach perfection if he does his duty as an act of worship to the Lord, who is the source of the universe.' (GITA, chap. 18)

It didn't have to be, our finite logic timidly suggests. But it was. Or maybe it did have to be. Two things, anyway, are certain. THIS comes from THAT, and THAT *is* THIS. What we call 'the world' is perpetual Creation, and Creation and Creator are One. *Sarvam khalvidam brahma*: All this is Brahman.

> Without the Eternal, temporal things would not exist; without the Absolute, there would be no contingent order. . . . The phenomenon of the miracle is ontologically indispensable because the meeting between the Eternal and the temporal is possible and necessary; the archetype of the miracle is the irruption of the Absolute into contingency. And this irruption would not be conceivable if contingency were not, precisely, 'something of the Absolute'.
>
> ~ FRITHJOF SCHUON

HALLELUJAH CROSS-EXAMINED

Thou alone art,
Thou the Light Imperishable, adorable:
Great Glory is Thy Name.
~ SVETASVATARA UPANISHAD

Encomiums to God's glory are universal in scriptures, religious writing, especially psalmody, and in the orations of native peoples, and they are fundamental in our worship of the personal God. The Paternoster concludes with praise of His Glory. 'Thine is the Kingdom, and the Power and the Glory.'

In meditation, our entry into Reality, we become aware of an infinite splendor, a transcendent beauty and majesty, a sublime effulgence of unearthly light, indescribably magnificent, a shining Presence at once remote and immediate, supporting and pervading everything and yet absolutely untouched by anything. The name we give to this ineffable Presence is Glory. It is God. Not an attribute, but God Himself.

As seen from our side of the river, however. It is only through the eyes of humanity, the central consciousness of this Manifestation, theomorphic being—we are *imago dei*, 'made in His image'—that God experiences Himself as Glory. His appearance as Glory, the perception of this Glory, the worship of this Glory, and humanity, are like four 90-degree sections of arc flowing around the circumference of a circle, alternately differentiating themselves and dissolving back into the one circle, which is the Self, the immortal Atman. God's Glory 'appears' the instant of creation, the instant there is a world, and the instant He is worshipped by humanity, and these two instants, due to the centrality and totality of human consciousness in the Manifestation, are really one. Our worship of His Glory completes and speaks for the Creation—which is one of the many reas-ons why only religious experience is 'fulfilling'. ('It's only for the sake of the saints that there *is* a world, since they alone know what it is.' I can't recall the source of this quote.) Why it's the only way to go: the Answer to the question we are asking when we stare in silence at the sky full of stars or think about death and suffering or feel within our hearts, lying awake in bed, the baffled, vaguely anguished indestructible hope we never voice because we know it's built into the nature of things but will only be received as personal: the one true object of our continually misinformed pursuit of happiness.

At first, in this meditation, we are overwhelmed by the mere fact of the *existence* of this Glory. Its existence nullifies everything else. In a sense, God's Glory is invoked for that very purpose: to 'neutralize' or 'subdue' or 'escape' the current of forms, the fleeting content in the flow of time, to reduce it to the nothingness our intuition of the Absolute knows it to be. 'Be of good cheer, for I have conquered the world,' as Our Saviour reassures us in the High Holy Sermon. So there's an air of appeal here, supplication, petition.

Getting in deeper, we experience helpless awe before His utter transcendence. God is beyond the capacity of our praise, as He is beyond the capacity of our understanding, beyond what our minds can conceive. Our insignificance before Him carries a comforting feeling because it accurately defines and transforms into direct experience our true status in the universe. We feel 'at home.' We are defined, situated and, ultimately, redeemed by His Glory.

Finally, we realize that the divine Person we have loved and worshipped as 'mine'—my God, my Beloved, my very heart, my very own, my Teacher, my refuge and my hope, my True Friend—is indeed this very God of Glory, the transcendent One and Supreme Existence. *Parabrahman, Paramartha.* Infinite Truth: and yet, by the incomprehensible alchemy of the divine economy, *still 'mine'. Still My Beloved.* Mysterious, hidden within me: yet the infinite eternal Reality from whose creative power the universe proceeds. The combination of possession and awe, unpredictably, produces a contemplative serenity. The divine aspect finally experienced in this meditation upon the divine Glory is Peace.

His Glory is His existence, and He alone exists.

Before this universe came to be, I was.
When the universe shall have passed away, I shall be.
At the heart of the universe,
throughout the cycle of its existence,

I AM. I AM all this. Eternal,
without beginning, without end,
I AM.
~ SRIMAD BHAGAVATAM

I DON'T BELIEVE I RECOGNIZE YOU

The object of human worship, when and wherever He appears to our consciousness—always as if emerging into visibility through dissipating mists, having been there all along—is immediately recognized as such. We know in that moment, with a certainty experienced as serenity and joy, that this is the One, this is the Being Who appeared to them all: to Sankara, Saint Augustine, ibn Arabi, Plotinus, Eckhart, Rumi, Black Elk, Al-Ghazali, Boehme, and Ramakrishna, to all the saints and sages and to anyone and everyone who was ever blessed with the vision of God. We knew Him at first only in the reputation that preceded Him. Now, without a doubt and infinitely beyond any expectations we were capable of entertaining, the corroboration is before us: this is Him, He is here: this is God.

One would imagine that it only happens this way the first time, that subsequent visions of God recall to mind and are confirmed by reference to the previous ones and no longer to a reputation. To an extent this is true; the memory thenceforward determines our purpose in life, we long only to see Him again and to be with Him forever. But in another and deeper sense the vision of God is always unprecedented. He is infinite and eternal; our encounters with Him take place outside of time, in the timeless reality of His immutable being: in meeting Him we are absorbed into Him and partake of His changelessness. All encounters are the One Encounter, and not only within the individual life span but for humanity as a whole. It's not that this experience is *identical* to that of Ramakrishna and the rest: it *is* that experience, a single eternal Event in which time has collapsed and all 'moments' have become contemporary. It is Humanity that encounters God, and the Encounter is uninterrupted, simultaneous and unique. He is perpetually fresh, perpetually reborn, perpetually instantaneous radiance. The reputation is established here in the dream of time. The recognition is eternal.

We are approaching the inexpressible here, because we are trying to talk about the One without a second. The concept, 'recognition of God', reveals layer after layer of meaning. It is the recognition of Reality and of Truth; the dispelling of the illusion of separateness; the return to a Oneness from which we never really departed; the accession into the eternal divinity which is our true humanity; the explosive transfiguration, actual annihilation, of everything we had formerly regarded as real. Here in the 'world-appearance', in *maya*, we are one splinter among an infinity of splinters, all the separate moments in time and space into which Reality has been fractured. In the 'recognition of God' the 'hardness' of individuation within linear temporality and spatial extension melts away, leaving... what? The indescribable which the Vedic sages simply referred to as That. The Supreme Person whose recognition is the realization that no one else exists.

✱

GLINTS & GLIMPSES VII

'May I worship Thee forever'

The words come spontaneously, fervently to our lips as a response to the joy of worship. We want it to never end, just go on forever. Worship is bliss, being home.

And not only that. In worship we perceive His Eternity, and we realize that temporary or episodic worship is inconsistent with its object (we recall the Apostle's injunction to 'pray ceaselessly,' Brother Lawrence's 'practice of the presence of God'), that true worship, by its very nature, partakes of eternity. It's an eternal act, it occurs outside of time: it's an uninterrupted Reality within us by identification with which we become real ourselves, by neglect of which we become unreal. So we are requesting that our worship be authentic: that we may worship in truth.

❁

'Thou alone, Thou forever'

A central affirmation, and very powerful. The heart of the matter. To love Him is to turn our whole being toward His: on this point the sages are unanimous. We want everything other than the Beloved to vanish, because it is illusory, a Single Presence to became eternal in our hearts, because Reality is a single Eternal Presence. 'One without a second.' The Self.

'May there be none but Thee, nothing but Thee, no one and nothing but Thee, forever.'

This phrase summarizes the bhakta's whole life.

❁

'It's all One'

When you see it, you can say it. The invisible unity behind the visible multiplicity is hard to acknowledge, hard to understand, hard to believe. But this thing called 'Oneness' is universal in revelations, in the wisdom tradition, whatever name it may be given. You could say that multiplicity is physical, apparent, and Oneness is metaphysical, real. Whenever people timidly or defiantly affirm, as they do with increasing frequency in these unsettling ominous days of ultimate menace, 'We're all one,' referring to the human family, they're seeing metaphysical oneness, the oneness that embraces and dissolves distinctions, the prior and underlying oneness from which differentiation only apparently emerges. It's there, but not 'out there'. It's within things. Within us, Christ's Kingdom of Heaven. *Sivanandarasa.*

❁

'Thou and I are One'

The Person to Whom we are speaking here is Truth itself and must acknowledge the Teaching. What that means in practice is that it's possible, in meditation, as a spiritual 'strategy', to place the revealed Truth of the Vedanta, that *Atman* is *Brahman*, that idea, the statement of it, between ourselves and God and wait for His response, with no taint of presumption. (A completely different way of presenting ourselves before God than, for example, 'May I serve Thee,' but equally permissible, equally plausible.) It's 'His move,' in a sense, since realization of this Truth, of any Truth, originates in His act of Grace. We can reside calmly, with perfect serenity, in the contemplation of a spiritual Truth, awaiting the realization of it that is not in our power to bring about, and may or may not be granted.

❁

'Make me Thine Own: May I be Thine'

The *jnani* says 'I am He,' the *bhakta* says 'I am His.' Identity and Union. And really no difference, ultimately. Each is a *Via Sacra*. The following four assertions can be pronounced in any order. We can relish and revel in the varieties of joy.

I am Thine,
Thou art me.
Thou art mine,
I am Thee.

We can't by our own efforts become His, however. What we're actually asking for here in the *bhakta* emphasis is a crushing of the wayward will, a transformation and purification of our contaminated volition, which is really the ego. 'A man is, above all, his will.' The ego prevents us from being His. Destroy me, turn me inside out, do whatever is necessary, amputate whatever is holding me back, keeping us apart, but make me Thine! Liberate me for self-surrender, or, if I'm not capable of self-surrender, just snatch me out of my imprisonment in this dream anyway, by whatever means is called for. Despite myself.

❁

'OLD LOVE, NEW LOVE, EVERY LOVE BUT TRUE LOVE' — COLE PORTER AGAIN, FROM 'LOVE FOR SALE' (*THE NEW YORKERS*, 1930)

The love of God experienced in devotional meditation is so total, so overwhelming, so ultimate and definitive, we find ourselves murmuring, or thinking, 'Who could we love but Thee?' Even 'Who is there to love but Thee?' Rhetorical questions, the second more pointed than the first.

The feeling is one of finally having seen the self-evident truth after long years of pursuing phantoms in darkness, particularly the phantom of romance. We are, as it were, shaking our heads in faintly smiling disbelief: 'How could I have been so blind?' There's a trace of rue for the wasted time; compassion, for the suffering of people—you, husbands and wives, lovers and friends—who had to experience retribution, to learn life's lessons the hard way; rebuke, gentle rebuke, more reminder than censure, since the error has been seen and acknowledged. A savor of the wisdom that is peace. And the love we are feeling is like an ocean into which all these reactions sink and disappear.

Love, in the highest sense of the word, is synonymous with the love of God. We see the great truth; that alone is love which is the love of God. All earthly loves are merely aspirations toward their fulfillment in divine love. To have experienced the love of God is to know that nothing else, no other 'love', even remotely approaches it. It is to realize our oneness with the infinite Love that pervades and perpetually becomes the Cosmos, the Love that is God.

You could think of it this way:

It's as if we have within us a latent power, a potential experience, a capacity for fulfillment ('Love is in the depths of man as water is in the depths of the earth. . . .' (SCHUON)—whose unique mode of realization, as it appears to us and is described on our side of the river, is 'the love of God'. That's what we call it. The human ability to love, in other words, requires a 'proper object' in order to be realized, fulfilled, an 'object' commensurate with and implicit in its divine nature—just as the 'proper object' or fulfillment of intelligence is to know the truth and of the will is to do the good—and this 'proper object' of love is God and God alone.

In the absence of that object, in misdirected attachment to anything else, love is simply not itself. It's something else, trying but failing to become what it is meant to be. It will resemble what it's meant to be; we feel something like what we're meant to feel; but the experience will always be partial or qualified, even absurdly fragile in its dependence upon an ego with whose vagaries, explosions of self-righteousness, capricious unreliability, extravagance and impetuosity we have grown sufficiently familiar. Discontinuous and therefore containing the seeds of impermanence. The thought of these defects, these liabilities, limitations, blemishes, will haunt our minds and, in lucid moments, we'll realize that they contribute to an underlying uneasiness, restiveness, even fear, upon whose denial the 'love' relies. Earthly love, as we all learn sooner or later, is, although divinely enjoined and in the nature of things, ultimately unsatisfying, something we 'settle for', because it is finite and rela-tive, like everything else of this world. In earthly attachments love has been cheated of its proper object. The potential demands some-thing greater. Infinitely greater.

Divine love and earthly love are not mutually exclusive, nor is the former an indictment of the latter; they're merely distinct. Divine love is the fulfillment of our humanity, our consummation, our ascent to God, apotheosis, and we know this in the experience of it. Earthly love is its reflection, its manifestation 'here below', an expression of the 'overflow' of divine love into earthly containers, and this earthly love is not only sanctioned, it is commanded: conjugal love, love for parents, children, friends and saints, love of the neighbor and of all people in their courage, dignity, rectitude and affirmation of life—these societal loves have their proper place in the scheme of things. (Even love of *simpatico* entertainers: who was so hard of heart, among those the right age, not to have wiped away a vagrant tear when Lucille Ball died? We *loved* Lucy! Gene Kelly too.) But the inherent and imperious demand of essential love is for the infinite and the eternal: as if there were an inverse image of the infinite and eternal *within* our longing, as if that love 'in the depths of man as water is in the depths of the earth' is an inverse image forever seeking its complement—its 'original', as it were—which is God. We are only satisfied by union with something—really someone, because love seeks a 'person'—infinite and eternal, and that is God. We cannot, given the objective nature of this longing whose search for its proper object may be said to define human life, truly love anything else. The tone—ironic, forlorn, baffled, resigned—of so many blues and country and western ballads is justified.

The second rhetorical question, 'more pointed than the first,' as I suggested above, refers to the insubstantiality, or relative non-existence, of anything other than God. The emphasis here is on Oneness and the status of the world, the emphasis being not on the relative unworthiness of earthly objects, their inability, because finite and temporal, to be equal to love's inherent demand, but rather on their unreality altogether. The Presence of God with which we are rewarded in the act of loving Him—or the love we feel when rewarded by His Presence: the two sequences are simultaneous—reveals the existence or derivative reality of everything else. This is why we ask—in the upwelling of serene joy that accompanies having 'seen through' the illusion, having felt within us the miracle of Enlightenment—'Who is there to love but Thee?'

Either the world is unreal, because vanishing in every moment, or, equally true, and 'visible' as such in the moment of rapture, the world is God. The love of God is simultaneously the revelation that nothing else exists but God or that everything we have ever loved was God all along. In either case the point remains the same. We can love only God.

These rhetorical questions are a direct address. We are speaking directly to the Beloved, 'seeing' Him with the eye of the heart. Their whole meaning is contained in the presence in our souls of the word 'Thee'. In the quality of that Presence. As Kabir well knew and memorably expressed. God is the truth of the questions. He called them from our lips, called them back to Him from our hearts where He placed them before time began. Transfixed, tears of love filling our eyes, we could gaze at Him forever.

Love of God is the one essential thing.
—SRI RAMAKRISHNA

THANK GOD FOR THE TRUTH!

At the time of God's Presence, the time of Silence, the inexpressible Knowledge unveiled within us, indistinguishable from Bliss, can sometimes provoke, from what remains of 'us', from the mingled amazement and dazzled gratitude, the question, 'Where would we be without Thee?'

Destitute? Not even. We'd be nowhere. We would be nothing. The question emerges from a realization of our absolute dependence upon God for existence itself. It is accompanied by its complement, the blinding realization of His transcendent glory—to the degree that human beings are capable of conceiving it.

On another level, however, empirical rather than metaphysical, the question points at what has been called 'the misery of man without God.' It refers to the condition of the atheist or non-believer, terms which actually sound exaggerated and somewhat antique, since for the average citizen of the modern world 'religion' is no longer even a living issue involving opinions and positions; the subject no longer requires, nor receives, any thought. (As COOMARASWAMY remarked, with characteristic acerbity, 'Religion is no longer discussed in polite society'.) The religious argument, in other words, is as utterly absent from modern consciousness as, for example, the argument that the earth is flat. The question has been definitively settled, the rejected point of view now known to be simply one more of the innumerable pathetic or amusing fictions that demonstrate the helplessness and desperation of human inquiry during the eons of ignorance in which we languished prior to the advent of modern scientific method; although this magnanimous complacency, in the wake of so many puzzling and disturbing disasters in a society devoting an ever increasing percentage of its resources, intellectual and material, to preventing more, and in the midst of a systemic malaise so accustomed that few even bother to talk or write about it anymore, at least in any depth, at least as anything more than a nagging problem of insufficient information which computers will soon take in hand, now demands a little greater *esprit de corps* in its expression, more cunning and intricate devices of evasion manufactured by the 'entertainment industry', than it felt a need for in its jubilant mid-century heyday.

But I digress.

The question reflects simultaneous visions of the fullness of life with God and the desperation of life without Him. (How many people have never felt, at least in occasional attacks of candor, that their daily life, both at work and at home, is some strange punishment to which they have been mysteriously condemned and have no choice but to be patiently resigned, a sentence they are serving, each day of their life a day they have been *condemned* to live, simply in consequence of their own existence? How blessed are the few who learn the deep meaning of the first of the Four Noble Truths, the Truth of Dukkha, or Suffering!) Ultimately, nothing can sustain us, both in the day-to-day quest for a context large enough to give meaning to the full range and depth of our experience, and in the unavoidable summation that awaits us all in our mortality, the 'moment of truth', but the knowledge of His existence. Although the 'excuse' of atheists and non-believers incarcerated and educated in a totally secularized society carries a certain amount of weight, and our compassion is definitely elicited, their loss is nonetheless real and, given the nature of these things, has something absolute about it: tragic, catastrophic.

And this is so because that 'knowledge of His existence' translates into the ecstatic certitude, the breathtaking realization, that liberation, actual immortality, is accessible to us, because it tells us that *this*—this world, this life, this drama in time and space—*is not final*: that there is a Beyond, where alone finality is found because there it originates. Knowledge of God's existence, direct experience of Eternal Life: they are the same. 'In this world you will find tribulation, but be of good cheer, for I have conquered the world.' The thought of people we love walking daily and bravely in darkness through what Matthew Arnold called 'the gradual furnace of the world,' and then dying in ignorance, can break our hearts.

'Where would we be without Thee?'

A wasted birth. Listen: it has been said, as I have remarked already somewhere in this text, that it's only for the sake of the saints and devotees of God, for the illumined of every tradition, that there is a world at all, since only they know what the world really is, they alone inhabit and enjoy reality. That's the truth, and hard to say given the love we have for our friends and family. And it goes even further. As we flow in prayer and meditation toward God, the fullness of our humanity flows back into us from Him. We become, and we know we become, what humanity actually is: theomorphic, *imago dei*. Ignorance of the divine is not only ignorance of reality, of what the world really is, but ignorance of our true nature as well, entailing in turn, as its fatal consequence and the only terminal tragedy in our catalogue of destinies, the impossibility of striving for its realization.

This is an 'argument', however, and as His Mercy always outweighs His Rigor, and certainly over-rides our logic, it is, as it were, 'subject to review'. Someone's 'ignorance' is an inference and its 'fatal consequence' the logical conclusion of our finite and fallible understanding. The fact that there's no finality 'here below' determines more than we suspect. The final meaning, the final fate, the final judgment upon a life is not decided here but in heaven, and neither the criteria nor the evidence brought to bear are knowable in this world. The last moments and the twilight years of a human life are, with good reason, generally, perhaps even inescapably, private or dissembled, and they can make all the difference. Everyone has a secret life, a secret truth about them, known only to God. 'Though a man be soiled with the sins of a lifetime, let him but love Me, rightly resolved, in utter devotion: I see no sinner, that man is holy.' (GITA, chap. 9) We can't know whether that love is present in others, nor what forms of it are acceptable to Him. Look to yourself.

Back again to the question.

'Where would we be without Thee?' The basic feeling that motivates and is reawakened, prior to any interpretation, by the question, the 'heart' of the question drawn from us in devotional meditation and its real answer, is simply this: 'without Thee' we could not know this bliss: the bliss we felt right there in the divine Presence, inspiring the question, and which we realize immediately to be inseparable from, equivalent to, that very Presence. This bliss compared with which the greatest satisfaction and happiness the world can offer are nothing.

What motivates the question is the thought of that emptiness now made visible by stunning contrast, the emptiness of all earthly experience, the promises perpetually betrayed, the pursuit perpetually resumed, the vanishing of every moment leaving us always with nothing but the next vanishing moment, day after day… this is where we are without Him. The bliss of His Presence made visible the misery of His absence, 'the misery of man without God.' To know this Bliss is to know the Truth, and it is to know the Truth that we were made.

❁

A SEQUENCE ON THE HEART

The Heart is the only Reality. The mind is only a transient phase.
To remain as one's Self is to enter the Heart.
~ Sri Ramana Maharshi

❁

THE HEART

'Heart' is merely another name for the Supreme Spirit, because He is in all hearts.
~ Sri Ramana Maharshi

Independent of our awareness of the fact, we are a Center around which a world falls, or leaps, into place. The principle of centrality is implicit in consciousness. Or, shifting the emphasis, the existence of a world disclosed by consciousness implies the centrality of the latter. Or, shifting it once again, the existence of a world requires consciousness as its center.

In deep meditation, when the truths of which we are unaware, and inaccessible to awareness, in the waking state are revealed, the Center is directly perceived, directly experienced as both within and without, and spontaneously named—because the word is fundamental and powerful in this significance—the Heart.

The Heart is God.

❁

The heart is the same as Prajapati, the Lord of Creation.
It is Brahma. It is all.
~ Brihad-Aranyaka Upanishad

Suddenly Divine Presence, and the word comes simultaneously to our lips. *Thou, my heart.*

This Is the Heart: it carries its name with it. This is the fullest meaning, the ultimate reference of the word we have known all our lives in its lesser senses, its derivative senses, now before us. This is the archetype of the word, the Presence within the word, now unveiled, shining within us and before us. It is This that summons the word from us. It fills the universe.

As always, the sense of joyful recognition, as if by some inevitable blemish of the mind, some genetic amnesia of the species, we had forgotten this miracle, this great Reality, and now are seeing It again for the first time. *Mneme Theou*: the remembrance of God. Life flows from This, our lives, we can feel it. Not like a river, but as light and warmth radiate from the sun to saturate the whole fullness of three-dimensional space surrounding it. The Heart is alive: Life itself and the source of life and life wherever life is found. Joy and Love also, their source and their presence.

❋

My earth and My heaven contain Me not,
but the heart of my faithful servant containeth Me.
— MUHAMMAD

Intimacy, the intuition of Identity. The Heart is, as it were, the center of *my* center. This is my true Self, the core of my self, the depth of me. The One Heart is my heart as well: in beholding the Heart I behold myself. I had thought I was the ego, the physical being who bears my name, but all along I was This.

Heart of my heart:

There is a sense in this phrase of repudiating spiritual versions which emphasize the exclusive transcendence or otherness, and consequent absence here below, of God. (Rudolph Otto's '*die ganze anderer*'.) No; He is not 'out there' somewhere but right here within me, manifesting in this way almost as if to reassure me precisely on this point. So the feeling of confirmation in the words, merging into a dreamlike contentment, a silent blissful residence in their lingering echo. Heart of my heart. Nothing to fear, nothing to want or to hope for. Simply this serenity, this certitude, this tranquil exultation.

(At one time I considered never using 'heart of my heart' as a *mantra* in devotional meditation because I so often found myself automatically following it up with 'I love that melody, dum-da-dum-da-dum!' You know: 'The Gang That Sang Heart Of My Heart' by B. Ryan, 1926. A great and very catchy tune. But I decided that this was an indication of incomplete concentration, so I retained it for its additional challenge. Entering this '*mantra*' requires not hearing the lyrics of the song; success indicates a more thorough repudiation of the world, a greater freedom from it, a greater mastery of the mind. But I yet may have to give up on it. It might be, for me anyway, an unforgettable tune.)

❁

O Wakan-Tanka, behold the pipe!. . . . You have taught us that the round bowl of the pipe is the very center of the universe and the heart of man!
~ BLACK ELK

Heart of the universe, heart of my heart.

The Heart which is my own center is also the Heart of the universe, and It is God. I recognize Him here, the feeling is unmistakable, it's Him again. There in the silence and the candle-light: Him again. 'I' am not the Center, but God within me, Who is the heart of my heart, is the Center. He Whom I love beyond anything the word may be said to mean is the radiant Center of the universe, the Sun in whose light a universe is manifested, and He is in my heart. To know this is victory, the end of the Path. There can be no greater joy. The love of God reveals the splendor of heaven in the worshipper's own heart.

The Heart (*hrdaya*) has from Vedic times been a common symbol for the reality which both underlies the universe and the core of man's being. It is here that the macrocosm and microcosm, transcendence and immanence meet. The Upanishads declare that the Heart contains both Heaven and Earth, what is ours here and now and what is not yet ours. . . . The Heart is the Creator and Ground of all beings as well as the All.

~ MARK DYCZKOWSKI, *The Aphorisms of Shiva* [Shiva Sutras]

❁

This center which is here, but which we know
is really everywhere, is Wakan-Tanka.
~ BLACK ELK

In devotional meditation God is perceived as the living Center from which all manifestation is born and by which it is vindicated, the inner truth or sustainer, and praised for this emblem of His Glory. He is the principle of Existence, Existence Itself, and all that exists does so only by participation in His being. 'In Him we live and move and have our being'.

It can go this way:

First the Presence, recognized as God; then, almost instantly, the realization, the intuition of His aspect as the Heart; then the affirmation which, like all affirmations of His attributes, can only be uttered as praise. *Thou, the Heart, the All.* The feeling is wonder, a wonder so absorbed, so transfixed, that it numbs the interference of any other thought, as if we were murmuring, 'I knew you were God . . . but I didn't know *this*!'

We are perceiving, and we say to ourselves, to Him: 'Thou art the very heart of all things'. The *very* heart: the impact, the full significance, the realization, is focussed in that word. It reinforces amazement with conviction and a sense of conclusive confirmation. We repeat it, our souls transformed into gratitude, finality, infinite love. The statement is intensified. Heart becomes Quintessence.

❁

Bhrigu practiced meditation and learned that bliss is Brahman. For from bliss all beings are born, by bliss they are sustained, being born, and into bliss they enter after death.
~ TAITTIRIYA UPANISHAD

We are taught in the holy Upanishads that all things arise from Bliss, that Ultimate Reality, or Brahman, is Bliss. And I think we sense this without having to read it anywhere. I think we know it intuitively, even in the teeth of the apparently overwhelming evidence to the contrary with which every adult, looking up with an expression of haggard irony or baffled courage or simple grief from the great book of human misery, must eventually come to grips, and despite the prevailing alternative worldview supported by atomic physics, theories of stellar evolution and the awesome primordial deafening Big Bang reverberating to this day in the brains of contemporary sages.

Why 'intuitively'?

Because, notwithstanding this evidence and worldview, flying gaily and without hesitation in its very face, we are always seeking that 'Heart of Bliss'. Reaching for it, imagining it, speculating about it, even glimpsing it, whenever we manage to evade for a few precious moments the implacable surveillance of history and biography. We argue about it with our husbands and wives, we save money to purchase it, consult travel agents and the Internet to pin down its exact location and the times it is available, the discounts and restrictions, make reservations to fly to its attractions. We know it's there, somewhere, a potential we can actually realize, but we always associate it with the conquest of some elusive or expensive experience, we always think it's *outside*, in the world—and there we will never find it. There's the Great Mistake, the Great Wrong Turn the saints and sages have been warning us against from the beginning. The Immutable Reality, the Joy we actually are, the divine Intention for us, *that Bliss*, lies far beneath the treacherous kaleidoscopic surface where our desperate search is conducted. The Heart of Bliss is within us.

❁

Who could live, who could breathe, if that blissful
Self dwelt not within the lotus of the heart? He
it is that gives joy.

~ Taittiriya Upanishad

But the inescapable precondition for attaining that Bliss is renunciation of the world where we mistakenly sought it: renunciation of that misguided fruitless pursuit: seeing through the immemorial mystification. In other words, we misinterpret the very quest we are always engaged upon. We don't know that only the Ultimate Reality for which and of which we are made will satisfy our longing. We don't know that the happiness we pursue is not of this transient world, that nothing transient will satisfy us, nothing that comes and goes with time. We don't know that the Bliss we seek is God. And there has never been a culture in the entire history of humanity that more consistently, remorselessly, ingeniously and successfully than our own denies that truth, more inherently detests it. The Great Mistake is hammered into our heads from the moment we can hear and read and every day of our lives. It has to be, because it runs counter to the deathless truth: if the noise ceases, even for a second, if in meditation we can quell the racket in our minds, we hear the Music. And remember it afterwards. And pursue it.

'The Heart of Bliss' is a syntactical contraction of 'The Heart of (all things which is) Bliss.' The truth at the Center and Origin, directly perceived in meditation, is pure Bliss. We feel, in this moment of vision, that we could say 'I am seeing here the heart of the universe, shining within my consciousness, heart of my heart, and it is Bliss, infinite Bliss.'

All the agonized and contested distinctions that arise within *maya*, the *samsara*, conditioned and contingent existence, the world of forms—this I like, this I resent, this I am pleased with, this I can't escape, yesterday that reversal, tomorrow that maneuver, that I can't change, that I can deal with, this strategy worked, that one backfired, today here, next week there: the ubiquity of contingency, the endless definitions and confrontations, flux and consequence—all these distinctions simply disappear. Gone. Perception of the Heart of Bliss dissolves the world.

In the very instant that we perceive, with no shadow of doubt, that this, the infinite Bliss, is the Reality at the heart of all things, we also perceive, with the same shadowless clarity, that everything else, the whole world and our lives within it, is unreal. Either a dream, if we choose to see it that way, or simply a domain of mutually negating relativities, the 'pairs of opposites', energized by the chaotic, fanatic or administered passions of illusory egos and the mysterious redemptive inheritance of responsibility: that Great Drama which is the unfolding of *karma*, nothing more. The world, just before it vanishes altogether, appears for a fleeting instant, and to our compassion, as nothing but a poignant memory, a flicker in consciousness, clinging to us right up to the end and literally for its existence, like a spark from the campfire rising to its height and suddenly gone. All along, it was Bliss. We thought it was a world, but it was Bliss.

> When the universe is seen correctly, it is Atman and all bliss, but when it is seen incorrectly, it appears as the world, full of sufferings. He whose mind has world-cognition suffers, but to him whose mind has Atman-cognition, the world is a garden of bliss.
> ~ YOGA-VASISHTHA

❁

Spirit and Matter, God and the World, Heaven and Earth, That and This. We think to ourselves: 'It manifests here, but it's really there.' And where is 'there'? Beyond. Within. Eternal. And how does 'It' sometimes appear to us in meditation? Infinite Light, all-pervading; what the *Yoga-Vasishtha* calls 'the infinite consciousness.' Located in the Heart that is mysteriously identified with 'our own heart'. The Heart of Light.

> All this world is nothing but the one Supreme Reality which is Niralamba, devoid of any other support but Itself. The world shines by the light of this Reality. Know that the Yogi, whose mind is turned inward, dissolves all phenomenal objects, and merges itself in that Supreme Reality and becomes one with It.
> ~ DEVIKALOTTARA-JNANACHARA-VICHARA-PATALAM

We try to interpret what we see in meditation, sometimes in the moment, sometimes afterward. We try to translate the unutterable, bridge the gap between meditative and ordinary states of consciousness, express it in words. Anything that can help us to remember, because it can then help us to return, is priceless.

It manifests here,
but it's really there,
beyond, within, eternal.
The Heart of Light.

Those few words actually describe something like a 'total picture' realization. 'The Heart of Light' gives a name to what is actually seen. The words preceding that contain the explanation that leaps to mind simultaneously with the vision: we see it all in one instant. The invisible structure of things, the Truth. The spare precision of this 'explanation' has a tone of intensity, even suppressed triumph, like the announcement of a breakthrough discovery or long-awaited definitive solution, the presentation of something momentous, after which nothing will ever be the same.

Let's break it down.

'It manifests *here*.' The Absolute, the Brahman, God, or if we don't want to give It a name, simply the unmanifested Source of all this, the Origin, which, because It is inaccessible to the senses, must be 'elsewhere', has nonetheless burst into being *here*, where 'I' am, as this domain my senses *do* register, this place I call 'the world', *Creation*: this universe of things and beings in which I am a member of a preeminent subgroup, the celebrated human race, which experiences 'the world' as some kind of ultimate challenge in which the stakes are infinite, an opportunity which must be taken advantage of on pain of having lived in vain.

'But it's really *there*.' Now, because we have seen It in meditation, we begin to affirm what we know about It, beginning by picking up the central emphasis in the preceding phrase, Its 'location'. It is indeed *elsewhere*, an elsewhere indescribable in ordinary language simply because it is not *here*, within the spatio-temporal continuum to which all our terminology of location refers. The word '*there*' is like a pointing finger, directing our attention to the Reality.

'Beyond, within, eternal.' The Source of manifestation, of 'all this', is clearly outside of manifestation, outside everything we can know or name: therefore 'beyond'. It is 'within', which means both within *us*, but not physically, and in that 'other place' which can only be defined by negation: it is not *without*, not accessible to the senses, not knowable by the mind. It is, in the classic formulation, '*Neti, neti,' not this, not this.* Which is simply, this simultaneous immanence and transcendence, the usual double meaning of the word 'within' in religious usage, confirming our cosmic centrality and deiform nature.

And just as everything here is characterized by transience and mortality, so everything there is changeless and eternal. This is the universal teaching—attested in Revelation; confirmed by the testimony of the saints and the sages; self-evident to the Intellect, the intuition inherent in our deiformity, known *a priori*, in the sense of 'innate to the mind'—and in devotional meditation we perceive its truth directly. What is beyond this world and within the human soul is the immortal splendor of the Real. To realize our eternal oneness with It is the challenge and opportunity with which we are blessed by human birth.

'The Heart of Light'. This is what we saw, this is the name we gave to It. The Center is Light. 'Suppose a thousand suns should rise together into the sky: such is the glory of the Shape of Infinite God.' (GITA, chap. 11) Unfading, unfailing, all-pervading, the substance of all things as gold is the underlying substance in all the forms the gold-smith fashions. The Center and Source of manifestation appears to us, and within us, as a Heart of Light. Just a brilliant radiant infinite unutterably glorious *Shining.*

We know It for what It is when we see It. (To say the least.) It is my own heart, It is my mind, and It is the world. It is the Self, the blissful Atman, the great Lord of the Universe. God.

> Glory be to Him who hides Himself by the manifestations of His light, and manifests Himself by drawing a veil over His face.
> ~ JAMI

❁

'God of my heart,' 'Lord of my heart.' For a Christian 'Christ of my heart,' for a Hindu 'Krishna of my heart'. Phrases like these always come to mind in devotional meditation. Rise to our lips repeatedly, saturate our consciousness, our whole being, with infinite love, flow through us like an endless river of joy. The phrases and the feeling they express rebound on each other, generate each other, become inseparable. The secret of *mantra*. Sometimes we add the word 'forever,' sometimes 'my very own'.

> The Dwelling of the Tathagata is the great compassionate heart within all living beings.
>
> ~ SADDHARMA-PUNDARIKA

God is spontaneously associated with 'my heart'. The unstated feeling from which the above phrases emerge but which they despair of expressing—it would sound like 'I am helpless, I am choked, this cannot be uttered, I can only repeat these simple words, over and over'—is love, divine love, the great transporting love of God which is ours only as a gift of His Grace. When the word 'heart' comes to our lips in a religious context we are thinking of or experiencing love.

The suffix 'of my heart' is both an affirmation of supremacy, defining this love of God as my first or greatest love, and a reference to the center of my being, my heart. This supreme focus of my love has captured the center of my being, my heart, where true love originates. I am His. 'Forever' adds the sense of irreversibility, finality, indestructible commitment. 'Lord of my heart' suggests, in addition, a complete giving or surrender of that center, a self-effacement before God, a sacrifice of self to the Beloved Who is also Sovereign: 'King of the Universe', in the Judaic usage. Finally, 'Christ of my heart' or 'Krishna of my heart' shifts the emphasis to the Avatar, the form assumed for our sake by the Infinite Person Who is the universe, the Beloved in whose Holy Name we find God.

All these phrases vibrate with the feeling of sacred centrality and latent union whose association with the Heart, or with 'my heart', is basic in religious experience, and which originates in our intuitive awareness of our own centrality and its coincidence with the centrality of God. The Heart is the Center where God and humanity are united in love.

This is why we are sometimes moved to say, there in the candlelit silence, 'Love of my heart.' In saying these words we are greeting

Him as someone might greet a loved one returned after a long absence, a long and perilous absence, rising to our feet and coming forward with welcome open arms and a smile of joy, choking back tears or expressing the emotion openly, the love in our hearts permeating every atom of our being. It really feels that way, it really happens that way, because He's really there. He's really Someone we always knew but forgot, Who was always there but unnoticed: the 'return' is a recognition.

❁

When God's nearness takes possession of a man's heart, it overwhelms all else, both the inward infiltrations of the purposes and the outward motions of the members. Thereafter that man continues, going or coming, taking or giving: there prevails in him the purpose which has ruled his mind, namely, the love of God and His nearness.
~ Ahmad bin Isa al-Kharraz

When we experience God as more dear to us, more loved by us, than anything or anyone else, we spontaneously equate Him with 'my very heart'. We think those words: 'my very heart.' Its intuitively evident to us that a love so complete, so absolute and so unqualified can only originate in a prior unity, in Oneness, in an identity of the lover with the Beloved that has always been the case only we didn't know it, and that Oneness is directly experienced in devotional meditation.

We approach this sense of 'cardiac oneness' in earthly life as well, when we speak 'heart-to-heart', when we say, of a son or daughter perhaps, 'I love her as I love my own life,' or 'If she died, a part of me would die also': the loss is 'heart-rending,' it can 'break our hearts'. We love with our hearts, 'with all my heart', and we say that those we love are 'in' our hearts or 'live' in our hearts.

Love is on any level an intuition or expression of the Atman, the one Self in all. 'Everything is loved not for its awn sake, but because the Self lives in it,' as the Upanishad affirms. And on the highest level, in love of God, Love and Self-Realization are the same. 'I am the Self seated in the hearts of all,' says Krishna, the Lord of Love.

Divine love fills us completely, leaving no room for the self or the world. (Or, seen from the other direction, from the requirements of our practice, only when the self and the world are gone can divine love enter.) We are 'lost' in it. A rapt absorption *in* love of God and a rapt contemplation *of* the love of God becomes a single 'state of mind'. How can anything else matter, when *this* is possible? When this One, this incredible inherent object of all love *exists*?

You could say it happened this way:

Our languages have a word, Heart. It is continuously associated, in innumerable contexts, with four things: life, love, selfhood and centrality. Language, then, in an appropriate symbol, reflects humanity's knowledge that these four are closely related. Revelation, repeatedly in all religions, equates them all, and 'the heart' as well, with God. They are seen as divine qualities. Depth, as well, is associated with the heart: the divine is deep within us, deep within the universe: the Center is deep. When we speak from that deep place, we say we are speaking 'from the heart', 'from the depths of my heart', 'straight from the heart'. The word 'heart' comes unfailingly to our minds when we think about or try to articulate to ourselves our spiritual experiences.

Beneath the word, however—and this is the whole point—is the 'unvoiced' heart, the unvoiced *word*, which is not the Reality to which the word refers, but the state of awareness from which the word emerges as sounds stand out against and are defined by the eternity of Silence in which they appear and disappear, but with which they have nothing in common.

When the mind is absorbed in the Heart, the Self is realized.
~ Sri Ramana Maharshi

❁

O Arjuna, the Lord dwells in the heart of all beings,
causing all beings to revolve, as if mounted on a wheel.
~ Bhagavad-Gita, xviii.61

These are the words of Krishna, Avatar of the *Gita*.

In 'summarizing' his or her relationship to Krishna—the same possibility is present in a Christian's relationship to Christ, or anyone's relationship to any Avatar—the Hindu absorbed in devotional meditation might murmur, 'My Lord, my Heart, my Krishna.' These three terms, actually equivalent, would not be weighted equally. The first two are fulfilled in the third, the emphasis would be on Krishna. The One in Whom I see 'my Lord' and Who has become 'my Heart' is Krishna the Beloved, the Teacher of the Universe.

There is an enclosing, enfolding feeling in this 'summarizing' moment in devotional meditation, an intimacy, created by the word 'my'. Krishna, like Christ, is what is called a 'redemptive Incarnation'. In His aspect as redeeming Grace, Krishna of the Hindu religion is here to love us and to be loved, and in that mutual love, reinforced by His form as we see it in the traditional iconography and by His words and presence in scripture, He makes the more remote hypostases of the divine, such as 'Pure Consciousness' or 'Existence', the denotations of the Transcendent Absolute, accessible to our limited faculties. In our love for Him we love God, love the whole Reality of things; in His love for us we perceive God, perceive Reality. We even see, in Him, the Infinite. In a sense the Avatar makes a certain level of spiritual perception, the perception of formless 'abstractions', both possible and unnecessary. He is everything, all divinity is summarized in Him. Because we have seen and loved Him, we know that the Lord is in our hearts, that our hearts are the One Heart, that the Lord and the Heart are One.

However:

There is no world, there is no time. None of what I am writing here is literally true. To our eyes, and from our ordained aspiration to discover the truth of our being, a religious universe is unveiled, filled with its categories, doctrines and techniques. Religions, or systems of salvation, always appear native to the human world, a constellation of coherent affirmations simultaneous and coextensive with human experience. This is our side of the river, and our only hope. But the world is *maya*, and religion is a *upaya*, a Buddhist term which is sometimes translated 'saving mirage': for religions themselves are within *maya*. From the other side of the river there is no river: only that infinite Presence which is Brahman Supreme.

When we, who do not exist, perceive It within us, we call It the Atman. Where, within us? We answer, 'In our hearts'. But this is a figure of speech, a verbal convenience, a concession to the illusion of separate existence. Actually, It is everything and It is everywhere, and so am I. *Tat tvam asi*: That art Thou.

> God is said to reside in the heart-lotus. The heart-lotus is not a place. Some name is mentioned as the place of God because we think we are in the body. This kind of instruction is meant for those who can appreciate only relative knowledge. Being immanent everywhere there is no particular place for God. The instruction means: 'Look within.'
>
> ~ Sri Ramana Maharshi

✼

Find Buddha in your own heart,
whose essential nature is the Buddha himself.
~ Eisai

Try this: Say, or think to yourself, 'Thou, my heart.' Address your own heart as God. What happens, or can happen, then?

The Heart becomes personal, Thou, and disappears into God while still remaining itself, 'my heart'. It's important to remember that it is 'my heart' that is being addressed, not the 'Thou,' to think it that way, because the syntax permits both interpretations but only in the former sense is the identity complete. We look *through* the Thou, as it were, and speak to our heart. The heart is actually experienced then as personal rather than a symbol or concept, a thing of the mind: a Person within us Who is definitely not the person with whom we identify in daily life, definitely 'someone else', and yet just as definitely our self in a deeper sense, our *true* self which is now seen to be transpersonal and eternal: the divine Atman. This is the whole message of the Vedanta, and now we perceive it directly.

Through its ultimate compression of language this '*mantra*' presents, I think, a fairly intense reflection of our more intimate experience during meditation upon the heart, and a corresponding potential for recalling or even inducing it—which is, of course, the function of a *mantra*. When I experience my heart as a Person within me, as God, that simple human heart is ennobled, exalted—'crowned', in a sense—and transfigured into, or revealed as, the One Heart, the Center. The sense of the body as its container, and of the personality as an enveloping landscape, becomes dimmed: the Heart, which is God, alone seems real. The treasure we carry within us is so great that we disappear in the adoration of it, so lost in love that we aren't even aware that the illusion of the ego, that obstinate darkness, our 'faithful foe', has been dispelled.

> You must realize that you are one with the exalted Lord Who shines, self-luminous and all-pervading, in the innermost depths of the heart.
>
> ~ SRIMAD-BHAGAVATAM

❁

> *When can a man be said to have achieved union with Brahman? When his mind is under perfect control and freed from all desires, so that he becomes absorbed in the Atman, and nothing else. 'The light of a lamp does not flicker in a windless place': that is the simile which describes a yogi of one pointed-mind, who meditates upon the Atman. When through the practice of yoga, the mind ceases its restless movements, and becomes still, he realizes the Atman. It satisfies him entirely. Then he knows that infinite happiness which can be realized by the purified heart but is beyond the grasp of the senses.*
>
> ~ BHAGAVAD GITA VI

We must always pray for a pure heart—'Purify Thou my heart'—and we are truly doomed if we ever think this prayer unnecessary. In this petition, this plea, there is no realization, no vision. We are completely identified with the illusory daily lower self, the ego, duality prevails, and our supplication is humble and penitent—even, if we feel it that way, wretched.

No matter how sublime our spiritual experience, a part of us, gratefully, never forgets how much work yet remains to be done, how precarious and insecure—is it even imaginary?—our progress can suddenly appear, if the word is even applicable. We know full well what we are in daily life, the brooding resentment and flashes of ill will, the unworthy thoughts with which we salve our envy or guilt, our apparently indestructible fascination with lurid trash and weakness for escapist leisure, the nonchalant manipulation and dissimulation which has become second nature, the pure spite quietly simmering within us: the part of us as utterly untouched by spiritual endeavor as if we had never undertaken it. Not the great violations, not moral defection: just the daily corrosion. This self-knowledge demands appeasement, recognition; it demands to be comforted; it demands, above all, to be offered to God. We cannot purify ourselves except by His Grace, and we know this not from having read it somewhere but from direct experience of our helplessness. 'Purify Thou my heart.' This is the supreme request, because a pure heart is the precondition for receptivity to divine gifts, among which is our salvation, and therefore the divine gift *par excellence* as well.

There is great peace in this prayer, great relief. We know we are at one with God's Will for us. We feel we have made a complete confession, 'a clean breast of it,' and are therefore purified on one level in that very moment. We rest, because we have placed the future of our *sadhana*—in whatever sense we may reckon time on the Path: perhaps until the feeling of the prayer fades from our daily spiritual memory, or perhaps forever, because He has heard it—in His hands, where it always was anyway. If I may be permitted a crude but psychologically accurate metaphor, we feel reassured that we have covered all our bases, not as a calculated maneuver, of course, but in truthful recognition of two very fundamental human perils: complacency, and the related sin of pride. Both tend to sneak into our souls behind our backs. By praying for purity of heart we acknowledge our susceptibility and present our human condition to His Wisdom and Grace.

In addition to everything else, then, the heart, in its aspect as center, is the identity of the worshipper. Our ability or right to worship, to hope for acceptance, depends upon its purity. Purity here means *wholeness*: we must offer the whole self, withholding nothing, we must be undivided in our minds, making no mental reservations, we must throw ourselves at His feet and upon His Mercy, and we must do all this not for any personal gain or reward (without any 'gaining idea,' as Suzuki Roshi always put it) but because it is His Will, because it is simple obedience to the Lord of the Universe whose Will for us is our only hope: because human beings are *supposed* to do this in the same way that stars are supposed to shine and flowers to bloom. We must be one with His Will, we must locate and identify our true nature, our essential destiny, as it is intended in His Conception of us: that divine Conception, in both senses of the word, which is our timeless reality and our continuous birth within His infinite Beatitude.

The lower self has a heart too, in other words, with its own dignity and integrity, its own beauty. A humble heart. ('A humble and a contrite heart,' as Kipling worded it.) That heart is our awareness of a fulfillment in which we will disappear, in which we will die, like the metamorphosis of caterpillar into butterfly. We must pray for that death. The being who must die must pray for its death. 'Purify Thou my heart.' Knowing its role and accepting it, the ego pleads for the cleansing transformation in which it will be extinguished, in which everything *personal* will be extinguished, leaving only what we really are, and always were, and which alone *is*.

This prayer comes from the depths of the heart in the lower self. We feel that the tarnished heart for whose purification we are praying is different from us, another heart, before us as on an altar, above us somewhere, a tainted treasure, different from the heart in whose simple single-minded contrition the prayer originates. It suppresses a potential in the universe. We can see that clearly. It's the only blemish in an infinite perfection, the sole denial of an infinite Truth. Yet its our own: it's my heart. We pray for it.

If you think deeply about spiritual moments, tenaciously, you always reach a point where there's nothing more to say, where the mind stops, The mind stops and you're there, in the wordless Truth. We have to move with those moments, follow their lead, listen to them, plumb their depths, because it is only deep within them that He, Who is all we have in this life, is found.

Blessed are the pure in heart, for they shall see God.
~ MATTHEW 5:8

PART THREE

I SUGGEST THIS PARRY FOR THAT THRUST

'I am Thine.

We surrender. Not because we have no other choice, but because we realize that 'I am Thine' was the truth all along anyway, and now we are confessing it, acknowledging it, accepting it. Embracing it.

The feeling is one of self-abandonment to God, a complete giving up of the self, the ego. It's as if we are saying 'I am convinced, my reservations have fallen away, I turn my back on my "self". I turn my back on all that. I wish only to be an instrument of Thy Will, that my life and Thy Will be one.'

The pain of our lives is the burden of selfhood: the erroneous belief in, and identification with, an individual agency behind the scenes, ME, 'possessing' desires, making decisions, initiating actions, experiencing joy and suffering, satisfaction and frustration, victory and defeat (the notorious and illusory 'pairs of opposites') and the vigorous 'acting out' of a life based upon that belief and identification. The whole momentum of the dream we call 'my life', propelling us up and down the roller coaster of a 'personal biography' which is really nothing more than the sporadic and fragmentary appearance in consciousness of habitually repeated thought patterns—mental events, drowsy or feverish, cranky or placid, stagnant constellations and explosive rearrangements that exist no place but in the mind—originates in that one fatal belief, that single primordial error: the conviction of autonomous selfhood. The whole of Buddhism rests upon the negation of, and alternative to, that error. 'When the ego dies, all problems are solved.' (Ramakrishna) Therefore the priceless and compassionate instruction of the saints, the resignation of our lives to God.

I am Thine. The words come to our lips in devotional meditation, the thought to our minds. Sometimes it feels like a surrender, sometimes like a simple statement of fact; always, there's a sense of inexpressible joy and relief, a sense of melting. We've put the burden down, we've given ourselves to Him.

And every time we put it down we think that maybe some day when the time comes to lean over and gloomily pick it up again—as it always does, the world never forgets, it always comes back to reclaim us—we'll be able to halt in mid-motion, stare at it, and finally decide to leave it lying there, just stand up and walk away, despite the shocked disbelief, changing rapidly to rage, on the face of the astonished world: stand up, walk away, and be nothing but His servant forever. *Always taking care of business*, but with no will of our own. No goals, no purposes, no passions, no enterprises. No hope of approval, no fear of consequences: invulnerable: the same smile for everyone. In a word: no ego.

What we're after is a permanent state of potentiality, a permanent readiness, preparedness, such that every time the world, meaning the ego, comes knocking at the door, insistent and imperious, or slips into the room behind our backs, we can send it off simply by recalling, affirming, 'I am Thine.' We no longer belong to the world, we belong to Him. It's a strategy of emancipation, not from the rivers and mountains, the stars, the sea and the terrain, the weather and the seasons, because He is one with His Creation, Creation is Revelation *par excellence*, but from the world of human affairs: the world of the ego, the world in which our egos are entangled with other egos, millions of them, the overwhelming majority of whom, of course, don't even know of our existence, but who have plans for us, whose plans will reach out to us, whose multitudinous unpredictable enterprises encompass our participation, shape our very lives: I'm talking about History, Society, the Collective: as I'm sure you have realized. There's no question here, of course, of unilateral assertion: we become His by His Grace, we become His when He accepts us. And one essential goal of our practice is to make ourselves worthy of that election.

Images of returning home to love and welcome rest after a long and fruitless journey. Safety, the certainty of forgiveness; recognition that our misadventure was preordained and universal, just one more blind recapitulation of the path to submission. Images of returning to the earth, to virgin nature. Static repose, contemplative serenity. Watching the waves surge, flatten and recede. Watching the play of light and shadow off somewhere in the woods. Being still, being silent in the autumn sun, lost to ourselves and any human drama. Retreat to a refuge where the noise can't reach us: God.

I am Thine. He is the Master now and we the servant, an instrument of His infinite Will and Wisdom. How do you do it? How do you know His Will? Always put others first. Give: don't want.

I am Thine. We abandon the life that was never real and enter the Peace that was always there, unnoticed, unsought, unimaginable.

YOU CALLING *ME* A PHARISEE? SURE! WHO ELSE?

Anyone who has ever tried to meditate, or simply to seriously concentrate, to 'contemplate' a sacred symbol or concept for any period of time, has learned, to his or her baffled consternation, irritated dismay and even fury, something about the nature of the mind. It has a mind of its own.

The difficulties encountered, broadly speaking, fall into two categories.

First, the mind drifts away from the focus we have chosen—an aspect of God or the divine life—in favor of the absurd, embarrassing or grotesque preferences and fixations with which we soon became familiar, the sly exchange almost invariably discovered after the fact. Happens to everyone.

Second, the mind, whose basket of surprises is never exhausted, seems quite capable of entertaining two thoughts at once, in a foreground and a background, so that the chosen focus will either be continuously blurred by the murmur of background thoughts, or will actually slip into the background itself, still present but merely as an intermittent drone or flickering silhouette behind the more compelling preoccupation—a compulsive monologue illustrating a tenacious dedication to one of the passions, such as resentment or ambition, or an obsessive absorption in some riveting triviality, or the probing review of a gripping episode in a movie seen ten years ago, opportunities like these are irresistible—for whose sake the mind relegated the worship of God to a position of secondary importance.

There's an enormous and sufficiently exhaustive catalogue of meditative techniques, especially in the Buddhist and yoga literature, designed to help us cope with these two persistent and depressing tendencies of the mind. (Basically, either let the mind wallow around in the nonsense while 'you' watch it, detached; or haul it back to task by maintaining vigilance and exercising discrimination and self-mastery.) I have referred, however, to these well-known challenges presented to the meditator only to distinguish them from another challenge which is not technical and which should not, and cannot, be approached as such. Controlling the mind is important, to say the least; but there's another demand to be met.

We want to be able to meditate, or pray, 'from the heart'. And this may itself be the content of our prayer or petition: 'May my prayer be from the heart.' Our prayer, our meditation, our worship, from the heart.

The question is one of sincerity, which is 'the mother of all virtues', according to the Prophet, may Peace be upon him. 'From the heart' means sincerity; and we may pray from the heart even in the presence of a background drone in the same sense as an athlete with a pulled muscle may nevertheless 'run a good race' by throwing himself into his effort with a fervor equal to that of his competitors whose legs are in perfect condition. What is at issue is purity of will, or sincerity of intention, and not a technical perfection or an objective achievement. Purity of will, as a matter of fact and in this sense, is the achievement. What 'from the heart' is really asking for, with a solemn dignity, almost matter-of-course—as if referring to a requirement so fundamental that expression of emotion would be superfluous, if not suspicious—is the gift of identification with, *and therefore discovery of*, the center of one's being: the person in the depths of the heart, the person within us who alone can truly pray.

This petition, while not actually a formality, is less intense in its utterance, but not less urgent in its meaning, than other petitions we have considered. It expresses a continually renewed resolve to detect and disregard the bland and specious reassurances of the lower self; to resist the tendency, always latent in prayer, to lapse into mechanical semi-conscious repetition of the words, or to be lulled into satisfaction with a merely external observance, with a 'posturing', as it were, of meditation.

In other words, you have to really be there: you have to mean it: you have to be serious. There is no authentic spiritual engagement without sincerity, and no sincerity, for that matter, except as a gift of Grace, because, as we recognize at the very outset in our life of prayer and meditation, purity of will is not attainable by our own effort. Paradoxically enough, we have to pray for the ability to pray. It's not an infinite regression, God doesn't play games. (Games are played in spiritual life, and in tropical variety: but not by God.) We simply acknowledge a prerequisite and will its fulfillment.

To have been rewarded with the gift of prayer from the heart is no guarantee that the gift will be offered again, or that anything like a permanent receptivity has been granted or attained. The possibility of relapse is always present, we always slump back into worldly consciousness, and the plea ought to be continually renewed, as a daily reminder of the danger of self-deception. Prayer from the heart, since it reveals the divine Presence which made it possible, is a supreme spiritual experience: it is a vision of the beatific Mercy concealed behind the veil of the world. In this sense it is a mystery, as are all occasions when the barrier between heaven and earth has been pierced, or, more precisely, shown to have been illusory.

The person within us who can pray from the heart, the worshipper, is always there. Not 'uncreated', like the Self, still a created being, but the highest point, or extreme reach, of Creation. Why so? Because this 'person' is Creation's longing to reunite with its Creator, to realize the Eternal Identity. This 'person' is the awareness of God: God's Self-Awareness within 'us'. The person we think we are, on the other hand, who has been saying 'I' and 'me' a thousand times a day for so many years, is precisely the illusion that must be renounced in order that the prayer of the heart may be breathed into us, and drawn from us, by His infinite Mercy.

I MUST HAVE BEEN NOWHERE AT THE TIME

The word 'where' cannot be applied to Him—
Time and space are merely His Dream.
But He was right there in the room with me;
I knew He was there in the room.
Before that the all-pervading Presence,
Then suddenly: right there. In the room.
Only a few moments. Then He left.

The word 'where' cannot be applied to Him—
Time and space are merely His Dream.
Right. I know it. His Dream.
I want Him to come to me again.
I want to be with Him again,
There in the room, in the shining silence. . . .
Just the way it was that time.

The word 'where' cannot be applied to Him—
Time and space are merely His Dream.
He came to me that way more than once.
I can't remember how many times.
(Was it over half a dozen?)
I can barely bring myself to say this:
But sometimes I think He'll never come again.

The word 'where' cannot be applied to Him—
Time and space are merely His Dream.
Is it possible that after knowing Him
He gradually disappears from your life
And you never see Him again?
What if I become the only one
In the world that ever happened to?

The word 'where' cannot be applied to Him—
Time and space are merely His Dream.
The fact is, He's right here right now.
He's always right here right now.

But I don't feel it. I know it with my mind,
But that's all: I don't feel it.
I'm hearing September Song on BBC.

The word 'where' cannot be applied to Him—
Time and space are merely His Dream.
These words are merely His Dream.
How much longer am I going to live?
I know I can wait forever to see Him again.
As a matter of fact, that's what
I'm always doing: waiting to see Him again.

The word 'where' cannot be applied to Him—
Time and space are merely His Dream.
Every morning and every night, in meditation,
And during the day whenever I can,
I say His Name, I invoke His Presence.
And I'm blessed. But it's been a long time
Since He was right there in the room.

Where? Where is He, that One,
The Great Dreamer Who enters His Dream?
I am His Dream. There's really nothing
To be so concerned about here.
I am His Dream, and my longing
For His return is also His Dream.
But there in the room: was that a dream?

❁

GLINTS & GLIMPSES VIII

'Beloved One—Thou art the Beloved of us all'

All human love is a quest for God, no matter how grotesquely or pathetically misdirected. All those people out there, chasing rainbows—they're really chasing Him. They just don't know it. They caught a glimpse of Him once, when they were kids lost in reverie, or walking along the beach, lost in the sky and the sound of the waves, or in a human face, in one of those suddenly gripping flashes we get, or maybe it happened outside of time altogether, in the eternal Oneness from which they've only apparently separated themselves, and they've never forgotten it. And they don't *remember* it either, but on a deeper level it's really *all* they can remember, the feverish all-consuming relentless unconscious passion of their lives, and they've been running after it ever since. This is everyone. *Imago dei*, seeking itself.

❁

'May I be one with Thee'

Extinction *in* God rather than union *with* God through loving self-surrender. The river flowing into the sea.

Consciousness, or at least intuition, of separate existence as both a burden and an illusion is fundamental to any kind of spiritual engagement. If you haven't become urgently aware of the crucial enigma and dilemma presented by your own 'selfhood', if you haven't recognized that the ego or the personality is the real problem, the cause of all our suffering, the real issue, the crux of the treachery in all human enterprise and destiny, the place where we can and must address the riddle of ultimate meaning and significance in our existence and solve it, you have yet to enter upon the Path, yet to embark upon the One True Great Adventure, you're still playing around in the world, or, in the Buddha's metaphor, 'asleep in a burning house'. 'May I be one with Thee' emerges from that recognition, and from knowledge of the only way out—whether 'Thee' is Someone or No One.

❁

'O Thou, Thou, Thou'

'Thou' is a very powerful word, on a par with the Names themselves. It appears all through the world's liturgies and scriptures, of course, in all the prayers, and it can stand quite well alone as a very strong focus of spiritual concentration. Kabir extolled it:

Kabir saying 'Thou, Thou' has become Thee, and is not Me.
Glory to Thy Name!
Whichever side I look, there art 'Thou'.
Kabir saying 'Thou Thou' has become Thee, is merged in Thee.
Thou and I are now one, and the mind no longer turns away from Thee.

It's as if we are so overwhelmed by love and adoration that words fail us and we can only helplessly repeat the supreme pronoun, the mysterious unique word that refers to the One but in which two are implicitly present and simultaneously implies two but in which One is experienced. You can say it and think it, experience it, either way. The word contains Love, Lover and Beloved at once, it's really quite magical. He is present in the word as someone being addressed by another, present *in* that address, in the invocation itself, the relationship, the encounter. It's an 'encounter' *within* a Oneness. Thou, uttered from the heart, induces a state in which He is present, not separate from us—which of course is always the truth, always 'the case'—and yet still being *addressed*. A marvellous word! Truly a great *mantra*. A wild ecstasy.

❁

'May I not fail Thee'

The fear, the chilling apprehension, of disappointing God, 'letting Him down', can serve as a very strong motivation in our spiritual life. The language is figurative, of course, since God does not experience disappointment or lament the defection of servants. It's we who will feel disappointment. Real remorse.

The enterprise in which we do not wish to fail is spiritual fulfillment, God-Realization, the one purpose for which we were created. In earthly life, letting people down, especially people who counted on us and trusted us, who relied upon our fidelity and integrity of character, is a very bitter, even shattering experience. (Recall Conrad's great novel, *Lord Jim*.) We can't look ourselves in the face after a defeat so intimate and definitive, we're so ashamed. We've lost our reputation, our good standing, our good name. 'May I not fail Thee' harnesses to our spiritual vocation our fear of this kind of humiliation. The shame of failing God would be painful indeed. Shameful, terrifying, devastating, suicidal. Desolation Row. It's a matter of the stakes.

❁

MANY PEOPLE DON'T REALIZE HOW IMPORTANT THESE TWO WORDS ARE

Mercy and Grace. Two very basic words in the divine vocabulary. In devotional meditation we learn what they mean, by direct experience. They're what metaphysicians call 'hypostatic Faces' of God, and when God becomes present to us as those Faces—always spontaneously, unpredictably, for 'the Spirit bloweth where it listeth'—we immediately become and understand what we are in our corresponding identity. Everything we really *are* is 'our half', as it were, in a relationship with an aspect of the divine Being, with one of God's Names. We perceive God as Mercy, as Grace, and we think, or murmur to ourselves, 'Thou art Mercy,' 'Thou art Grace,' the words propelled into our minds by sudden insights into our true condition triggered by that very perception. We realize who we are, what we are, what happened in the universe, in the context of this principial relationship.

Broadly speaking:

The perception of God as Mercy and Grace is an experience of the Love that is God flowing into the universe, sanctifying and redemptive, flowing into our hearts and dissolving their inveterate uncertainty, dissolving the puzzling anticipation of despair that haunts us in His apparent absence, filling us with His gift of reassuring peace. Everything can be traced back to Him and everything will culminate in Him. We live in His Love. We experience His Love directly, know the 'perfect love (that) driveth out all fear,' and we enjoy the peace and bliss that enter immediately upon the disappearance of that great invisible internal enemy. Fear, that all-too-familiar subtle ineradicable undercurrent of uneasiness, is what we are after the Fall and in our Ignorance, in the error of assumed autonomy. Divine Mercy alone, The Grace of God, and nothing in this world, can remove it from us. Don't be impressed by what you see around you: it's an ocean of bravado.

More narrowly now, getting into it. Mercy first.

We realize, in dispassionate appraisal, that we are defined by a condition we inherited simply in virtue of our humanity; that this condition is somehow compromised, wounded, imperfect at present but, we suspect and hope, capable of perfection; that we cannot enter upon the path to recovery until we are released by forgiveness, forgiveness for being what we are generically and have been individually; that this forgiveness emanates from the creative Agency behind the universe in which we inherit the imperfection, the flaw, the wound, and that it is given, instantly, upon our recognition of the need for it: the two, recognition and condonation, are simultaneous. We are a being in need of healing, in need of restoration to an original or intrinsic perfection, we are candidates for reinstatement, and our recovery requires some kind of forgiveness, a pardon originating in a universal benevolence or infinite clemency which becomes operative, at least to our awareness, as soon as we perceive and acknowledge our absolute dependence upon it. This insight into our true condition *qua* human emerges from our direct experience of the forgiveness, of Mercy. It happens, it can happen, our understanding is illuminated, Light breaks in, right there in an ordinary room of our ordinary home where we live our ordinary lives. Practicing devotional meditation.

This particular insight sounds very Christian. But only because the Revelation of God in Christ emphasizes the perspective of sin and redemption. Imperfection is interpreted, and experienced, as Sin, and consequently Guilt, and recovery as Redemption through reception of and participation in the sacrificial Atonement on the Cross. Actually, since all Revelations are addressed to a fallen humanity—a more fundamental point can scarcely be imagined—no matter how 'fallen' is defined, whether as sin or disobedience, ignorance or concupiscence, rebellion or even curiosity, the insight into our true condition accompanying the words 'Thou art Mercy' is neither restricted nor theological. It is simply a conclusion of the contemplative intelligence aided by revealed Wisdom: in a word, the fruit of meditation within a sacred tradition. The Hindu as well as the Christian prays for Mercy, the latter addressing the plea for intercession to Christ, the former to any of several major avatars and hundreds of minor ones.

Now Grace.

Grace is a broader category. The insight here is the realization that *everything* is God's Grace: the universe, our awareness and love of it, our existence and our joy in existence, our intelligence and our capacity to have experience, our awareness of and capacity to worship Him, and the insights such as this one with which we are blessed in devotional meditation. The 'overflowing' or radiation of the Sovereign Good into a Cosmos, into Manifestation, is Grace. 'I was a hidden treasure, and I wanted to be known, so I created the world.' (*Hadith qudsi*—word of God not contained in the Quran—and probably the most well-known of such *hadith.*) 'Just as an artist cannot contain his delight within himself, but pours it out into a song, or a poem, even so Parama *Shiva* pours out the delightful wonder of His splendor into manifestation.' (Jaideva Singh, *The Shiva Sutras.*) Our presence as self-awareness, 'I Am', and illuminating consciousness, which is our participation in His Being and His infinite creativity, is His Grace. ('The highest attainment, however, is that of *Shiva*-consciousness, in which the entire universe appears as I or *Shiva*, and this comes by Saktipata—the descent of divine *Sakti* or *anugraha*, Divine Grace.' Singh again.) Grace is within the Self as the potential for music is within a violin. The world is the song Krishna is playing on His flute, or the dance of *Shiva* . . . or, in one version, 'His Laughter.'

And finally, Grace, as well as Mercy, is an illusion, for our status as recipients depends upon our erroneous conviction that we are separate beings. Grace, in other words, is a relationship within *maya*, the universal illusion or relative world or world-appearance. The Personal God, the Beloved, is the highest manifestation of Brahman, the Absolute, the famous 'one without a second', to the individual soul who has not yet realized Oneness, or who is not at the moment realizing Oneness, and Mercy and Grace are the relationship of this God to the soul, in all the ways in which both have just been defined. The highest Truth is always non-dualism, the end of the Path is always non-dualism, absolute Identity: there is nothing but the Self, the One without a Second. Grace and Mercy only exist 'from our side', and our side, and we ourselves, are a dream.

Think of it this way:

By His Grace we have been given all this: a universe, ourselves and each other, music and rivers, sons and daughters, laughter, the colors of things, the birds, the hills and the sky, a past and a future, snow and stars, waves and mornings and meadows filled with wildflowers, shells, fishes and rainbows, the great life we call our world. And by His Mercy we are forgiven our enthrallment to all this, and offered the immortality we lost, and lose again and again, when we turned from Him to embrace His incomparable Dream.

So as you can see, He has withheld nothing. Withheld nothing. What is our life but a choosing from among His gifts?

Finally, I should add that this has been one interpretation of Mercy and Grace among others, one experience. There are others, varying from tradition to tradition and within traditions as well. The words are often used interchangeably. The general meaning shared by all interpretations affirms God's inexhaustible generosity and benevolence and our utter dependence upon it.

God is always the active agent; our apparent initiatives are always enabled by Him. The distinction between, on the one hand, the generosity by which we are granted this world and our hope within it, or Grace, and, on the other hand, Mercy, a generosity by which we are offered deliverance from our exile here below, in this world of transience and insubstantiality, is, it seems to me, metaphysically founded on the provisional truth that Heaven is not Earth. At the point where the difference between them disappears, a 'point' which is actually eternal because All is *Atma*, because Self -Realization is not an attainment but an unveiling, by no one, of what has always been the Reality, Grace and Mercy disappear as well. There is only God.

All of which becomes clear, and discursive thought vanishes, and the circle closes, in the wordless infinite Bliss of His Presence.

Thou art Mercy.
Thou art Grace,
May I see Thee.
Face to face.

AND THERE IT IS! RIGHT THERE WHERE YOU FORGOT IT!

Here's another little rhyme. A *mantra*.

Heart of Love,
Heart of Light,
Thou art within me,
Day and night.

It can serve as a reminder: this is something not to be forgotten and a joy to recall. You get a distant look in your eye, a faint smile, and then you light up: 'What joy in Thy remembrance!' (SRIMAD BHAGAVATAM) The point of impact, as it were, where the assertion is focussed and completed, triumphantly 'satisfied', is in the last line, where the familiar all-inclusive feeling of the figure of speech 'night and day' is reinforced by the tone of conclusive finality in rhyme words. A warmly reassuring reminder.

We might repeat it to ourselves during the day, when we sometimes find ourselves ambling thoughtlessly, plodding despondently, hurrying frantically or stalking grimly from one post to the next in our round of responsibilities. The customary circuit of the stations of the Cross. It tells us that even now, in an improbable moment when God is the very definition of 'remote', nothing has changed. The divine Reality is unmoved (in both senses of the word), indeed untouched, by the daily current of vicissitude—which is, in reality, nothing but a stream of consciousness belonging to no one which becomes 'ours', i.e. pretends to have a personality, precisely because we forget to keep an eye on it, thereby violating the Buddhist injunction to sustain mindfulness. We suddenly remember the Truth, and the Person within us Who *is* the Truth.

Heart of Love: devotion to God, the fervor for union, sacrificial adoration—the way of the *bhakta*. Heart of Light: knowledge, the Intellect, spiritual vision—the path of the *jnani*. The two Royal Roads. Each is a 'heart' because each is central to our true being and central in the universe, the divine Center from which the universe emanates: 'Thou,' because each is God.

Our centrality as illuminating love and our identity in the depths of our being with the Supreme Person, *Paramatman*, is always the reality, always what is actually 'going on' beneath the surface of dissipated consciousness and transient events. But, with an apparently irresistible regularity, we forget this truth: we became *distracted*, in all the related meanings of that richly significant word.

The little rhyme is a reminder, a vehicle of reawakening. Say it now! What have you got to lose? Maybe, by a sudden gratuitous infusion of Grace, because the time for you is ripe, you'll feel and know its truth and be transformed forever!

> It is of course nothing new that you gain. God is already within you, but you had forgotten Him and so temporarily lost Him. When any external matter enters your eye, you feel terrible irritation. When it is removed, your pain is removed and you feel as if you had gained something new. In fact, you did not gain anything new. You only got back to the normal state you had lost temporarily.
>
> ~ Swami Ramdas [1886–1963]

AND WILL IT BE PERSONAL OR IMPERSONAL TODAY?

Experience of the Pure Consciousness, of absolute Oneness, the Self, can seem to confirm the non-dualist argument that the personal God we love is, like we ourselves, merely an appearance within *maya*—although a 'special' one, as the non-dualist readily concedes. Non-dualism implies, in other words, that the whole 'affair' between devotee and God, worshipper and worshipped, lover and Beloved, is illusory—a 'stage' on the Path prior to the final blinding ego-extinguishing Self-Realization in which there is only the 'One without a second', in which all dissolves into Brahman, the infinite Oneness.

However: once having known and loved God, Whom we perceived with unassailable clarity as Reality itself, it is totally impossible to turn from Him, impossible to imagine living without

Him: terrifying to entertain, even momentarily, the thought of it. Any suggestion that His Glory might be diminished, in any way, by the least fragment, is utterly unacceptable: unthinkable.

So what ought we to do when, as some sometimes happens, the spell of Non-Dualism—either in the wake of direct experience or as a water-tight metaphysical 'argument'—has temporarily anesthetized our capacity for devotional worship? When it seems impossible to locate, and ridiculous to *wish* to locate, a separate ego, an 'I' which we know to be ultimately illusory, to play the role of a worshipper. From the purely intellectual point of view, given the sublimity and prestige of Non-Dualism, the dilemma may appear absurd. But on the level of our actual experience it is quite real indeed, assuming, if the period of His absence lengthens, an urgency truly desperate.

The scriptural description of the two Paths, the Path of devotion and the Path of knowledge, is found in the opening of Chapter 12 of the *Gita*, where Krishna, the Avatar of the *Gita*, explains the difference between devotees of the Personal God, 'those whose minds are fixed on Me in steadfast love, worshipping Me with absolute faith,' and aspirants to non-dual Realization, 'those others, the devotees of God the unmanifest, indefinable, and changeless . . . omnipresent, constant, eternal, beyond thought's compass.' The paths are said to be distinct, with *jñana*, the Path of non-dual Realization, more difficult, but leading to the same summit. The frequently quoted Hindu saying, 'I would rather *taste* honey than *be* honey,' testifies to the continually arising 'need' in this tradition, and privilege, to distinguish, and even attempt to choose, between the two paths. Nor should the earthiness of the metaphor here, which is more an unembarrassed confession than an apology, detract from its penetrating insight into the humbly honest rationale behind a preference for the Path of Devotion. It can appear as an option for greater intensity.

Kabir's well-known and equally homely metaphor, 'The formless Absolute is my Father, the God with form is my Mother,' illustrates one style of reconciliation. It suggests a summary and probably disdainful dispensing with fruitless hair-splitting: the two perspectives are merely two experiences, equally legitimate, of the Divine. Since both views are true, it follows that any sense or episode of entrapment in one or the other must be countered, and the balance redressed, or else, quite simply, we will lose contact with the total Truth whose realization is our birthright.

Most people never get to the point where any of this is a real issue in their lives. But some have. It crops up in scripture and in the testimony of the saints and sages. It may even happen to you. And if it does, you'll certainly he able to deal with it on your own. It'll be *your* 'problem'! Whoever *you* are!

'OH HOW I LONG TO BE IN THAT NUMBER!'

The saints.

Sometimes I wonder what they were like. These were real people, not the stereotypes they tend to become in pious memory, and not the featureless interchangeable mystical giants looming behind the words we read like images sculpted from mist. Wouldn't it be incredible to see a photograph of Rumi, or Shankara, or Nagarjuna, or Augustine? To go back in time and see them walking around, talking, smiling, reflecting, explaining? The saints and the sages! The creativity of the revelations, the people who fleshed them out and kept them alive. The teachers, the proof, the glorious affirmation. We owe them everything.

You could think it this way, this would be the essence of it: 'As these, Thy blessed saints, have known Thee, may I know Thee.' Those words, that sentiment, that petition incorporate us into the relationship of Grace with a unique and intimate emphasis. The saints may not have started out as we did (Who knows how they started out?), but we know where they arrived, and something of the arduous journey.

Christians in the second century undoubtedly had it the worst, and the Jews off and on for millennia, but even in propitious settings, hospitable to spiritual types, the aspirants to gnosis must have paid a price. The world exacts its price; that's a part of the picture, the way of it with 'worlds'. Our identification with their sacrifice is one thing that brings them closer to us in these times, although, since what is lost is actually nothing and what is gained, although invisible, is everything, maybe 'sacrifice' is the wrong word. (I'm reminded of the parable of the mendicant's conversation with a king who alludes to the former's great renunciation. The gist of the mendicant's reply is 'My renunciation is trivial compared with yours. I have merely renounced the fleeting transient pleasures of a fleeting life, while you have renounced immortal bliss in God!') It's actually detachment, stubbornness, indestructible resolution, magnificent self-mastery, indifference to consequences and an unassailable cheerfully defiant resolve that we identify with: the retort to *contemptus mundi*, to 'the world, the flesh and the devil'. (Love that *contemptus mundi*! What could be more invigorating?) They had to swim against the main current. They had to deal with people who told them, with that genuine and intelligent concern so much more difficult to handle than snap judgments or mindless condescension or simple scorn, that they were crazy or useless or self-indulgent or 'going too far', or 'proud'. They had to have had moments when they wavered and quickly prayed for strength to persevere. Consider RUMI:

> Always flee from whatever you deem profitable to your lower self: drink poison and spill the water of life. Revile anyone that praises you: lend both interest and capital to the destitute. Let safety go and dwell in the place of fear: leave reputation behind and be disgraced and notorious. I have tried far-thinking intellect; henceforth I will make myself mad.

And THOMAS A KEMPIS:

> Unless I prepare myself with cheerful willingness to be despised and forsaken of all creatures, and to be esteemed altogether nothing, I cannot obtain inward peace and stability, nor be spiritually enlightened, nor be fully united unto Thee.

And SWAMI SIVANANDA:

> All that one calls honour, name, or reputation must be considered by the spiritual aspirant as filth or poison, whereas he must

> accept dishonor and scorn in the way that one wears a golden necklace. That is how he can reach the goal with certitude.

And Seneca:

> You are not yet blessed, if the multitude does not laugh at you.

These attestations sound exaggerated to our ears, partly because hyperbole is favored by the saints, maybe to drill it into our heads, and we make the mistake of taking them literally, but more so because in this despairing century—or in locations, geographical or cultural, where despair is less scandalous—there is actually a growing receptivity, I think, to spiritual vocations, or at least a sincere curiosity. The emptiness, the vacuum of meaningfulness in contemporary life, the growing sense of being trapped in some sort of ineluctable precipitous momentum generated by an agency and agenda devoid of human concern, all contribute to something like a reinstatement of spiritual values and a validation or at least understanding of, if not sympathy with, those who try to adopt them.

I think it's a matter of seriousness. 'The world', the *official* world, not necessarily individuals, watches everyone very carefully. The more serious we are about striving to bear witness to, and affirm in the way we live our lives, the unreality or ultimate inconsequentiality of worldly affairs, the more thorough-going the detachment to which we aspire, the more isolation we will experience, and the more 'the world' is going to feel snubbed, and resent it, and try to make us feel guilty or silly or irresponsible. 'The world' is reluctant to let people hand in their resignations: renunciation, by definition, is defection. The saints, however, with their testimony, step forward then as our company, 'our team', they stand beside us. In addition to showing us that it can be done they show us that we're not alone. On the other hand, however, and as our decent wonderful friends engaged in the great struggle we entered upon in the glorious sixties will properly remind us, there's work to be done and outrages to which we must declare our opposition, no matter how 'unreal' we know the world ultimately to be. There's a skill to be cultivated here.

What the saints looked like or experienced, and what 'the world' felt and always feels compelled to say about their choice, these are dialogues of the everyday consciousness and with our children and friends. In meditation the saints became what they always were: holes in the curtain, through which the eternal Radiance bathes our world with Its love and truth. In devotional meditation we become one with them in God and in the love of God, one in the Self, and then we see that there never were any saints, or, if this formulation is disturbing, that what they were they are now, within us, outside of time.

Our Lord Himself spoke to His disciples on this subject, in words we all have to face in the depths of our hearts, and come to terms with on our own. Negotiating a life span is a deadly serious business; taking it as such is the only way to go.

> If the world hate you, ye know that it hated me before it hated you. If ye were of the world, the world would love his own: but because ye are not of the world, but I have chosen you out of the world, therefore the world hateth you.
>
> ~ JOHN 15:18–19

THERE'S A LOT YOU CAN SEE WITH 'A FAR-AWAY LOOK'

A *mantra* is a word, name or phrase which refers to God or divine truths and can be employed to recapture and reexperience the state of mind in which God was Presence and Truth was known. This is customarily a meditative, or 'superconscious' state, and the *mantra* is primarily a meditative technique. Many have been suggested already in these pages.

But the gift of *mantra* is by no means restricted to our formal meditation. We can also repeat them, and enjoy a comforting if less intense recollection, in the mix of turbulence and monotony, stimulation and reverie, alarm and relief, that constitutes daily life in these times.

Each repetition plucks us momentarily from the ego-stream we wade into shortly after waking up, and re-enter after morning meditation, diverting the mind from its accustomed states, the worrisome preoccupations, itchy irritability and stupor of resignation, punctuated by nervous releases, which usually characterize company time and domestic life. We look up, as if from the grimy bottom of a mine shaft, our faces suddenly bathed with light, and recall the true heaven we inhabit beneath the relentless transience that defines our apparent exile. This relative world, this mortality, this conditioned existence, this entrapment in personality and biography, all are suddenly revealed in their unreality, unmasked. We recall who we are, where we are, what we are. We glimpse the Infinite which is alone joy—'There is no Joy in the finite'—and the Absolute in which we are the deathless Absence which is pure Presence. The 'far-away' look in our eyes is an image then of the eternal Truth: what we are seeing with that look is right here within us.

And then back to company time, where the gist of the traditional Instruction is something like this:

Do your level best, try to love everyone you see. Be compassionate, be cheerful, strive to be unobtrusively virtuous. Always draw attention to the moral dimension in human affairs, to the questions of right and wrong, justice and fairness upon which, surprisingly enough, nearly everyone is always dwelling anyway behind the social masquerade and the conviction of helplessness, Because we are blessed with human birth we have an intuition of the Absolute and are therefore innately aware of an aspect of our lives, centering in Biblical language around the concept of 'righteousness', that is somehow decisive; we know that where ethical issues are concerned the stakes are real and there's no way to bargain or play games. In other words, during company time—a familiar enough term, referring, in the present context and in conformity to an insightful popular usage, to *samsara*, the round of birth and death—try to talk about God without anyone knowing it. A matter of wit and humor, style, character type: the cultivation of a shrewd single-minded diplomacy with the uneasy rabble of personae inhabiting everyone's daily highjinks. And uphold the immortal Dharma which, insofar as it has any to speak of, is the world's only hope.

There's a saying, I think it's Buddhist, about the sages living and working and walking around in the world but never forgetting the jewel in the lotus of their hearts. I can't find it anywhere. ABU SA'ID IBN ABI'L-KHAYR, however, the 11th-century Sufi master, said essentially the same thing:

> The true saint goes in and out amongst the people and eats and sleeps with them and buys and sells in the market and marries and takes part in social intercourse, and never forgets God for a single moment.

But we're not saints. We forget repeatedly, reliably, with inveterate consistency. Our gratitude goes to the ancient nameless technicians of the sacred who discovered within their hearts the holy *mantras* of their faith and realized what miracles could be performed by mere words.

> Mantra is a combination of words that stands for the Supreme Reality. It is so set that by the utterance of it, a rhythmic sound is produced which has a marvellous effect on both the mental and the physical system. The sound of the Mantra produces mental equilibrium and physical harmony. It tunes the entire human being with the eternal music of the Divine, bringing the soul in direct contact with the in-dwelling and all-pervading Reality.
> ~ SWAMI RAMDAS

❁

GLINTS & GLIMPSES IX

I think the enormous invisible pervasiveness of the worldview in which religious experience is patronized or invalidated, the 'conclusion' at which the modern world has jubilantly arrived in the wake of Science's awesome achievements, justifies an occasional jab in return. Human souls are involved here, real people. Resisting the blanket repudiation of the social environment, and identifying and prevailing over its myriad forms of subtle distortion and hostility, is by no means an insignificant aspect of commitment to spiritual realization. The stakes are Infinite. You're among people all the time: strike when the iron is hot. Big strikes, sometimes little strikes, pointed inquisitive remarks, inscrutable smiles, serious statements delivered light-heartedly, unconcealed detachment from worldly affairs... Bearing witness admits of infinite variety.

❁

'My soul is Thine'

In devotional meditation, suspended like a cloud in the calm bliss, we realize that we are and always have been nothing but a ray of the divine Reality, the divine Light, nothing but an imaginary drop in the ocean of His Being. We have always been utterly immersed in God, we have never existed as a separate entity. The contamination of personality was always, all along, an illusion. The soul, the core, the heart, was always His. Separation from God was a fantasy, entertained by no one. 'All along it was Thee: there has never been anything but Thee.'

'My soul is Thine' can also refer to and recreate the moment of self-offering, the hallowed moment or state when we actually feel in ourselves a complete self-surrender, a 'caving in' of the ego. We lay down the burden of self, that essence of all misery, we perform the great world-transcending act described and enjoined in the famous 66th verse of Chapter 18 of the *Gita*, 'Abandon all dharmas and take refuge in Me alone.' ('Dharmas' here meaning 'all actions, righteous or unrighteous.' Swami Sivananda commentary.) In the fine Juan Mascaro translation, 'Leave all things behind.' They were never real anyway.

The next time anyone comes to tell you, with delicate indirectness, how much money they are making, or, definitely directly, how much fun they are having, you can answer this guiltless affront to our stubborn, astute and hardwon perspicacity, this ingenuous simple-minded discourtesy to the traditional wisdom and mindless disregard for the collective experience, with a smile, a smile which, on the outside, in compassion for their helpless innocence, their victimization, must congratulate with warm enthusiasm their success, but on the inside, in sober awareness of their probable but not certain fate, can only be grim: these souls, unless they catch on, are lost. It's a case of the water after drinking which we will thirst again, or of what those who sow the wind will reap, or of where, shown the two options, we will choose to lay up our treasure.

I love the word Grace. *All is Thy Grace*. Love the kind of universe it implies, reveals. This universe. When you know that there's nothing but God, and that the illusion of our separate existence originates in an infinite self-giving (*yajna*, the Primordial Sacrifice), an infinite creative love, an infinite overflowing of infinite Bliss, you feel joy and peace. Everything's OK. You feel that now you can live out your so-called life in what is without a doubt the intended state of mind, the properly human state of mind.

From a certain perspective (and it's always 'from a certain perspective' in the great spiritual summations) salvation begins with, and depends upon, the recognition of Grace.

❁

Neither God nor Truth nor Joy nor anything real in any way whatsoever will ever appear on television or a computer screen—which is why prolonged intercourse with either of these celebrated final nails in our coffin induces complacent stupefaction. It's not the device itself; it's the whole thing, the event, the 'person-before-the-device,' that makes the angels stare a moment with pity, then turn away with helpless resignation.

❁

GETTING UP EARLY ENOUGH TO MEDITATE, AND SIMILAR CHALLENGES

An American swami of the Ramakrishna Order once told me that the Order regarded strength as the most important asset in a spiritual aspirant. The reason is obvious. Determined perseverance, or strength of will continually reasserted, is what keeps the whole thing going, the precondition. Keeps us on the Path. It takes strength: stubborn, I-don't-care-what-the-consequences-are strength. You don't stray, you don't temporize, you don't bargain, you don't compromise. Will Power, unquenchable zeal. In it for the duration.

The prayer would be: 'O God, forgive my weakness, and grant me strength.'

And there are nuts and bolts involved here.

It takes strength to get out of bed an hour and a half early every workday morning in order to have time to meditate. Every day, every morning, the same strength. The body, that synonym for self-indulgence, never aspires a millimeter above its true nature and will offer the same whining protesting drag when the alarm goes off, the same flat refusal and cunning arguments, right up to the day you die. Expect nothing else. It wants to curl up under the delicious warm blankets and go back to sleep, and you'll have to haul mercilessly its dead weight out into the cold, ignore its unvarying protests, dress it, attend to its needs and walk it over to the meditation room every morning for the rest of your life.

In the beginning you'll depend upon sheer will power. Eventually, however, it will become easier, because you'll be able to depend upon fear. A new ally to lend a hand. Fear of the consequences of self-betrayal and Self-betrayal which are shame, bitterness and remorse. You will be disgraced and discredited, even contemptible, in your own eyes, your self-respect will be tarnished forever, your whole life, your reputation, blighted by this single stupendously consequential ignominious defection. You will be weakened, irreversibly, and you will experience self-hatred for having botched your one chance: the one hope, the one thing needful, the one true purpose, the one and only absolute meaning in human life, the one fulfillment of human birth. These apprehensions of the price we will pay for preferring sleep to worship are not overstated—how could they be?—and will vanquish, with appropriate ruthlessness, the body's inveterate sloth. The prospect of sham before God, your peers and yourself will get you out of bed in the morning. And other places as well.

So: first will power, then the reinforcement of fear. And finally, anticipation. To meditate is to prepare a reception for the Guest Who is Bliss: for God, the Beautiful One, the Glorious One, the Self of the Universe. He might come, He might not, as we know from experience: 'The Spirit bloweth where It listeth'. Even if He doesn't, we'll know the joy and peace of obedience, of having a clean slate. But if He does answer our invitation—it's really we, of course, who are answering His—the meditation room will become heaven. We get out of bed because we remember what has happened before, and can happen again. We remember Reality, and how much we love It, how life without It is not worth living.

So much for getting out of bed. What else?

It takes strength to overcome glumness. To simply be happy with your lot and play the hand you were dealt rather than always trying to exchange it for better cards. Human beings seem to be plagued by a strange chronic intermittent predisposition to squirm with discontent, to be harassed by the feeling that something, often unidentifiable but readily invented, is not quite right in their lives, that something is out of kilter or doesn't sit well or is subtly poisoning everything else ('Am I imagining all this?' we think. 'No, I'm not! I'm right!') and has to be exposed and confronted, dealt with or eliminated, or at least located. We become restless, morose for no reason or a thousand reasons everyone who pretends to love us has conveniently ignored. Maybe our whole scene is One Giant Mistake. We fall prey to sullen moods and sulky withdrawals into fruitless brooding, we slump into gloom. I exaggerate, I hope; but only to jog your memory, to make your familiarity with this recurrent fever more accessible to you. No one escapes.

This pall of discontent, this capitulation to the permanent mindless hunger of the lower self, to the illusory dissatisfactions the ego is perpetually weaving around itself and then pointing to with resentful indignation, is the smoky atmosphere in which *karma* is created, in which we forge and tighten the chains of our own bondage. It is inconsistent, to say the least, with the spiritual life to which we aspire. And just as it takes strength to rise up physically out of bed, it takes strength to pull ourselves out of this mental morass, to rise up spiritually towards God. We are always being dragged down—or, more accurately, falling down under our own weight—into identification with the moronic insatiable lower self, identification with concupiscence, with the stream of inexhaustible cravings, frustrated fantasy scenarios and habitual responses and patterns called, in Sanskrit, *samskaras.* If we think of our 'character' as the terrain, the *samskaras* may be compared to the channels, or the whole ravine, carved by the stream. But as intimate and dynamic agencies the *samskaras* are the stream itself, the stream of *consciousness*, one thought after another, one emotion after another, which we are continually reassembling and behind which we impute an ego or 'self'—the fateful elemental error, comparable to the Fall in western traditions, which gives rise to the illusion of separative existence—we spend, or waste, an entire lifetime thinking of as 'me', when there's actually nothing there at all.

It takes strength to drag ourselves, in defiance of the ego's gravity, up out of this clinging muck. Out of the sunless ravine of the lower self to walk in the light again. It takes vigilance: what the Buddhists call mindfulness. It takes tenacity, because we fall back repeatedly. It takes, above all, a capacity for detached compassion: this lower self is to be pitied as well as repudiated. If we view it with contempt or hatred it still holds a grip on us; but in the generosity of compassion we establish ourselves at good distance from it, and in meditation we clearly perceive its unreality.

But he lower self always returns, with its clamorous complaints and pathetic celebrations, its gloom and discontent, its wild or complacent illusions of success, at least until we are firmly established in sainthood, and the strength to rise above it will always be demanded of us. The pathos of human experience and the life of the lower self are one and the same. What else are all the novels, plays and movies about? But we are Light, and our inheritance is the Light.

Strength: where else is it needed? Anger deserves a special mention. I'm tempted to say a special citation: it takes real strength to resist anger, 'the wise man's faithful foe.' Krishna warns us against it in chapter III of the *Gita*, along with lust, which, in a house-holder's life anyway, is a challenge to self-control rather than self-denial, as it is for the monastic. (And who's to say which is a more difficult, treacherous path!) The issue of lust is less momentous than the ubiquity of titillation and the conflicted legacy of Puritan Christianity might lead us to believe. Anger is much the greater enemy. Lust at least is precisely restricted; anger assails us anywhere and everywhere.

It takes strength also, or skill as a form of practiced strength, to handle personal relationships impersonally, with detachment from and compassion for both our own inevitable feelings and the feelings of others, while still appearing to have personal investments. (I sometimes say, to people who will appreciate the unanswerable roguish irony, 'I *pretend* to have feelings in order not to appear inhuman!') Our friends and loved ones want us to be motivated, and hopefully occasionally overpowered, by feelings; they'd like to think of us as passionate, which they equate with being human. (Which is right on the mark—'spot on', as our English comrades would say—in the *Kali-Yuga*, one of whose characteristics is the dominion, within the person, of appetite and impulse, 'willfulness' and spontaneity, in the absence of a traditional wisdom, authority, paradigm or Way.) But we love them, and it's actually easy, once we master the knack of it, and once our 'eccentricity' has been accepted as incurable, to live out the *karma* we share with them and never for a moment forget the Truth. I love my children beyond expression, and my partner in life and my friends and the kids in my class: I'm only human, as you are. But I never forget.

We pray for spiritual strength because we are correctly taught that it comes from God, we have nowhere else to turn in our helplessness, and because His unfailing and ever-renewed Promise, which is Existence itself, breathes it into our faith. When great strength is demanded and exhibited, however, we don't always or necessarily experience it as pouring into us from without. To say the least. It can feel very much indeed like our own, summoned up with grim and tremendous effort from resources deep within us which we can quite well imagine running dry, at least temporarily. From our side of the river perseverance on the Path can seem to require 101% of our strength, with God supplying the 1% and we supplying the rest. It takes all we have. Actually, however, what we are experiencing as 'our strength' is the continuous reintegration of the world into its own reality, which is God and from which it was never in fact separ-ated. The sincerity of our prayer plunges us into the great flow of things, the truth behind the scenes, enables us to go along with the flow without being shaken to pieces from resisting it, we 'triumph' through surrender. We enter the current of His Grace, the identity of the world with God, the movement of things which in traditional language corresponds most closely to the Tao, the Way of Heaven and Earth. 'The universe is ruled by allowing matters to take their course. It cannot be ruled by interfering.' Strength is our absence, in the world, our absence as agency, our absence as a separate being, our presence in God.

Spiritual strength was never really ours, anymore than anything else is ours. Or, coming at it from another direction, spiritual strength is only as real as the world and the ego. Or yet again, spiritual strength is His infinite Will, misread as our own. In any case, the exertion, like the need for it, and like bondage itself, exists only in our imagination. Where it is vivid enough.

WHO PUT THE SERPENT IN PARADISE? AND *WHY*?

Sometimes we perceive the Presence as Infinite Wisdom. From *our* side of the river, in *our* language, we perceive *That*, which is God, the unknowable Absolute Reality, as 'Infinite Wisdom'. The 'perception' is the rising to our minds or lips of the words: we *call* It, *see* It, spontaneously, 'Infinite Wisdom'. We may just murmur, lost in rapt adoration, adrift in the Void of Light, 'Thou Infinite Wisdom, Thou Infinite Wisdom,' or 'All resides in Thy Wisdom, all is held in Thy Perfect Wisdom.'

This conviction emerges because the mists of worldly concerns have been dissipated, unveiling our spiritual intuition, the Intellect, the *buddhi*, to which it is obvious that the Impersonal Absolute, Brahman Supreme, must coincide with infinite or perfect Knowledge, must *be* Infinite Knowledge: nothing else is possible, nothing else makes sense, any alternative proposal seems clearly inane, preposterous, and we see that clearly: with the crystal clarity, the absolute certitude, that is experienced as divine Bliss. The transcendent Source of Being is Perfect—'knows' what we cannot know, knows infinitely, and *is* what It knows.

Then problems arise.

The influence of a wise and beneficent Providence, an visible all-knowing all-loving Guiding Hand, an Infinite Benevolence, is rather difficult to discern in this world, and Paul's argument that 'all things work together for good to them that love God' (Rom. 8:28), although not cheerfully mindless like Pangloss's conclusion that 'all things are for the best in this best of all possible worlds,' sounds rather insufficiently concerned or thorough-going to our ears, even rather callously partial and elitist, and not even quite accurate for those blessed few to whose felicity Paul alluded. A bit too casual. Too sweeping. Maybe just simply not true.

For people of good will with reservations about religion any reference to 'divine wisdom' inevitably raises the question of God's inability or unwillingness to 'do something about' what we perceive as evil, His strange 'permission' of it, from Hiroshima and Auschwitz *ad infinitum* to the death of a child in a burning house to the birth of the blind and the deformed to the entire uninterrupted 'massacre of the innocents' on all levels of outrage that defines our modern world. We're talking about the problem of theodicy: the 'defense' of God in the face of what is manifestly, to our eyes, evil. Evil, monstrous, atrocious, horrific, obscene. For atheists, of course, the question doesn't exist—or, more precisely, atheism seemed the only answer to it.

The theodicy discussion rapidly becomes intricate, scholastic (in the modern pejorative sense of the word) and eventually embarrassing, and the intelligence that demands this intricacy, and is as innocent of embarrassment as it is ignorant of the direct experience it won't deign to pursue, will never be satisfied. Evil cannot and should not be argued away, nor a benevolent Providence demonstrated, by tormented redefinitions. There is evil in this world, on the relative plane where we must love one another or die (as Auden put it on September 1, 1939), and no need to pretend otherwise. At the same time the existence of God requires no 'proof'—being evident to the human Intellect, which is in itself proof, as is Existence, and given in direct experience to those who sincerely seek Him—and is in no way contradicted or compromised by fatal household accidents, earthquakes, cancer, squalor, war or crimes against humanity. How to reconcile this disturbing apparent contradiction in the universe without throwing up our hands and simply writing it off as a 'paradox'?

God definitely 'watches over us' (He sees a black ant crawling across a black rock at midnight on the darkest night of the year,' as I believe I read somewhere in the Koran), but not in the manner demanded by His sincere critics or by the exaggerated anthropomorphism of the very faithful who see and praise divine intervention, in the form of warnings, lessons and acts of protection in every detail of daily life. The problem is not one of defending or justifying God, which is a pastime for fools, nor of 'explaining' (or explaining away) evil as if evil has some special status: the question 'Why is there evil?' is obviously not essentially different from the question 'Why is there good?' or 'Why is there anything at all?' As FRITHJOF SCHUON puts it, 'The question: "Why does evil exist?" really comes down to the question of knowing why there is existence; the serpent is found in Paradise because Paradise exists. Paradise without the serpent would be God.' And less metaphorically:

> Manifestation by definition implies imperfection, as the Infinite by definition implies manifestation; this ternary, 'Infinite, manifestation, imperfection' constitutes the explanatory formula for all that can seem 'problematic' to the human mind in the vicissitudes of existence.

In other words, evil *as such* is metaphysically necessary in a manifestation, in a created world, simply because the manifestation is not God but the radiation into Being of His transcendent Infinitude and must display contrasts, the famous 'pairs of opposites', the infinity of the possible, if it is to display anything at all—which does *not* mean, however, that *particular* evils are either 'willed' or 'permitted' or that God is 'unable' to do anything about them, but rather that

> Being, which coincides with the personal God, cannot prevent evil because, as we have seen, It cannot abolish, and could not wish to abolish, the Infinitude of the pure Absolute. . . . He cannot abolish evil as such—and He does not wish to abolish it because He knows its metaphysical necessity—but He is able and wishes to abolish particular evils, and in fact, all particular evils are transient.

The 'problem' is rooted, in other words, in a confusion about the relationship between the Impersonal Divinity and the Personal God, and in a piety which is nourished by anthropomorphism and 'intercessory longing' alone—piety which is nonetheless perfectly legitimate, whose 'wrestling' with the theodicy question is an aspect of that priceless proximity to God, a gift of Grace, known as Faith. Metaphysical discrimination, gnosis, is neither 'final' nor 'superior' nor for everyone.

Let's stop at this point. We are on the verge of intricacy, probably over it. We have a right to ask these questions, to demand a theodicy, because our intelligence is total, but ultimately the discursive answer, even Schuon's, is proven limited by that very totality of which causal reasoning is only a part. The truth is not thought, not 'grasped,' but seen, felt, directly experienced, known by identity.

Our perception in devotional meditation of Divine Wisdom originates in an intuition of the Perfection from which this imperfect universe emanates, and in whose light its contrarieties are resolved back into the unity of their Source, the unity in which they 'reside' or are 'held'. That Perfection, which could just as well be experienced as Love or Peace, Truth or Pure Awareness, is here experienced as Wisdom. And what does that Wisdom mean? That all is for the best? Hardly; the expression is as shallow in print as it is cheap when it comes from someone's mouth. That nothing here below really matters? No; if nothing really mattered why would we be instructed by Revelation in charity, compassion, the holy Dharma?

We are His Knowledge of us. The world is His Knowledge, as He is the Self of the universe. The vision in which He is revealed as Perfect Wisdom is the vision of His infinite Transcendence. Everything is His Knowledge, contained in Him, existing in Him, defined by Him: 'In Him we live and move and have our being.' Yet He transcends all: He is, in Schuon's term, Beyond-Being. Within His Knowledge all things—the mountains and the sunrise, good and evil, the thoughts of a snail or a hawk—are of a piece, inhabiting the same plane, the same level, woven of the same substance: Being. His alone is the privileged vantage point: His Infinite Transcendence.

Our submission is our wisdom, experienced as recognition and worship of His. As Dante put it, 'In Thy Will is our peace.' We are here to ask questions, else discriminating intelligence and the power to act upon its conclusions would not have been given, to extend an affirmative and helping hand to others, to 'love one another as I have loved you,' as our Saviour instructed us: not to make demands of That but for Whom we wouldn't be here at all.

NEARER TO YOU THAN THE NECK OF YOUR CAMEL!

When we are told that 'God is everything' or 'All this is Brahman' we tend to stress the outer dimension. We think of an objective reality, a world, which is God mysteriously transformed into solid objects, into the material world surrounding us on all sides: God is the hills and the trees, that house out the window, that wall, this blue cup on the table.

Almost true. The error creeps in with the word 'transformed'. God is not transformed into the world: God *appears* as the world while remaining forever unchanged, undergoing no transformation whatsoever, just as the rope that appears to be a snake is never really anything but the rope. (Every time I come across that simile in Hindu texts I recall a map I once saw showing the incidence of reptiles in the world; where snakes are concerned, India is most definitely the heartland.) In other words, *objectivity itself is the illusion*:

the world is *maya*, an appearance in consciousness, neither subjective nor objective but rather that unity of subject and object, perceiver and perceived, cognizer and cognized, inner and outer, which is the Self, universal Reality. The celebrated Oneness. 'All this is Brahman' because Atman and *maya* are One. This is the Big Secret the sages learned from direct experience in meditation, and explains their incorrigible cheerfulness, their courteous indifference, their peaceful inward smile, their compassion.

Let's take a look now at the inner dimension of that unity. Round out the picture, as it were, by opening our eyes to yet another domain where we may adore the world as God and God as the world.

Inner life—human experience, the 'inside' of things, the event in our minds, the thrill, the reverie, the resounding, the 'feel' of it—is also God. The intangible thread of drama and meaning running through the heart of human affairs, what we think is happening to us in our lives, the way we'll remember it all, the continuous interpretation accompanying and defining the events as they unfold—this too is God. All the inner states, the 'moments', the precious irreplaceable lived and relived moments which are the very texture of our lived experience. The point, of course, is to be careful not to identify with those moments in a personal way, but to realize and rejoice that they also are God, the Self we truly are, the inner dimension of His dream that is our world. His dream, 'our' dream, for we are the Self. 'Our' moments are His dream, and His dream is ours. The divine intimacy is absolute Oneness, seamless Identity.

So it's appropriate, and illuminating, and emancipating, to praise and worship this aspect of His Glory: 'All the moments, all the moments, Thou art all the moments.' And we may do so both in that direct way, praise and worship, focussing on God, and indirectly by recalling some of the actual 'moments', not as specific events, although they may come to mind, but rather as archetypes, the great universal themes and passages, the memorable and definitive moments in the human drama. They are adored as the Beloved: as His Life which He has given us to experience as our own. (Realize this insight just once and you'll never be the same again!) We love humanity as the living being of God, and we love Him as we love ourselves, this human presence, this miracle in which we are both the dreamer and the dream. In the words once again of Our Redeemer, 'Love one another as I have loved you.' Walt Whitman comes to mind.

What are those moments?

They're the moments in which we love humanity, in which we feel deeply the momentous depth of the human presence, the inescapable fact of is significance, of our significance. Everyone has, and must draw upon, their own store. I think sometimes, for example, of partings. The unvoiced confusion of feelings written on the faces at railway and airline terminals, the sudden realization of how much this person has meant all along; the acceptance of loneliness, fragility and danger, and the recognition of how large a role hope and faith play in our lives. The adjustment of a collar, the abrupt embrace, the last-minute promises and reassurances, the clinging gaze while someone walks away out of sight. The moment in their minds, overwhelmed, the moment in mine, contemplative and respectful, the moment in yours, reading these words—any moment where life wells to the surface, showing what it always was, where we feel deeply and unselfishly, where we see the heart of humanity and know once again what it's really all about, where we see the truth of ourselves, our helpless grandeur, our original purity, our strange ineffaceable identity with impersonal love behind the innumerable masks we wear. That feeling and that vision are His Presence, His Eternity. He is the tissue of our lives, the substance, the link, the unity.

He is all the moments. *Thou art all the moments.* This realization subtracts away the last and deepest layer of illusory identity within us, our identity with inner life, with our personal drama, leaving only the immortal Witness, if our realization leads 'away from the world' towards the transcendent 'Brahman without attributes', or, if we tread the path of devotion, the pure love of God Who is *all this.* The taste, or *rasa*, of the first is Peace, the second Bliss. But each shines within the other.

I HAVE GREAT NEWS: I LOST MY LIFE!

The original, central and fundamental 'point' in the path of devotion might be epitomized like this:

I have no 'life'. I am no one. Thou art all.

The quotation marks around 'life' indicate that a specific usage of the word is intended. Definitions 3 and 7 in *Webster's Collegiate* give it perfectly: (3) 'The series of experiences, of body and mind, which make up the history of an animal from birth to death.' (7) 'An individual human existence; as, each day of one's *life*; also, a biography.'

This is what we are appealing to when we say, as we do almost every day, 'my life', what we are thinking within every memory, emotion, intention or act of cognition that makes up our stream of consciousness, and it's the single uninterrupted assumption in which every action of our waking existence is born, unfolds and is remembered. It's bedrock, the bedrock assumption. It's the *me*. I am living 'my life' and 'What I do with my life is my own affair' and 'That's the story of my life' and 'It was a turning point in my life' and 'I had the time of my life' and 'It was the happiest day of my life' (or the worst) and 'It was one of the most beautiful moments in my life' and 'I've felt that way all my life' and 'I'm not going to go on living my life this way' and 'No one's going to tell *me* how to run my life' and so on. We have to get this notion of 'my life' out of our heads. There's no such thing. This is the very heart, the very core of the Teaching.

But the only way we can know it, and believe it, make the truth our own, is in direct perception. What is it that, all along, has seemed to be 'my life'? How did the error come about, and who made it? Who am I? These questions are answered in meditation informed by apprenticeship to the Vedantic revelation, the Holy Truth of the Upanishads, and what we learn there in direct experience and self-confirming bliss is:

1. All consciousness, all awareness, is God;
2. There is only one Self in the universe;
3. That Self *is* the universe;

4. It is Infinity and Eternity, beyond all manifestation, in which universes appear and disappear forever like the myriad instantaneous jewels of light that scintillate on the surface of the ocean at sundown;
5. 'I am the Self-Awareness of the universe that is the universe';
6. Tat tvam asi: That art Thou!

So we affirm, 'I have no "life",' emphasizing the word 'life' with calm disdain. We affirm, with insistent solemnity, 'I am no one.' And with over-powering love and adoration filling our hearts, for we are addressing God here, 'Thou art all.' Will we realize, directly experience the truth of these affirmations, merely by uttering them? Maybe, maybe not. Sometimes yes, sometimes no. More often not and no. It depends upon the presence or absence of a certain fullness of self-giving in the heart, of self-abnegation through total transfixed absorption in the contemplation of divinity, of *That*. Which in turn depends upon Grace, upon a gift beyond our power to elicit. Never give up.

BACK TO UNREALITY!

There is, disciples, an Unbecome, Unborn, Unmade, Unformed; if there were not this Unbecome, Unborn, Unmade, Unformed, there would be no way out for that which is became, born, made and formed; but since there is an Unbecome, Unborn, Unmade, Unformed, there is escape for that which is become, born, made, and formed.

~ UDANA

The Portal of God is non-existence.

~ CHUANG TZU

Phrases like these come to mind, in the Silence: 'There is only God.' 'There is nothing, There was no one, There is only the Light.' 'There is only the Beloved.' 'Nothing has ever happened: There is only the Self.' 'All is God.' These are direct perceptions.

The metaphysical 'explanation' informing the realizations expressed in these phrases has already been discussed in these pages. It's the essence of the Vedanta, the Truth that is taught, and in devotional meditation it's directly perceived. Reality is directly perceived, entered: we drown in It. The prevailing feeling when the Reality is experienced as impersonal is Peace: the Peace of the Void in which the Illusion appeared and now vanishes. The prevailing feeling when the Reality is experienced as personal is Love: love of the One Who is All. That Peace is Bliss: that Love is Peace. Transcendent impersonality is also the Beloved Who is God.

These realizations definitely precede, and escape, their cognitive analysis, although many gallons of ink have been enlisted in many languages in feverish or methodical attempts at explanation. The Void, the Light, the Self, absolute Oneness, the unreality or non-existence of the world and the sole reality or existence of God, the identity of God and the world—all these are the familiar paradoxical verbal formulas, the 'raids on the inarticulate,' with which we try to communicate what is essentially incommunicable and can only be known through direct experience; and this proviso itself is sufficiently familiar to devotees of the Word and the texts. The truth reveals itself to those who long for it, as they say; if you want to know what an apple tastes like your strategy is fairly obvious.

> The Self reveals Himself to the one who longs for the Self. Those who long for the Self with all their heart are chosen by the Self as His own.
>
> ·~· MUNDAKA UPANISHAD

So let's assume the incommunicable realization has already occurred, at least once but hopefully more often, with a certain regularity, or been irreversibly intimated, and examine the essential characteristic of life *post facto*—I am tempted to say *postexilic* since our life in this world, in the conviction of worldly finality, or *maya*, *maya* being ultimately a state of mind, is truly a form of exile or captivity, a Babylon of the mind.

This essential characteristic is *detachment*.

> Like two golden birds perched on the selfsame tree, intimate friends, the ego and the Self dwell in the same body. The former eats the sweet and sour fruits of the tree of life while the latter looks on in detachment.
>
> ~ Mundaka Upanishad

The memory of Reality, and of the peace, bliss and love we experience in contemplating It, conduces to a detachment from empirical circumstance: an internal 'far-away look in the eye' in the midst of the perpetual agitation and dissipation with which we are assailed. We know now that we are really one with that Reality: that peace, bliss and love are not only Its essential nature but our own as well. We can consciously, when we choose, 'rest in the nothingness,' the infinite space in the mind (*akasa*, in Sanskrit) that is Pure Consciousness or Awareness, the 'place' where the world will appear when we emerge from meditation but which in meditation is empty, pure potential, the Self.

There is a larger scale.

It's difficult to view European and World history in the twentieth century, and the state of 'the planet', with detachment, and the attempt or claim to do so can seem unworthy, irresponsible, despicable, even inhuman. The issue, however, is not one of arbitration. There's nothing 'worldly'—or ignorant or 'unspiritual' or 'materialist'—in being moved, and moved very deeply, by historical events, as long as we remember that, no matter how tragic or atrocious, they are finite and relative and have no bearing upon the Reality. Nor is there any conflict between sustaining detachment and seeking wherever possible to assist in the relief of suffering, as long as we remember, to paraphrase *Brihadaranyaka*, that it is not for the sake of humanity and the earth that humanity and the earth are loved, but for the sake of the Self. The only error is to concede any transcendent, or even durable significance to the stream of events, the 'current of forms', known in the West as history and in the East as *maya*. (A sufficiently amusing correlation.) There are meanings within the drama, which is why a Gandhi entered into it, but the impersonal compassion, the focus on spiritual rectitude, which motivates our participation saves us from identifying with those meanings: we act in the world not for the world's sake, but for the sake of *dharma*.

Having seen the Reality we are free to act for the good of all beings, but we will no longer believe that they possess autonomous existence, nor that their destiny lies in this world, nor will we accord finality or absolute significance to anything that happens here. The one Self that dwells in all beings is untouched by the drama that unfolds within It, and you are that Self, and that Self is Love.

> The Self reveals Himself as the Lord of Love to the one who practices right disciplines. What the sages sought they have found at last. No more questions have they to ask of life. With self-will extinguished, they are at peace. Seeing the Lord of Love in all around, serving the Lord of Love in all around, they are united with Him forever.
>
> ~ MUNDAKA UPANISHAD

The phrases that come to our lips in the Silence emerge from visions of the incommunicable Truth, like the sputtering astounded exclamations of a diver gasping to the surface after glimpsing the silent otherworldly beauty of the seabed kingdom. Let's return to that Truth. The communicable, no matter how profound or uplifting, always goes stale with repetition and threatens to sound jejune: it is finite ('There is no joy in the finite'), settled, ready to be filed away. But the incommunicable is eternal delight, because it stems from the Infinite ('There is joy only in the Infinite'): indeed it is Heaven. Here are some reports by those who returned and tried to tell us where they'd been, what they'd seen:

> Brahman is where reason comes to a stop. There is the instance of camphor. Nothing remains after it is burnt—not even a trace of ash.
>
> ~ RAMAKRISHNA

> Things are all made from nothing, hence their true source is nothing.
>
> ~ ECKHART

When you talk about the Void (*sunyata*), do not fall into the idea of vacuity.
~ Hui-Neng, the Sixth Patriarch

This is the state of perfect union, which is termed by some a state of nothing, and by others with as much reason termed a state of totality.
~ Father Augustine Baker

The soul can only be pure and white like snow if you make a void in yourself, or on the contrary if you lose yourself in the totality of creation. All colors merge to produce white, which is the color of the Formless.
~ Ananda Moyi

Nothing is born, nothing is destroyed. Away with your dualism, your likes and dislikes. Every single thing is just the One Mind. When you have perceived this, you will have mounted the Chariot of the Buddhas.
~ Huang Po

The Self is the only Reality. If the false identity vanishes the persistence of the Reality becomes apparent.
~ Sri Ramana Maharshi

Carry 'Nothing' in the heart. It is 'Everything'.
~ from The Ten Virtues in Japanese Flower Arrangement

There is no need to pray for the disappearance of the world from your life, or for its transformation into God, for:

In the beginning was Allah, and beside Him there was nothing—and He remains as He was.
~ Muhammad

The beginning is Atman, the middle is Atman, and the end is Atman. What appears other than Atman is mere illusion.
~ Yoga-Vasishtha

I am the Lord, and there is none else.
~ Isaiah

> Thou art the All and the All is in Thee: and thou Art, and there is nought else that IS save Thee only.
> ~ ACTS OF PETER

What we should pray for is self-extinction. 'When the ego vanishes all problems cease,' as Ramakrishna Paramahamsa said. The plea for unity is a plea for the destruction of privative I-consciousness. The unitive vision means just that: Unity, Oneness, One without a second. The stipulation is as rigorous as it is paradoxical. Reality is not 'seen' by anyone: It *is*. 'The knower of Brahman *becomes* Brahman.' 'He is a knower of the Self to whom the ideas 'me' and 'mine' have become quite meaningless.' (SRI SANKARACHARYA) It can flow through the mind like a wave, a gentle swell, or like a long breath we take, inhale and exhale, during which there was extinction of the ego leaving only the indescribable Presence which is the All, the distinc-tion between inner and outer utterly annihilated, after which, stunned, smiling with ineffable joy and peace, we know with abso-lute certitude and say to ourselves: *That was It*. We could appropri-ately conclude with the quotation with which we began: 'The Portal of God is non-existence.'

✿

GLINTS & GLIMPSES X

Be very selective about whom (if anyone) you share your spiritual life with, very circumspect, very wary. Wait till they come to you. Don't make people feel awkward. Make no claims. What transpires between you and heaven is incommunicable, but it can be alluded to indirectly, discreetly. Tact, respect, compassion: skillful means. 'You must never tell this holy truth to anyone who lacks self-control and devotion, or who despises his teacher and mocks at Me, but the man who loves Me, and teaches My devotees this supreme truth of the Gita, will certainly come to Me.'

❁

'Who am I before Thee?'

Sometimes we feel that way, as we should, and as have multitudes before us. It's a genuine 'station of wisdom.'

But the feeling of utter insignificance we experience in the divine Presence serves not to 'show us our true place,' to humble us, but to make us aware of the nothingness of the ego, the illusory lower self with which we have mistakenly identified. And since there is nothing other than the Self, 'our' identification with a separate ego is really an identification with nothingness. (And by no 'one'!) It's the ego that 'feels insignificant,' that is humbled, that finally perceives, with rueful contrition, its own non-existence, its groundless pride, its need for forgiveness. And the ego realizes, right then and there, that that forgiveness is always granted, that it was granted forever, before the beginning of time, for all eternity.

Who knows these things, who realizes any of this? Impersonal Bliss.

✲

'Thou art my only hope.' Perennial insight.

Here, in this world, living the spell-binding drama of the precious tenacious non-existent ego, we mess around awhile, making the most of it, accepting finally that no one will ever *really* understand us, enjoying the ups and enduring the downs, eventually come to understand and accept that close to 100% of earthly affairs are not all that important, weaken gradually, break down, developing our particular mix of those debilitating diseases and 'conditions' associated with middle and old age, and then die, 'go to our reward.'

We should love it all, of course, passionately, desperately, even sincerely, but as a dream, a marvellous unsurpassable dream, a perpetually vanishing infatuation. And God is the exit from the dream, the only way out. The *awakening*. God, the Dreamer, your own immortal Self.

✲

The greater the reality of the divine in our lives, the reality of God, the less urgent, the less real the issues and miseries of our *karma*: our so-called *troubles*. Not apparently but actually. God heals by revealing the unreality of our suffering, not on its own plane, 'this world', where it is real enough, but in His Presence. In this sense meditation truly is a 'pain reliever.'

The world disappears into God. That's what happens. (As, for Christians, the universe vanishes into Christ.) In His Presence there is only His Presence. When we offer our sufferings to Him, we find that our hands are empty.

✲

'May I be acceptable to Thee'

Humility. It's as if we go back to square one, as if all our *sadhana* has come to nothing, and we ask for nothing more than permission to begin again as if it were the first time. We present ourselves before Him as nothing but a human being, simple humanity in the unredeemed state, fallen, ignorant, wretched, lost, turning to God for the first time, with no claim but sincerity and not even certain of that. We throw ourselves on His Mercy. May I be acceptable, just acceptable. And my presumption be forgiven.

❁

'May I be pleasing to Thee'

More ambitious. You can imagine a smile of approval. (An encouraging pat on the back would be going too far.) To have pleased God is a very great thing. Insofar as the expression is figurative, it means conforming to the Law, the Dharma, obedience to His Will, fulfilling the implicit divine intention without reservations or dissimulation. This sentiment is properly accompanied by a searching self-analysis, a frank acknowledgement of all those stubborn little rotten spots, and a commitment to improve ourselves. We're always short of the mark, always *possibly* worthless, because our greatest strength is weakness. (Recall to what Jesus equated 'all our righteousness.') We'll never reach a point where it's all settled, where we don't have to *try* anymore. The feeling here can be wistful or fervent.

❁

I SAW IT WITH MY OWN EYES! IT'S BEYOND BELIEF!

I remember sitting at my desk in the Custodian's Office (the CO) at the Occupational Development Center (the OCD) of the Oakland Public Schools (the OPS), where I worked as a custodian (updated word for janitor) for nine years, speaking to a man from India who had mistakenly wandered into my room seeking information on computer classes. Learning that I was a student of Indian religion, he sat down across from me and enthusiastically, as I recall it, revealed that he was himself an ardent practitioner of his country's religion and had contributed toward or worked on (or sponsored in some way: I didn't get this clearly) the construction of several shrines. Before he left he confessed to me—I guess we had been talking about Indian conceptions of the deity—with a smile of anticipatory joy, and as if to impress upon me my timidity of ambition in being content with a God beyond the reach of the senses, 'But I want to *see* God! I want to see Him as clearly as I see you sitting across the table from me!'

And sometimes we do pray, from the depths of the heart, 'May I see Thee.'

It's most definitely not a matter of 'seeing is believing'. The plea is rather for intimacy, for totality of presence. We want Him to fill completely, saturate, every sensory realm, we want to perceive Him and only Him with every instrument of perception we possess, be aware only of Him at all levels of awareness and cognition, simultaneously, without distraction and forever. His Total Presence, our total absence. This longing is symbolized in the image of seeing God with our eyes, as we see everything else, because what we see is present to us in a manner more impressive, continuous and apparently independent of our contribution as perceiver than the other senses can offer. We can gaze at things, linger over them, examine their unveiled actuality. Whatever exists in the visual field is in a sense possessed or incorporated by us, open to us, known: known in its *truth* and *real*. If we actually saw Him we could swoon with bliss (like Udhava and so many others in the Krishna stories), or die, literally, into infinite Love. It would be the definitive End of everything mundane, transient, illusory, including ourselves.

So we imagine the Divine Form, as It is described in a traditional sacred iconography, materializing before us, and the divine Countenance smiling at us, as a kind of consummation of our devotion, a reward. Longing for a Supreme Presence of the Beloved, we forget, sometimes even deliberately, that theophany is always with us—for the world is God—and allow our imaginations to run a little wild, justifying what we suspect to be extravagance by an appeal to the promise that 'With God all things are possible.'

The sense of personal Presence is emphasized more strongly when we add, as we sometimes do, 'face to face'. 'May I see Thee, face to face.' 'Face to face' suggests nothing intervening, genuine encounter at last, after the overcoming of some prior artificiality or separative contrivance which had frustrated the fulfillment of a relationship: now, finally, things are as they should be, we are united, we have met each other, we are together. I am in the Presence of the Beloved One of my heart, He has come to me. And in a mysterious but unmistakable sense, come *back* to me, for 'May I see Thee' is really a poignant retroactive epitome of our spiritual life since the expulsion from Eden, a memory of the 'Perfection of the Beginning,' our joy before the Fall. It rends the heart. Separated from His Glory, we appeal to His Grace. Our references to 'progress' are always hollow or ironic because in our humanity we know full well what really happened.

We cannot but feel the deepest compassion for all those who, in these times, and victims of these times, do not 'believe in God.' And I'm deliberately using here the figure of speech which always sounds so pathetic because the very conception of spirituality being affirmed or renounced, 'belief', is already so impoverished. We feel this compassion most keenly in the depths of prayer, in the joy of our own address in love and His response in Presence. The thought of people we love dying without having had even the vaguest inkling of the divine Reality in which they lived and moved and had their being is heart-breaking. It's that 'waste of a human birth' we are warned about throughout the Vedantic literature, that catastrophe.

So like Black Elk and Saint Francis, and echoing liturgical supplication in all faiths, we pray for the whole world: 'May all see Thee.' We pray for the enlightenment of all, since to see Him is to know the Truth. Presence and Truth: the two saving manifestations of the Absolute. The very thought of them is joy.

AT A LOSS FOR WORDS

Everything,
the whole universe including our own existence,
is a gift we didn't have to deserve.

You might have thought of this already,
and stared for a moment in wonder at the world—
wonder and love, stunned appreciation, wordless gratitude—
but then you probably moved on,
forgot about it immediately,
didn't follow it through
(distractions, pressing concerns, a tight schedule,
the light changed to green, the phone rang,
any one of the assured interruptions):
you didn't realize that it could have been
the beginning of something incredible,
the turning point in your life.

You didn't know what you saw,
what you felt, was Grace.
That's a religious word.
We don't use it anymore.

We speak a language,
we hear a language,
in this world, in these times,
in which certain things can't be said anymore,
not because the words aren't there,
but because they've lost their meaning,
they've been invalidated.

Their use is indulged, with
the automatic generosity of democratic institutions,
in the special sectors established
for those who still appeal to them.
(Have they lost their meaning
because they make people feel embarrassed,
or do they make people feel embarrassed
because they've lost their meaning?
Which came first? What happened?)
It's a blind-at-the-center language now.
A language that betrays our only hope.

Listen to the ancient voice,
the ancient language, it's your native tongue.
Speak it. If only to yourself.
It'll be heard. It's the real language,
the original language.
When you speak it from the heart
it is always heard,
and the hearing is the answering.

YOUR FACE IS AN OPEN BOOK!

'All Faces are Thine'

Through His manifestation as a universe He has become all of us, the whole human family, and that includes, in a quite concrete and physical sense, our faces. All these faces, all the faces that have ever been, the billions of them, no two alike, are His. 'All faces are Thine' focusses our devotion on the miracle of the human face.

The character, the actual person, the living presence and the memory—its all in the face. Our experience as human beings, in a language only other human beings can read, is written on our faces. Our stories and Our Story, Humanity with a capital H, are told by our faces. Each face is a world, a private world and the common world as well. No image we ever see has anything approaching the impact, the depth, the expressiveness, the unfathomable significance, of a human face. What we see on faces is, in a sense, infinite, or at least beyond the power of words to convey.

Consciousness itself, peering from the eyes, becomes a tangible presence, the Consciousness that is the Self. The human face is a symbol, and even a concrete demonstration, of theomorphism. The expression 'made in His image' doesn't refer to our physical characteristics; but our faces are an image of our humanity, and therefore, if not an image of God, an image at least of our theomorphism. We can see divinity in the photographs of Ramana Maharshi, and catch glimpses of it on the faces of people who are experiencing contemplative serenity or joy or unselfish love, on the faces of people who have won wisdom by suffering with patience and courage. We can see it in the pure innocence and trust of children. Even the face of grief is divine. In Buddhist iconography the divine imprint is unmistakable: eloquent without parallel.

The presence of these dimensions of divinity are more primordial on human faces than in the words that refer to them, more primordial than language. More is communicated by our faces than by our words; when we remember people, recall them to mind, their lives and personalities, we visualize their faces.

And all this reading of faces takes place *between* us, between human beings, there's nothing 'objective' on a human face; it requires two of us, it occurs within us, and it proves our oneness. A human face and the consciousness that 'reads' it are one. The human face is a daily miracle, the closest we ever get to seeing Him with our physical eyes. (We look at someone's face and see Him shining in the depth of their eyes: in the consciousness, the mingled infinite remoteness and absolute immediacy of the consciousness, the simultaneous transhuman presence of person and world. They look at us and see the same thing. What's happening here?) Meditation on this *mantra* is love of humanity as divine and God as humanity. We become lost in love of both as One. We remember faces, we review our gallery of unforgettable expressions, of untranslatable eloquence, and love Him in them, love them in Him.

IS TODAY TUESDAY?

'Every day is the same day.' When you see it, you see it.

The Eternal Now. The annihilation of time, as the deliberate focus of a meditation, has been, in my experience, rare; it seems most often to be an unpredictable gift of grace, already 'there' and then discovered.

The sense of linear temporality is always modified or dimmed or blurred to some extent in deep meditation and, as I have suggested, occasionally even completely dispelled, but most of the time it lurks somewhere in the background, as it were, a vague, barely audible 'ticking of the clock' emerging into consciousness at varying intervals like a seal swimming off the coast. Unless we direct our attention specifically to piercing the mystery of time—piercing through the illusion of duration to the reality of an eternal present in which all things apparently located at different points on a one-way temporal continuum are perceived to be contemporary and simultaneous, or in which the timeless archetypes shine through their temporal manifestations—or unless our attention is directed there for us in the unpredictability of His dispensation, we don't see the Reality, the Eternal Now in which we are always immersed, *and which we are*, with anything but a flickering regard. And in another perspective it's really a matter of degree: sometimes the sense of timelessness—watching the waves roll in and withdraw, listening to the rain—is more vivid than at other times (like when we're put 'on hold', or trapped in traffic).

In any event, it's probably harder for people living in these times, in the Kali-Yuga, to experience the truth of timelessness than ever before. We are locked into the fabrication of linear temporality with an implacable vengeance: by the omnipresence of clock-time and its innumerable reminders, by the pace and density of 'schedules', a pace and density that technology has accelerated to a point literally lethal, as we approach the 'nanosecond' world (we never have 'enough time'), by the suffocating ubiquity of artifacts, images, activities and voices that remind us continually of the hour, the day, the date, the year, the feverish presence of 'history', by countless habitual maneuvers and figures of speech, all reflected in our increasingly conscious and desperate awareness of a deadly inexorable escalating velocity of the whole nightmare. Time speeds up in the Kali-Yuga. 'Definitely an overkill situation,' as the generals, speaking crisply and confidently, would put it. We have to turn away from 'civilization,' which is increasingly characterized by the quantification of everything, to Nature, for intimations of the great truth about Time, to catch glimpses, precious glimpses, of the Eternal Now which is Reality: to see each morning as the one morning, the one eternal morning in heaven and our hearts.

Timelessness is heaven. To look up for a haggard moment from the rat-race and remember it is enough to bring tears to your eyes.

Here is no place,
Now is no time,
There is nothing,
I am no one:
The Beloved alone is Real.

The bhakta's *Advaita* is to see the Beloved everywhere, in timeless rapture. And this One we see everywhere, Who is everything and everywhen, resides in our hearts. Inner and outer are One. How can I fail to see it? How could I have forgotten again? How many times am I going to think this is the world and I am 'me', moving through 'time,' and forget that All is Thee in the Eternal Now that I AM?

SONNET 30 AGAIN!

Friendship comes closer to being 'sacred', in the minds of many people, than just about anything else here in the dream-world. Someone who betrays a friend is universally regarded as the lowest of the low, even lower than a liar. And this is as it should be, of course. We're here for each other; love of the neighbor clearly implies solidarity. Years ago, when I was working in the missile factory in San Leandro, someone did something ugly and underhanded to someone else in a tight group of friends who worked there. The fellow who told me about it, one of the group, was so shaken he could barely be coherent. He tried to convey to me, to impress upon me, holding my eyes with his, how absolutely fundamental friendship was to him, that nothing was more serious. Commitment, fidelity, sincerity, the qualities that hold things together here, had been outraged; the world was tipping a bit on its foundations. I still remember his face, the mixture of anger and confusion, the helpless dismay.

God reveals Himself to us in meditation as the Friend, with a capital F. The word appears frequently in Sufic literature: 'I am the place of abode, the beginning, the friend and the refuge.' Krishna speaking. We see Him then, in devotional meditation, as the true Friend, the only true Friend, the one Who will never fail us, the only one we can truly count on, knowing and willing only what is best for us: identical with our day-to-day and eternal perfection and fulfillment.

We gaze at the mental image of Him with rapt adoration, pure love. The reassurance we feel, the confidence. the serene fearlessness, flow into us from Him. We realize—another of those 'How could I have been so blind?' moments—that He has always been there for us, and always will be. We realize that He loves us eternally, and that in that love we *are* eternal. We realize our own eternity.

There's an anthropomorphic aspect here, obviously, but what we actually experience, appearing to us as this Friend, is more like an immanent divine Wisdom, the loving presence within us of an infinite Wisdom. Again, it's in the word, the word 'friend'. It's as if the word is suddenly *entered* by the divine Presence and explodes before us, within us, into its true full significance. The same way it happens with the words 'Beloved,' 'Teacher,' 'Lord'. The *mantra* miracle. He is present in His Names. *Thou art my Friend, my true Friend: Thou hast ever been with me.*

FOURTEEN *MANTRAS* IN PRAISE OF THE LIGHT

'ALL IS LIGHT, THE LIGHT IS ALL'

Light is probably the most common symbol, in all religions, for the Reality, the Absolute, for God—although in a very real sense it's more than a symbol, it's a description. 'I am the light of the world,' He said. In the Vedanta, the Light, of course, is the Atman, the Self, Pure Consciousness. In meditation we realize that there is nothing else but the Light. We *see* the world as Light and know that the Light is everything.

> There is only light and the light is all. Everything else is but a picture made of light. The picture is in the light and the light is in the picture.
> ~ NISARGADATTA MAHARAJ

'LIGHT OF LIGHTS, LIGHT OF LIGHTS'

Invocation, celebration, adoration. We see it shining before us, within us, filling the universe, all-pervading, eternal Reality. In the *Gita* It is 'brighter than a thousand suns'. *Jyotir Uttamam*: Light Supreme.

'THOU ART LIGHT, THOU ART LIGHT...
SHINING FOREVER IN THE HEARTS OF ALL'

The emphasis here is on our oneness with all beings through our oneness in God. His manner of being within all of us, as the light of consciousness, is His manner of making all of us one, and in a shared world. He has given Himself to us in our hearts, as Light: therefore the universe and each one of us and God are One. What more can be said or known?

> Light is my very nature; I am no other than light. When the universe manifests itself, verily then it is I that shine.
> ~ ASTAVAKRA SAMHITA, Janaka speaking

'WHAT ART THOU BUT LIGHT?'

A moment of awe. The light of awareness is absolutely unreachable, indefinable, inaccessible, incomprehensible because It is *not a thing*: not an *object*. It's unlike anything else, unlike any *thing*. All other interpretations of the ultimate Reality must bow before this one. Sourceless all-pervading Light, the sourceless all-pervading Light in which a universe appears: that is Brahman Supreme of the Vedanta. The Presence, 'my' Self, is Light.

> Then, last of all, meditate on the oneness of the Self with God, the one blissful existence, the one I AM. With mind thus absorbed, a man sees Me alone in himself, and sees himself in Me, the Self of all—light joined to Light.
> ~ SRIMAD BHAGAVATAM, Krishna instructing Uddhava

'THOU ART THE LIGHT WITHIN ME'

My own awareness, than which nothing could seem to be more intimately 'mine', is actually God. At first we perceive this supreme truth as if 'we' are an observer of it, and with calm bliss contemplate and affirm it. The feeling is overwhelming love for God: who could have foreseen this, this incredible dispensation? who could have guessed in advance what salvation would look like, anticipated this miracle? But whose 'love for God' is this? My entire 'I' is Thou.

> Obeisance to Shiva Whose body is unique, perfectly full consciousness, unobscured by the radiance of His own eternally manifest Light.
> — SHIVA SUTRAS

'ALL IS THY LIGHT'

An affirmation, in direct address, tranquil and worshipful, of the Vedantic Truth. This is a static residence; a place of rest for the mind, of pure contemplation, of infinite peace.

> He, the Supreme Consciousness, is the Light of all lights. It is He Who manifests the universe, It is His Light that animates nature. The sun, the moon, the stars are but faint reflections of His supreme Light.
> — SWAMI SATPRAKASHANANDA

'LIGHT ETERNAL, LIGHT DIVINE'

This Light does not fade, nor was there ever a time when it wasn't shining. Past and future exist only in this Light, and they exist there simultaneously, in the Eternal Present. The light of consciousness annihilates time, the *illusion* of time; everything is always present to It, always *now.* We do not appear at a certain time in the world: the world appears eternally in us. If not for the eternal Light which is my real Self, there wouldn't be any world in which my apparent self could appear. This is why the Zen masters ask the question 'What was your original face before you were born?' Why Nisargadatta Maharaj asked 'Who came first, you or your parents?' Why Jesus said 'Before Abraham was, I am.'

> God is the Light of the Heavens and the Earth.
> — KORAN

'Thou art the Light Divine'

The personal God, or the Avatar, is identified with the Light, the Light is perceived in Its personal aspect. The emphasis here is on realization of the direct equivalence of the personal with the impersonal, making our experience complete. There's also a sense of pronouncing the highest praise, of having finally realized what He really is: Thou, my Friend, my Teacher and my Beloved, are the infinite Light as well, and quintessentially. Or, Thou, Who have appeared before me as my Friend, my Teacher and my Beloved, are actually the Light within me, my very Self.

> Once, while I was meditating in the temple, screen after screen of Maya was removed from my consciousness. Mother showed me a Light more brilliant than a million suns. From that Light came forth a spiritual form. Then this form melted away into the Light itself. The formless had taken form and then melted again into the formless.
>
> ~ Sri Ramakrishna

'O Thou Who art Light'

We identify Him by His supreme attribute, but here we are 'calling upon' God as well as invoking Him. The feeling is focussed in the silent space after the words are uttered, as if we would like to request or affirm something but no words are adequate, or are too caught up in contemplation of His infinite perfection, His essential miracle, to complete what we were going to say, and we fall silent into a state of mute adoration. What could we say? The invocation of His Presence is the obliteration of ours. To summon Him is to rescind ourselves. And we could just as well say 'recall' instead of 'rescind': it's both. He is everything real, the one real part of 'us.'

'Beloved Lord, Beloved Light'

The divine is loved in all Its manifestations, as the Lord, Who is God Omnipotent, or as the impersonal Light, the Self of the universe, and as the universe itself, Creation. There's a suggestion here, through the juxtaposition of Lord and Light, of the light of Wisdom, the Lord as the illuminating Wisdom that perpetually conceives, sustains and permeates the universe, guaranteeing its harmony and coherence, its meaningfulness. The Logos, *sophia perennis et universalis.* 'The Light shineth in the darkness, but the darkness comprehended it not.'

> I am the light of the world
> ~ John 8:12

'Truly this world is Light'

The world is here perceived as what it is: Pure Consciousness. The words come to our lips, or voiceless in our minds. We see it, we know it, the question is settled (in that moment!) forever.

This doesn't mean the world is insubstantial; but its substantiality is itself an appearance in consciousness. Nor is it the case that a mental world is constructed from sense data, but rather that sense data, which exist only in consciousness, are the apparently 'objective' world. The world and ('my') knowledge of the world are one and the same.

None of this analyzing, however, nothing like it, runs through the mind when, in meditation, the world is directly perceived as Light. And no discursive analysis, neither this one nor any I have ever seen (even the work of the great Wei Wu Wei, the *terrible* Wei Wu Wei as he calls himself, *although he almost gets there!)* is equal to experience of Reality. 'Mind and speech return baffled from That', as we read somewhere in the Upanishads. In the old figure of speech, 'the finger is not what it's pointing at.'

Spiritual truths are never known the way the discursive intelligence knows facts, because the knower of spiritual truths, in the act or state of knowing them, is not the everyday self, and for this very reason the everyday self can never know them. It's as if we were magically enabled to perceive the world as a cat perceives it, with cat-consciousness, and then, back in our human consciousness, tried to explain to other humans what it looked like.

Meditation is transformation into a knower who is one with the known: into what we were and are all along, as the sages tirelessly point out, but cannot realize due to our misidentification with an illusory self, an 'ego'. ('Nirvana there is, but no one who attains it.') There is only the Light.

> There is no such thing as an 'objective world' for the Buddhist, since we can only speak of the world of our experience, which cannot be separated from the experiencing sub-ject; secondly, the state of enlightenment is no temporal state, but an experience of a higher dimension, beyond the realm of time.'
> ~ WISDOM OF LAMA ANAGARIKA GOVINDA.

> The Self is the Heart. The Heart is self-luminous. Light arises from the Heart and reaches the brain, which is the seat of the mind. The world is seen with the mind, that is, by the reflected light of the Self. If the mind is turned in towards the source of light, objective knowledge ceases and Self alone shines forth as the Heart.
> ~ SRI RAMANA MAHARSHI

'THAT LIGHT, THAT IS THE ONE BLISSFUL EXISTENCE, THE ONE I AM, THE REALITY'

A slightly altered borrowing of a passage from Swami Prabhavananda's excellent abridgement of *Srimad Bhagavatam*.

The Light has been perceived, realized, we can see what It is and here we are 'describing' It, defining It to ourselves. The *mantra* emerges from that experience. The feeling, again and of course, is that inexpressible Bliss, within and without. There is nothing but the Light, nothing but that incredible Ocean of Light. We see the truth with calm and lucid clarity. Meditation means going deeper and deeper, allowing the depth of things to draw us nearer and nearer: there's a Center, a perpetual Origin, a Source, a Heart.

I AM (is) what 'becomes' the world, because It always 'was' the world, and what the world 'becomes' when we realize Who I AM. But all along I AM (is) really all there is. The world we love so much, whose irresistible magnetism elicits from us such wildly inconsistent responses, is nothing but the Self. Its birth, decay and death is no more real than your own birth, decay and death. There is only the Self, the Light.

'Thou art Pure Light'

With no admixture, no attributes, no personal aspect. The God we worship, the Thou, is Pure Light, pure Illumination. What we experience could be described as the Empty Now of Pure Awareness. An emptiness as undifferentiated as the taste of ice water. We realize that every instant in this dream world is absolutely fresh (deliciously fresh!) because it is made of the Light, and the Light is the eternal present, the Light of I AM is the perpetual fountain of Now. Furthermore, the Light doesn't 'know' its ephemeral contents as distinct from Itself: the Light knows Itself only and always as Light: Pure Light.

> *Now I shall tell you the nature of the Atman.*
> *There is a self-existent Reality, which is the basis of our consciousness of ego.*
> *That Reality sees everything by Its own Light.*
> *That Reality pervades the universe, but no one penetrates It. It alone shines. The universe shines with Its reflected light. Its nature is eternal consciousness.*
> *This is the Atman, the Supreme Being, the ancient. It never ceases to experience infinite joy. It is always the same. It is consciousness itself.*

Here, within this body, in the pure mind, in the secret chamber of intelligence, in the infinite universe within the Heart, the Atman shines in Its captivating splendor, like a noonday sun. By Its Light, the universe is revealed. You are one with the shining Light that casts this shadow of a world.

~ condensed from SHANKARA

'THIS UNIVERSE OF SOULS, THIS UNIVERSE OF SOULS, LIGHTS WITHIN THE GREAT LIGHT. O GOD, THOU ART THE GREAT LIGHT, THOU ART THE GREAT LIGHT'

An outpouring of love. Love of the humans, ourselves, the theomorphic beings, *imago dei*, love of the universe that is one with them, that is their radiance, love of the One Radiance that is All. The universe is not made of 'things' and 'events': it is made of human souls, and these souls are like jewels or stars, like the myriad coruscating reflections of the sun on the moving surf, points of light within the One Great Light that is our Beloved, our God.

In the precious golden case of inner consciousness is the Supreme Brahman, ever pure and partless, the all-white Light of Lights. Hence, the knowers of the Self know That.

~ MUNDAKA UPANISHAD

SATCHIDANANDA

'Consciousness is Bliss'

It's possible, in meditation, to become aware of Awareness, to *be* self-aware Awareness. Pure Consciousness. Without any content. This contentless Awareness, the Ultimate Reality of Vedanta, *Paramartha Tattvam,* is experienced as Bliss, which is consistent with the teaching. The state, however, can't really be encouraged, much less reawakened, by this *mantra*, which is more like a reminder of it, or a recollection. OM, the divine *pranava*, the word that is God, is the *mantra* of the Pure Consciousness: 'OM is Brahman.' But we can repeat 'Consciousness is Bliss' anyway, as a reminder, try to establish serenity, receptiveness, and then wait to see where the mind decides to go. It might slowly, 'thoughtlessly', spiral inward toward the eternal Joy. Or it might suddenly sink its teeth into the latest fierce obsession. In which case you'll have to start all over again, maybe try something else.

'Existence is Bliss'

Bliss, like Consciousness. Existence is really dynamic, not static; things aren't just 'there'. Existence is the perpetual Self-Manifestation of God, it's an activity, it's what continuously 'stands out' against and triumphs over nothingness. Shakti, the Power of Shiva: Maya, the Power of Brahman. Existence *happens*.

We can feel this perpetual triumph within us as Bliss. Everyday exclamations like 'Its great to be alive!' are expressions of the same feeling. It *is* great to be alive, great to *be*. Simply to *be here* is Bliss—if you look at it without allowing one-sided prejudices or fleeting dissatisfactions to jaundice your vision. We can focus our minds on this truth in meditation, focus our minds on the miracle of Existence, and if we can succeed in abandoning all personal considerations, letting them collapse away within us, just see Existence for what it is, in itself, we can taste the Bliss of which it is made, which it *is*. And when that happens we know, without the shadow of a doubt, that this is the true perception, that we've seen into the heart of things. Existence-Consciousness-Bliss, *Satchidananda* of the Vedanta: the Reality.

❁

Remember this Promise of SRI KRISHNA:

Verily, having obtained the human birth
which reflects My image,
and having surrendered yourself in love to Me,
you will ascend in your own being to Me,
the all-blissful universal Self.

Lightning Source UK Ltd.
Milton Keynes UK
UKOW01f1601170616

276499UK00001B/281/P

9 780900 588525